Children V

Paul Cavadino is Chair of the Penal Affair.   ......num, an alliance of 31 organizations concerned with the penal system, and Clerk to the Parliamentary All-Party Penal Affairs Group. He is co-author of *Introduction to the Criminal Justice Process, Criminal Justice in Transition, The Youth Court One Year Onwards* and *Bail: The Law, Best Practice and the Debate.*

Children Who Kill

An examination of the treatment of juveniles
who kill in different European countries

Edited by

Paul Cavadino

WATERSIDE PRESS

In association with the

British Juvenile and Family Courts Society

Children Who Kill

Published 1996 by
WATERSIDE PRESS
Domum Road
Winchester SO23 9NN
Telephone or Fax 01962 855567
INTERNET:106025.1020@compuserve.com

In association with The British Juvenile and Family Courts Society
(BJFCS)

ISBN Paperback 1 872 870 29 5

Cataloguing-in-Publication Data A catalogue record for this book can
be obtained from the British Library

Printing and binding Antony Rowe Ltd, Chippenham

Cover design John Good Holbrook Ltd, Coventry.

Children Who Kill

CONTENTS

Part III: Canada

Part IV: The Way Forward

Foreword

This invaluable book contains a wealth of information, and the stimulating views of experts drawn from a wide range of disciplines, on the way in which different countries deal with children who kill.

Its genesis goes back to August 1994 when Avril Calder, the then Chairman of the British Juvenile and Family Courts Society, attended a congress of the International Association of Juvenile and Family Court Magistrates in Bremen, Germany. For the previous 18 months the United Kingdom had been in the grips of the Bulger case. The video film of that little boy being led by two older children from a Liverpool shopping mall to his death had gone round the world. The world's media followed the subsequent trial of the two boys assiduously. At the congress the Chairman was asked constantly about the Bulger case and picked up adverse reactions about the way in which the two boys were dealt with by the English system.

There were many professionals in the United Kingdom who were uncomfortable about the process. A time honoured way to throw light on one's own practice is to look at the practices of others. The British Juvenile and Family Courts Society decided to make a comparison possible by setting up a conference to study a range of European systems, focusing on the specific issue of 'Children Who Kill'.

This book brings together the papers presented at the ensuing conference which took place in London in November 1995. The event attracted delegates from seventeen European countries, as well as from Canada and the United States. The participants were truly representative of all the professionals involved with children, their families and the law. The conference provided the opportunity for a well informed debate about diverse approaches to dealing with children who commit grave crimes. The contributions from many jurisdictions assembled in this publication show how varied the approaches are, their similarities and differences, their advantages and disadvantages. The book aims to bring this information to a wider audience in a clear and concise fashion. It should provide a context for further discussion about the extent to which different approaches best meet the needs of the children, their victims and families, and the wider society.

The style of the contributions varies: some were detailed, closely referenced, written papers prepared in advance of the conference, while others are edited transcripts of the contributors' addresses. Some speakers focused their contributions tightly on the issue of children who kill, while others ranged more widely in describing the juvenile justice systems of their respective countries.

The British Juvenile and Family Courts Society appreciated the willingness, warmth and generosity shown by the many people who responded to invitations to speak, or who contributed in other ways to the success of the conference. They gave freely and wholeheartedly of their time and expertise. The ability to organise a European gathering of this kind was facilitated by the many contacts afforded by affiliation to the International Association of Juvenile and Family Court Magistrates. The Society was much encouraged by the support of many European colleagues and was especially pleased that the Council of Europe and the British Association for Central and Eastern Europe sponsored the attendance of delegates from Eastern Europe. The European dimension was much valued by all present, particularly by the Society's multi-disciplinary membership who supported the event enthusiastically.

The Rt Hon Sir Stephen Brown
Sheriff Principal Gordon Nicholson QC

Patrons
British Juvenile and Family Courts Society
September 1996

CHAPTER 1

A Case for Change

Paul Cavadino

This paper will examine the statistics on the number and children and young persons found guilty of murder and manslaughter in England and Wales over the last 15 years; summarise the available evidence on why children kill; describe the way in which this country deals with children who commit homicide; and compare our approach with that of other European countries.

How Many Children Kill?

Inevitably, any case in which a child kills is likely to attract extensive media attention. This can give the impression that the number of such cases is rapidly rising. However, this impression is not borne out by the facts. The number of children and young persons who were convicted of murder or manslaughter in England and Wales in the period from 1979 to 1994 was as follows:

	Murder			Manslaughter		
	10-13	10-16	10-17	10-13	10-16	10-17
1979	-	6	20	1	7	19
1980	-	5	16	-	5	10
1981	-	5	11	-	9	16
1982	1	15	22	-	7	9
1983	1	6	11	-	8	19
1984	-	5	13	-	6	14
1985	-	6	12	-	7	12
1986	1	6	8	-	8	15
1987	-	4	14	-	11	18
1988	1	3	7	-	6	13
1989	-	5	11	-	9	23
1990	-	8	11	1	2	9
1991	-	7	13	-	8	15
1992	-	4	11	1	5	8
1993	2	13	23	1	5	12
1994	2	10	16	-	3	8

In total 108 young people aged ten to 16 inclusive were found guilty of murder and 106 of manslaughter during this period. Two hundred and ten young people aged ten to 17 were convicted of murder and 220 of manslaughter. Children under the age of 14—who, understandably, receive most media attention—totalled eight convicted of murder and four of manslaughter.

The figures show no clear trend, fluctuating up and down from year to year. The average annual number of people under 18 found guilty of homicide (murder or manslaughter) in the first five-year period covered by the statistics, 1979-83, was 29; whereas in the most recent five-year period, 1990-94, the average number was 25.

Why Do Children Kill?

There are many different reasons why children kill. Contributory factors which produce the types of disturbance which can lead children to kill include serious physical abuse; sexual abuse; exposure to repetitive or extreme violence (including witnessing such violence); parental mental illness; parental rejection; neurological abnormalities; conduct disorder; substance abuse; and, in a few cases, mental illness. The combination of factors is different in each individual case. Although homicides by children are relatively rare, these conditions, unhappily, are not—which suggests that a substantial number of other children may potentially be capable of killing. The combination of factors of the type listed above with other circumstances, such as the meeting and friendship of two young people with complementary disturbed personalities and in adolescence the escalation of behaviour through gang participation, can lead to killings by such children which would not otherwise have taken place.

In *The Case of Mary Bell*,[1] Gitta Sereny analyses one of the two killings by children which have aroused the greatest attention and debate in the course of the last 30 years—the case of Mary Bell who, in 1968 when aged 11, was found guilty of having at the age of ten killed two small boys, one aged four and one three. The book describes in detail the bizarre upbringing of a child who was 'emotionally abused for years by a seriously disturbed mother'—a mother who immediately after the birth cried 'Take the thing away from me' and jerked her body away when the new-born Mary was put into her arms. Following medical evidence that Mary Bell was suffering from psychopathic disorder, she was found guilty of manslaughter by reason of diminished responsibility. The trial judge, who wished to make a hospital order, was unable to do so because no suitable hospital place was available, and therefore sentenced her to detention for life. Released from

10

detention in 1980 at the age of 23, she is now living under a different name in the north east of England with a teenage daughter.

The 1995 edition of Gitta Sereny's book contains an appendix about the second of this country's two most publicised cases involving child killers—the murder of two year old James Bulger in 1993 by two ten year old boys, Jonathan Venables and Robert Thompson. Miss Sereny describes Robert Thompson's abandonment, together with his five brothers, by his father; his mother's subsequent problems of deep depression and drink; the bullying and physical ill-treatment of Robert by his older brothers; and his ill-treatment in turn of his younger brother. She discusses Jonathan Venables' early years spent in an 'atmosphere of tremendous maternal tension' and his repeated manifestations of seriously disturbed behaviour as a schoolchild. Finally, she considers the implications of the sexual element of the crime, observing that 'children who abuse other children have almost invariably been abused themselves'.

A recent study by Dr. Gwyneth Boswell entitled 'Violent Victims'[2] examined 200 cases of offenders sentenced as juveniles under section 53 Children and Young Persons Act 1933. Of the total sample, 100 had been sentenced for murder under section 53(1) of the Act and 100 for a range of other serious crimes, including manslaughter, under section 53(2). The study found that 72 per cent had experienced emotional, sexual, physical and/or organized abuse as children. This is undoubtedly an underestimate because other cases, where suggestions of abuse were recorded in the files without professional corroboration, were not included in the figures unless there was direct evidence of abuse from an interview with the offender.

Fifty-three per cent of the sample had experienced the loss of a significant figure to whom they were emotionally attached, via bereavement or cessation of contact, which was estimated by professionals or by the offenders themselves to have had a distinct impact upon them and their subsequent behaviour. Dr. Boswell observed that such loss 'constitutes a major source of childhood trauma which, depending on how it is handled, may later contribute to disordered behaviour, including aggression and violence'.

In 91 per cent of cases there was recorded or personally related evidence of abuse and/or loss, with 35 per cent experiencing both. Dr. Boswell commented:

> The findings in this report reveal that a high proportion of young people who have committed violent or murderous offences have themselves been the victims of childhood trauma in the form of abuse and/or loss and frequently both. This does not mean, of course, that all youthful victims of trauma will become violent or murderous offenders. That is liable to

11

depend on a whole variety of other variables . . . Self- evidently, however, many members of the current survey had not been effectively helped to think through, interpret or resolve the traumatic event(s) which had occurred in their earlier lives. Whilst this may move the debate one step nearer to potential cause it is probably of most help in considering the kind of work that still needs to be effected with these young offenders. The growing body of work on post-traumatic stress disorder confirms that children suffer the after-effects of traumatic stress in a similar way to adults, and that one way in which unresolved fear or grief can manifest itself, particularly in males, is in later aggressive or violent behaviour.

She recommended that when the cases of children and young persons who commit violent offences come to light, there should be a consistent system of professional assessment with investigations routinely made into abuse and loss experiences amongst other background factors. Such an assessment should aim to offer

. . . an appropriate programme of action which will specifically seek to ensure that the young person does not repeat their violent behaviour. In cases where unresolved childhood trauma is found, post-traumatic stress counselling should form a significant part of that programme.

Or, as Gitta Sereny puts it:

How can any individual - whether child or adult - who has been subjected to traumatic events which have affected his development and behaviour, be expected to come to terms with them, with his fears, with his actions and with himself unless he be permitted and helped to face up to these memories?[1]

Childhood trauma leads to violent behaviour not only in childhood and adolescence, but also in adult life. In a report prepared for the Reed Committee,[3] Robert Johnson, then consultant psychiatrist at Parkhurst prison, described the 'buried terror syndrome' induced by child abuse in the context of his work with seriously violent adult prisoners. The terror experienced by these men had become deeply buried for fear that bringing it back to the surface would lead to its re-enactment. Any likelihood of this happening would precipitate an extreme and possibly violent reaction. The psychiatrist's job was to identify the terror and show that it was now obsolete, a process which could ultimately lead to a recovery from violent behaviour. However, many of these men had spent decades in institutions without the questions being asked which could lead them to an understanding of the roots of their violence.

In a letter published in *The Guardian* on 22 February 1993, Dr. Johnson wrote:

Last week I was asked to evaluate a violent prisoner who was becoming increasingly bitter and aggressive. "Were you happy as a child?" is my standard question. "No," he replied, "my father tried to kill me." At the age of three, his father suspended him from a 200ft bridge by a rope round his ankles to within a few feet of the water below. His mother pulled him back up.

If human beings, especially in infancy, were made of wood, then we could expect them to absorb such incidents as a matter of course, and proceed through this best-of-all-possible worlds like the rest of us virtuous souls. Since all children are highly impressionable, how can we possibly avoid some savage social penalty in later life? This man was serving a life sentence for a violent crime, and believed he would commit more. Unless the childhood damage can be addressed and repaired, how can we expect civilised friendly behaviour from such aggrieved individuals?

Without exception, all long-term violent prisoners who have agreed to discuss such painful topics with me have confirmed a history of sickening child abuse. Many have also averred that they would have benefited by skilled caring intervention at a much earlier age.

In a civilised society, reparative measures such as these would be explored and implemented as a matter of urgency, if only to allow us all to sleep more soundly at night.

How Do We Deal With Children Who Kill?

The age of criminal responsibility in the British Isles is unusually low by European standards: in England and Wales it is ten years old.

Children accused of murder or manslaughter are tried and sentenced by the Crown Court. During the trial of the children who killed James Bulger (two boys aged ten at the time of the killing and aged 11 when tried), most foreign commentators were amazed that children of this age should be dealt with by an adult-style Crown Court criminal trial. Many observers questioned whether such young children were really able to comprehend the complexities of a lengthy criminal prosecution and trial; whether they should have appeared in the full glare of media coverage of Crown Court proceedings; whether they understood all the issues and language used, in order to give clear instructions as necessary; whether their decision not to give evidence arose from fear of speaking in such a public forum; and whether it was right to lift reporting restrictions after conviction, thereby allowing their names and photographs to be widely publicised with the difficulties which this would pose for their eventual rehabilitation.

As the recent report of the Justice working party on 'Children and Homicide'[4] commented:

> Crown Court procedures expose children to a public hearing, as opposed to the private hearing conducted in the youth courts. If cases are particularly notorious, the media may be present in large numbers . . . Language and procedures are complex and likely to be perceived as threatening, and . . . the participants wear strange ceremonial costumes. These surroundings may engender a fear of giving evidence, which is an experience even adults may find traumatic, and must contribute to the difficulty of understanding procedures which baffle many adults.

The working party identified a further unsatisfactory feature of the process as follows:

> Dealing with juvenile homicide in adult courts, where cases may take many months to come to trial, inevitably means substantial delays in providing the psychological help required by many of the young people; effective therapy can only begin after the verdict because of the need to preserve the integrity of the evidence, and the fear that treatment may affect it . . . neither the interests of the victim, the public, nor the defendant are well served by protracted delays. It is unacceptable for the family of the victim to have to wait up to a year or more for a hearing which is a critical point in their process of bereavement. By the same token for a child who may be in desperate need of therapeutic help to be unable to receive it, for fear of compromising the legal process, is equally unacceptable.

The Bulger case took nine months to come to trial, during which time the defendants received no treatment in case it prejudiced their pleas. As the mother of Robert Thompson said to Gitta Sereny:

> I think Bobby needs help, and he's been needing it for a long time. I asked them – give him help; they said he can't have help because he hasn't been found guilty. I said, if he isn't guilty, he needs help, now. But I might have been talking to the wall; nobody listened.[1]

When a child or young person aged under 18 is found guilty of murder, the mandatory sentence under section 53(1) Children and Young Persons Act 1933 is detention during Her Majesty's pleasure—the juvenile equivalent of the mandatory life sentence. Since 1983 the procedures following the imposition of such a sentence have been as follows.

As in the case of adult life sentences, a minimum term known as the 'tariff' is set which the offender must serve to meet the requirements of retribution and deterrence. The trial judge makes a recommendation to the Home Secretary on the appropriate length of the tariff period. The Lord Chief Justice also makes a recommendation: in the absence of any mechanism for appeal against the tariff, this is intended to help provide a check against inconsistencies as between different judges. However, the Home Secretary does not have to accept either of these judicial recommendations. In the Bulger case, for example, the trial judge recommended an eight year tariff period; the Lord Chief Justice recommended ten years; but the Home Secretary fixed the tariff at 15 years, stating that he had taken account of 'the judicial recommendations as well as all other relevant factors including the circumstances of the case, public concern about the case and the need to maintain public confidence in the criminal justice system'.

At the end of the tariff period, the Parole Board considers the case and makes a recommendation as to whether the offender can now safely be released. However, the Home Secretary is not obliged to accept a recommendation for release.

Most practitioners in both the criminal justice system and the child care system regard these procedures with grave disquiet. The feature of the process which is widely regarded as the most objectionable is the role of the Home Secretary in setting the tariff and making release decisions. Setting the tariff is a sentencing decision—yet it is taken not by the trial judge who has heard all the evidence, but by a politician in his or her office with no hearing, no right for the defendant to be present or represented, and no right of appeal. This procedure contravenes all the basic requirements of natural justice. When politicians make these decisions, there is a danger that they will be influenced by electoral considerations and the prospect of headlines in the tabloid media rather than the merits of the case. This is disturbing enough in adult cases. In the case of children and young persons— where justice demands that the process should take account of their immaturity and their capacity for change, as well as their degree of psychological disturbance—it is indefensible.

In February 1996 in the cases of *Hussain v United Kingdom* and *Singh v United Kingdom*, the European Court of Human Rights held that the system for making release decisions at the end of the tariff period on juveniles sentenced under section 53(1) of the 1933 Act contravenes Article 5.4 of the European Convention, and that such young people are entitled to have the lawfulness of their detention reviewed by a court or court-like body. The Government has said that it will abide by this decision, which will involve legislation to replace the current system with one in which some form of judicial hearing (e.g. a panel of the Parole Board sitting according to a judicial procedure) makes release decisions. As an interim measure, the Government announced in July

1996 that from August 1996 offenders detained during Her Majesty's pleasure will be entitled to an oral hearing before the Parole Board, to be legally represented and to cross-examine witnesses. It was also announced that the Home Secretary will 'normally' accept the Parole Board's recommendations for release in these cases.

The judgment does not affect the procedure for setting tariffs, which is likely to be the subject of a separate decision by the European Court in the near future. (As this book went to press, on 30 July 1996 in *R v Secretary of State for the Home Department, ex parte Venables and Thompson* the Court of Appeal upheld the Home Secretary's right to set tariff periods in cases of detention during Her Majesty's pleasure. This overturned a decision in May 1996 by the Divisional Court, which had held that setting a rigid tariff was inconsistent with Parliament's intention in creating this sentence. The Court of Appeal nevertheless held that the Home Secretary had acted unlawfully in setting tariffs in respect of Venables and Thompson as the procedures which he had followed were 'seriously flawed' and 'lacking in fairness'. In particular, the Court held that he should not have taken into account public petitions urging that the two boys should never be released. The case will now go on appeal to the House of Lords.)

When a child or young person is found guilty of manslaughter, as opposed to murder, the judge has discretion as to sentence. He or she can impose a sentence of long term detention under section 53(2) of the Children and Young Person Act 1933: this can either be detention for life or detention for a fixed term. Alternatively, the judge can pass any of the other sentences available for children and young persons, including non-custodial sentences: a recent example of the latter was a supervision order passed on an 11 year old found guilty of manslaughter, who had dropped a slab of concrete from the top of a tower block in Leeds, killing a pensioner who was hit by the falling slab.

Young people detained under section 53(1) or 53(2) may be held in such place and under such conditions as the Home Secretary may decide. Those under the age of 15 are held in local authority secure units or in the Department of Health youth treatment centre at Glenthorne, Birmingham. Between the ages of 15 and 17 inclusive, young people can be held either in secure accommodation or in a Prison Service young offender institution. Between the ages of 18 and 20 inclusive they are held in Prison Service young offender institutions and, at the age of 21, are transferred to an adult prison. Dr. Gwyneth Boswell commented in her study:

> The child care system's facilities are such that they provide the best likelihood of treatment and educational facilities the young person is likely to receive throughout their section 53 career. Staff assert that this often

16

brings the offender to an optimum point for safe release or would do so given the continuity of another year or two in the same setting. However, at the age of 18 years, young people are suddenly effectively re-criminalised by their transfer to the prison system.[2]

Comparison With Other European Countries

In most other European countries, children aged under 14 who commit offences do not appear before the criminal courts. They are dealt with in civil proceedings by family courts (usually sitting in private) which are concerned with the need for compulsory measures of care. This can include long term detention in secure accommodation but this is arranged under the auspices of a care order rather than as a custodial punishment imposed in criminal proceedings.

The *Appendix* to this paper lists the ages of criminal responsibility in Council of Europe countries, from which it is clear that our age of criminal responsibility is unusually low. In Holland, the age is twelve; in France it is 13; in Germany, Austria and Italy it is 14; in the Scandinavian countries it is 15; in Spain and Portugal it is 16; and in Belgium it is 18. In Eastern Europe, it ranges between 14 and 16. There has been a trend internationally towards raising the age of criminal responsibility in recent years—for example, in Norway from 14 to 15, in Canada from seven to twelve and in Israel from nine to 13. In a report of January 1995, the United Nations Committee on the Rights of the Child recommended that 'serious consideration be given to raising the age of criminal responsibility throughout the areas of the United Kingdom'.

In her book, Gitta Sereny reflects as follows on the 1993 trial in the Bulger case:

> For me, sitting through an almost exact replica of the 1968 trial, much of it had a distressing quality of *deja vu*. And during the breaks and the sixteen evenings of the trial days, I found, yet again, that every lawyer, every court official, virtually every police officer and every member of the media I spoke with had grave misgivings about the case and, yes, the venue of the trial.[1]

Our system of sentencing is also strikingly different from the rest of Europe. According to the Justice working party report,[4] outside the British Isles only two European countries, France and Holland, have indeterminate sentences for convicted juveniles. No other European country has indeterminate sentences which are not judicially supervised. In France and Holland such sentences are reviewed either annually or biennially by the judiciary—where possible by the judge

17

who heard the case and passed sentence—who can order the young person's conditional release.

More detail on the operation of other European systems is provided in the papers of later contributors. However, even a brief comparison with the way in which other nations of Europe deal with children who kill shows that our system is an anachronism. It fails to meet the needs of disturbed juveniles; it fails to meet the requirements of natural justice; and it fails society by placing serious obstacles in the way of ensuring that these children receive the treatment they need if they are to overcome the violent tendencies which led to their offences. Other Europeans do not consider that their systems are without blemish, and a number of the papers which follow (in *Part II* of this book) are refreshingly self-critical. However, the procedures in this country are invariably seen by our European counterparts as astonishingly extreme.

Our anachronistic system should be replaced with an approach which is geared to the needs of seriously disturbed children. The age of criminal responsibility should be raised to at least 14: below this age children who kill should be dealt with by the family proceedings court as children in need of compulsory measures of care. (If, however, criminal trials are retained for children aged ten to 13, they should take the form of a tribunal sitting in private and presided over by a judge specially trained in dealing with children. Following a finding of guilt, no criminal penalties should be available. Instead, the case should be remitted to the family proceedings court for a decision on disposal.)

When young people are over the age of criminal responsibility, there should be early pleas and accelerated hearings with a view to the early initiation of treatment and therapy. Hearings should be held in private and presided over by a specially trained judge. There should be no mandatory sentences and courts should have discretion to sentence according to the circumstances of the individual case. When indeterminate sentences are passed, periods of detention should be determined and release decisions made by a judicial body, which should regularly review the progress of the case. Its decisions should be based on the progress of the treatment programme, the young person's development and whether he or she is now safe to release. Such an approach would be more just, more humane, and would better serve the needs of society than our present system, which is so markedly out of line with the rest of Europe.

Paul Cavadino is Chair of the Penal Affairs Consortium, an alliance of 31 organizations concerned with the penal system, and Clerk to the Parliamentary All-Party Penal Affairs Group

ENDNOTES

1. Gitta Sereny, *The Case of Mary Bell*, Eyre Methuen, 1972; republished 1995 by Pimlico.
2. Gwyneth Boswell, *Violent Victims*, Prince's Trust, 1995.
3. Robert Johnson, *Intensive work with disordered personalities*, unpublished, 1993.
4. *Children and Homicide*, Justice, 1996.

APPENDIX

Age of criminal responsibility in Council of Europe countries

Andorra	16	Malta	9
Austria	14	Netherlands	12
Belgium	18	Norway	15
Bulgaria	14	Poland	16
Cyprus	7	Portugal	16
Czech Republic	15	Romania	14
Denmark	15	San Marino	12
Estonia	15	Slovakia	15
Finland	15	Slovenia	14
France	13	Spain	16
Germany	14	Sweden	15
Greece	12	Switzerland	7
Hungary	14	Turkey	12
Iceland	15	England/Wales	10
Ireland	7	Scotland	8
Italy	14	Northern Ireland	8
Latvia	14		
Liechtenstein	7		
Lithuania	14	(Source: House of Lords *Hansard*,	
Luxembourg	18	27 February 1995, col WA82)	

CHAPTER 2

Children Who Kill

Gitta Sereny

I believe that it is absolutely necessary to change the judicial system in Britain as it concerns children who kill. Children as of the age of 10—in Scotland as of the age of eight—who commit murder or manslaughter are tried by a judge and jury in an adult court. They are not allowed to consult or be seen by therapists before the sentence, except by a psychiatrist to give an opinion on their ability and capacity to distinguish between right and wrong.

This conference takes place two days after the end of the trial in one of the most shocking cases which has ever taken place in Britain—the murders committed by Frederick and Rosemary West. I am not one of those people who think that all those who commit crimes are necessarily sick and should be in hospital. As far as adults are concerned, I think that there are some very bad people around. In my view Frederick West did us all an enormous favour in killing himself, and it is very sad that the prison to which Rosemary West has been taken will have to support her presence: the presence of such people, the influence and the effect on other prisoners, can be quite appalling.

However, it is important to appreciate that even these two terrible people had an extremely abusive childhood and very dysfunctional families. All my experience, and all the experience of people who have had as much and more to do with this subject than myself, shows that every single child who commits murder or is involved in very serious crime or very anti-social living—such as the 36 child prostitutes I worked with to write my book *The Invisible Children*—comes from a dysfunctional family. The machinery which society has created to care for people is unable to cope with these cases.

Children who kill are a rare phenomenon in Europe. You would not think so if you have read the newspaper coverage of the Bulger case; and at the time of the Mary Bell case, the same hysteria swept through the papers, through television and through the country. In the last 250 years we know of 27 cases of children under 14 who have killed other children in Britain (though there have been other murders by children of adults). I understand from my friends and colleagues in some other European countries that this is comparable to other countries in Europe, although it is true that the situation is now worse in America. I am going to talk mainly about two cases where children have committed apparently motiveless murders of small children. However, there are now other types of case, which are increasing. There was quite recently a terrible case in Sweden where two 15 year old skinheads killed a 14 year old child (and, even more recently, there have been several murders in Britain by teenagers *of* teenagers).

I attended the trial of Mary Bell in 1968, and afterwards I researched it for many months to see why it had happened. I also attended the trial in the Bulger case, after which I also carried out research to find out why it happened. These children—Mary Bell aged 11; Norma Bell, her neighbour, not related, aged 13 but with a mental age of about nine or ten; and 25 years later Robert Thompson aged 10 and Jonathan Venables aged 10—stood before a judge and jury.

The Mary Bell Case

When I went to Newcastle and lived through this the first time, I found it traumatic. Of course it was the first trial of its kind that I had attended—but then how many people have attended such a trial? No-one in either court knew anything about the background of these children. Mary Bell was a beautiful small girl of quite exceptional intelligence. Norma Bell was very pretty too but not intelligent. There was one enormous difference between these two children—namely, the people they were surrounded by. Norma Bell came from a family of 11 children, a close, loving, working class family. Her parents, aunts, uncles and the other children (who were outside the courtroom) were there every day of that trial. She was supported throughout. When she became restless, she was stroked. When she became tired, one of her parents whispered to her. When she cried, she was handed a handkerchief from behind her, where they sat

Although Mary Bell's father was there and, as of the third day, also her mother (who had to be brought almost by force), and her sad grandmother, throughout the many days of that trial that child was not touched. Only once when she became restless did her mother push her. Mary was a very isolated child. The court took an immediate liking to Norma Bell and a dreadful dislike to Mary Bell. Although I knew no more than anyone else did at that time, watching that situation I was absolutely certain that something dreadful had gone on in the life of that child. In every intermission and in the evenings I talked to lawyers, court officials, social workers and psychiatrists who were there, and this was when I saw that nobody knew anything about her background.

I was of course unable to talk to the families of these children until the trial was over. Norma Bell was acquitted. Mary Bell was found

21

guilty of manslaughter because of diminished responsibility and was detained for life. The judge explained of course that detention for life did not mean that she would actually be detained necessarily for life, and she was released 12 years later when she was 23.

In the first edition of my book *The Case of Mary Bell*, and in subsequent editions, I begged that the system should be changed. These small children should not have to face an adult court and a jury, whom I watched every day sit there uncomprehending when the children spoke and when it was intimated to them that they were facing a 'bad seed' or an evil being. Of course, nothing was done. The only thing that happened after the trial over the next two years was that a few more special secure units were opened, so that there was a little more choice should this happen again.

The Bulger Case

In February 1993 (after two other cases of children killing children, which, however, were hardly reported) it happened again. I do not suppose there is a person who did not see those pictures, which in February 1993 entered every home in the land, of three children: one little one, two bigger ones; the little one holding hands with one of the bigger ones; the other bigger one walking slightly in front but separate. But did people ask 'What made it happen?' Some people did of course, but not enough. They were 'evil'. If their families were talked about at all, they had done it because they belonged to 'them'—the poor, the unemployed, the disadvantaged, the people who drink, the people who do not know how to care for their homes and their children.

However true that may have been in part, this is not what causes children to be damaged. It is not because they belong to disadvantaged classes. I have worked with children who belong to the upperest of the upper classes and become child prostitutes. Of the 36 children with whom I worked for my book *The Invisible Children*, at least two-thirds were middle class children—and virtually every one of those children could have killed. Child psychiatrists will tell you that all of them have on their books children who could kill. This is a problem which goes much further than social class.

In the case of the two children who murdered James Bulger, the police who questioned them were convinced that they had always planned to kill a child that day. I am not convinced and never was. James Bulger was severely sexually abused by these two boys and he was dreadfully tortured before he died. Children do not sexually abuse unless they have been sexually abused. Children also do not cause pain unless they have had pain caused to them. There is a vast difference between the case of Mary Bell and the murder of James Bulger. There is one very strange feature of the case of Mary Bell. There is no doubt that she killed both or one of these children—but she did not hurt them. She had allegedly seen a film in which it was shown how one could kill very quickly and without causing pain, and this is what she did to both those children: they died in seconds, they suffered no pain, and she did not mean to cause pain. Robert Thompson and Jon Venables needed to cause pain.

Robert Thompson and Jon Venables were found guilty and were sentenced to detention. In December 1993 the judge, Judge Morland, recommended that they serve a minimum of eight years. The Lord Chief Justice a few days later recommended that they serve at least ten years. However, in Britain it is not the judge or the Lord Chief Justice who makes the final decision, it is the Home Secretary of the day; and in July 1994 the Home Secretary, having received a petition of 250,000 people organized by James Bulger's parents, decreed that these children would have to remain in detention for a minimum of 15 years. By the time their parole can be considered—which does not mean they will necessarily be released—they will be 26. In twelve years Mary Bell spent seven years in prisons, having spent the first few in a special unit. These children will spend approximately eleven years in prison. We know what happens to young boys in prisons: is this the right way? I am not telling you that I know what the right way is, but I know this is the wrong way.

The Need to Change

It is wrong to treat children as adults and to demand that they comprehend the thought procedures of adults. It is wrong to sit children in a dock for weeks on public exhibition. However talented police interrogators may be, it is wrong that they should question children for days on end about an act, a deed, a crime, without the training or authority for a parallel goal of understanding. It is wrong to use tricks, emotion or a parent to coerce the child to speak, for, however necessary and right it may seem in the essentials of the moment, the child will never forget. Truth must emerge not through the pressure of, or the longing for, love or approval but out of an inner need. The admission of guilt and the relief of remorse are only given to human beings through self-knowledge, and children—just as human, only smaller—have exactly the same needs as adults.

In a modern state at the end of the twentieth century it should be impossible for social services to remain unaware of crises in crisis families. It should be impossible for children who behave conspicuously

23

in school not to be noticed and attended to. It should be considered outrageous that either men or women caring for children on their own as single parents are not provided unstintingly with human and financial assistance. In both the extreme cases which I have talked about, all the relationships which normally nourish children's lives were limited, faulty or had broken down—and this applies to virtually every case of a child who kills or becomes totally asocial.

Ultimately the only people who can help us towards complete understanding, and thereby allow us to come much closer to achieving means of prevention, are the children themselves. It is only if, with their help, we learn to understand the impulses which preceded their acts that we may at some point in a more enlightened future manage to eliminate the circumstances which, in Britain alone, 27 times in the last two centuries have driven children to kill children.

Gitta Sereny is a journalist and author. Her books include 'The Case of Mary Bell', first published by Eyre Methuen 1972 and reissued in 1995—with a new preface and an appendix on the murder of James Bulger—by Pimlico.

CHAPTER 3

Sadistic and Violent Acts by Children and Young People

Dr. Susan Bailey

Where do we come from? Who are we? Where are we going? (Gaugin's triptych)

Surveys of the general population show that over 90 per cent of boys admit to acts that could have led to appearance in court. However, most are minor in their nature. Delinquent acts by young children are less frequent, more likely to be associated with psychological abnormalities that are persistent and reflect both social dysfunction and individual psychopathology. However, the rate of grave offences committed by children and young adolescents, in particular juvenile homicide, has not risen to any significant extent (McNally, 1995). Nonetheless sadistic violent acts carried out by children and adolescents bring with them a surfeit of public and media interest and reaction—a response that at times risks becoming a voyeuristic end in itself.

Thomas Hobbes in the *Leviathan* (1651) described the human condition in its natural state as 'solitary, poor, nasty, brutish and short'. Interpersonal violence spans a wide range of human behaviours, at its extreme violence ending in death seeming to represent one of the terminal disruptions in the equilibrium of any society.

Kraft-Ebbing (1886) suggested that 'mastering and processing an absolutely defenceless human object is the key element of sadism'. Since Brittain's classic paper 'The Sadistic Murderer' (1970) there has been a growing professional awareness of the extent of sadistic and aggressive behaviour in normal populations and a growing understanding of adult sadists especially of those already detained in maximum secure health settings. MacCulloch *et al* (1983) argued cogently that it is precisely the wish to control that is the primary motivating force in sadism, defining it as the 'repeated practice of behaviour and fantasy which is characterised by a wish to control another person by domination, denigration or inflicting pain for the purpose of producing mental pleasure and sexual arousal'. The range of controlling behaviour forms a continuum from subtle verbal control through graduations of psychological control to physical interventions ultimately rendering the victim unconscious or dead.

The debate continues as to whether it is the genetic alphabet rather than cultural differences that are the key determinants in the evolution, pattern and act of violence. Whatever the balance, it remains a fact that policies that follow from social explanation will require money and political will as any underlying risk status, however it has arisen, is ultimately expressed in the social context.

Perspectives

The media
It can be argued that individual case reports by journalists can and do inform as in Patrick Wilson's review of 'Children who Kill' (1973), but most individual case reporting only serves to escalate society's ever pervasive fear of crime at the hands of the young. Such fear without apparent hope of safe resolution then serves to increase the groundswell of negative feelings towards the non-offending majority of children and adolescents, some of whom through the very developmental process of adolescence already perceive themselves as alienated from the rest of society.

Body and mind
In the eighteenth and nineteenth centuries physiognomy and phrenology were tools used to study violent sadistic young criminals, examining death masks of murderers' heads in an attempt to explain criminal acts (Attick, 1970). In the 1960s researchers sought to link the commission of violent acts to chromosomal abnormalities, in particular XYY syndrome. Over the last 30 years authors (Bender, 1959; Lewis, Pincus and Bard, 1988) have delineated a range of neurological abnormalities in children and adolescents who have made serious fatal, non-fatal and sexual assaults on others evidenced by findings of organic brain damage, history of head injury, abnormal EEGs, past and present seizure disorder, deficits on neuropsychological testing, and soft neurological features—findings echoed in a UK series of juvenile homicides (Bailey, 1996).

Homicidal children and adolescents often fulfil the criteria for conduct disorder (Myers and Kemph, 1992) with associated learning difficulties and language delay (Hays *et al*, 1978). Psychotic disorder in juvenile homicide is unusual but paranoid ideation not uncommon (Cornell, Benedek, 1987). Substance abuse, in particular alcohol abuse and latterly drug abuse, is common and becoming an increasingly significant trigger in serious acts of violence by adolescents (Labelle *et al*, 1991).

Psychological theories and explanation of violent and sadistic acts in the young are substantially more common than those based on physical characteristics. The three main frameworks—psychodynamic, behavioural and a humanistic existential perspective—although widely divergent in their theoretical origins, share common threads and strands. Each points to a final common pathway of abnormal behaviour that arises from the child or young person's maladaptive attempt, whether consciously or unconsciously, to deal with their own ultimate sense of personal failure.

Psychodynamic explanations of child and adolescent aggression (Glover, 1960; Bender and Curran, 1940; Satten, Meninger and Rosen, 1960; Easson and Steinhilber, 1961) have related the violent act to a powerful sense of unconscious guilt. McCarthy (1978) postulated that such young people are not merely lacking impulse control, acting out Oedipal guilt or expressing poorly controlled rage. They are characterised by a vengeful narcissistic rage, expressed through violent acts as attacks on a poorly integrated self object, deprivation and rejection by early objects providing the framework for the narcissistic disturbance. In tracing the growth of healthy narcissism and regulation of self-esteem Kohut (1972) stressed the importance of the parent's availability for the self-enhancing mirroring process.

In violent sadistic youngsters, later parenting styles serve only to perpetuate their narcissistic vulnerability and feelings of shame and inadequacy. The violent act enables and comes to represent not only an expression of immediate rage but a defensive response to lowered self-esteem and an attempt at repair of the self. Miller and Looney (1974) delineate not just loss of control but the young persons' tendency to dehumanise their victims allowing a pathological projection of an unacceptable part of the self on to the then victim. Narcissistic rage invokes not only a need for revenge but a compulsion to pursue it, developed through the sadistic fantasy. The violent act, loss of control and sadistic fantasies serve to restore omnipotence to the young person in an attempt at reparation of the self. The important implication for successful interventions with such children and adolescents is the need for a dual focus not only on the evocation of the individual's rage but, if a safe resolution is to be achieved, on the presence of the underlying narcissistic disturbance.

Attachment

Bolwby (1953) clearly recognised prolonged separation from the mother during the first years of life as a primary cause of delinquent character formation. Insecure attachment is more deserving of attention in the specific areas of child and adolescent sadistic violence. Chronically inconsistent or rejecting parental behaviour leaves the child in a constant state of uncertainty about both the physical and emotional availability of the parent, leading to the experience of frequent and intense anger. Over time the relationship model has as its core anger and insecurity, leaving the child at heightened risk of aggression. Entering adolescence they view themselves as less competent and, critically, less in control, seeking control through domination and via deviant fantasy. In contrast competent adolescents are able to seek autonomy that both meets their own needs and respects the needs of others.

Sociocultural

Contributory socio-cultural factors (Walsh Brennan, 1974) have included severe physical abuse (Lewis *et al*, 1985), sexual abuse (Ressler, Burgess, Douglas, 1988), exposure to repetitive or extreme violence (Pfeffer, 1980), parental mental illness (Hellsen and Katila, 1965) and gang participation (Busch, 1990). More recently increasing concern has centred, particularly in the United States, on the availability of weapons especially guns (AACAP, 1991) and both in the United States (Heath, 1986) and United Kingdom (Bailey 1993, Newson 1994) on the quantity and level of response of children to media violence.

It has been argued that the analysis of patterns of violence within a given society at any one point in time provides a unique method of demonstrating many of the characteristics of that society (Buchanan, 1977). Critically the sociological literature has analysed the victims themselves through the concept of precipitation and victim participation (Mendelsohn, 1963).

Profiling and Clinicians

In the United States and more recently in the United Kingdom, criminal profiling has become an integral part of the criminal investigation of grave crimes. Willmer (1970) described the perpetrator as an emitter of signals during the commission of a violent act. Such criminal profilers and investigators have joined with mental health professionals (Ressler *et al*, 1980) using their combined knowledge to enhance the descriptive knowledge of both abused and abuser and to develop the cognitive behavioural strategies used in the treatment of the traumatised now to help in turn the young violent sadist to work through his or her own cycle of past trauma and current violence (Burgess and Holmstrom, 1974; Hollins, 1990).

Each perspective groups individuals into categories and subsequent taxonomic schemes helping in the understanding of human violence in order to clarify treatment methods that can eliminate high risk behaviour. Changing established violent and sadistic behaviour in the young has to move beyond changing obvious developmental factors in their background. Success and safe resolution must involve changing the way the young person has grown to think.

Lessons from Adulthood

In a survey of forensic psychiatrists (Spitzer *et al*, 1991), 90 per cent (87) of the cases reaching diagnostic criteria for sadistic personality disorder had childhoods characterised by a history of emotional abuse, one or both parental figures being repeatedly hostile, demeaning or neglecting. 76 per cent (74) had been physically abused, multiple incidents resulting in bruises or permanent injury, and 52 per cent (48) had experienced multiple losses, death or abandonment by parental figures, the latter consistent with the psychoanalytic view of the importance of object loss in the development of the disorder. Forty-one per cent (30) had been sexually abused. The key criteria for diagnosis were the use of physical violence/cruelty to achieve dominance over another, humiliation of people in the presence of others, harsh treatment of those under their care, pleasure in the act of psychological or physical harm to animals or humans, lying to cause pain, control of others through fear, restriction of autonomy of those in a close relationship and a fascination with violence, injury and torture.

Ressler, Burgess and Douglas (1988) in their description of 36 adult sadistic murderers identified the following most consistently reported internal factors reported over the three developmental periods of childhood, adolescence and early adulthood: day dreaming, compulsive masturbation, social isolation and poor body image. Most consistent external behaviours over the same developmental periods were lying, rebelliousness, stealing, cruelty to children and assaults on adults.

MacCulloch *et al* (1983) teased out the following core features from both their own special hospital series of sadistic murderers and Brittain's original series. Developmentally these men had had ambivalent relationships with their mother, authoritarian punitive fathers but additionally were themselves socially alienated from others. Their personality development was one of introspection, solitariness and obsessionality, rarely displaying actual violence but dwelling on hidden themes of aggression. They grew to feel sexually inferior to other men and had developed a substitute rich and deviant fantasy life. Few were described as psychotic but noticeably they displayed increased anxiety and depression as a resistance to increasingly violent, sadistic and murderous drives. Critically the grave offence often followed an episode that had led to lowered self-esteem, the planning of the criminal act making them able to feel superior, the actual crime bringing with it a sense of feeling better with normal behaviour after the act.

The adult literature points to antecedent history in late childhood and early adolescence of behavioural try-outs for a final violent sadistic act. Often, because not overtly sadistic or violent, the significance of apparently trivial components of stealing had been overlooked e.g. conduct disordered youngsters engaged in burglaries retaining keys and photographs, using these as a focus for developing sadistic fantasies. Failing to make such connections, the thinking patterns and early fantasies of these youngsters had not been explored with later grave consequences. Liebert (1985) has pointed out the resistance among both criminal investigators and clinicians to uncovering the sexual basis for grave acts committed by young people, particularly when conventional evidence for a sexual motivation may be lacking at the scene of the crime.

In a series of child and adolescent murderers (Bailey, 1994) it became apparent that a third had been sexually abused. Males described uncertainty about emerging sexuality and identity, negative experiences of sexual experimentation with age similar peers and inappropriate sexual experience with older females and males. In a third of cases there was both a sexual and sadistic motivation to the offence but, more importantly, undetected and previous `offence' behaviour of a violent, sadistic and sexual nature. In a series of 121 sex offenders (Dolan, Holloway and Bailey, in press), a third had used physical violence or threats (Wassermann, Kappel, 1985; Fehrenbach, 1986). Their sexual offences were not isolated incidents involving normally developing adolescents and many had a previous record of similar or less serious offences. The psychiatric interview of young sex offenders in the case of non-contact as well as contact type offences should always include an enquiry into the presence of rape fantasies and other concurrent violent behaviours in addition to the paraphilias.

The Evolution and Role of Fantasy

Fantasy has its origins in day dreaming, defined by Singer (1966) as any cognitive activity representing a shift of attention away from a task. The fantasy itself is characterised as an elaborate thought with great preoccupation and anchored in emotion. The young person may be aware of images, feelings and internal dialogue, and the fantasy provides a normal way for the child or young person to obtain and maintain control of an imagined situation. Rate of fantasy development and frequency differ considerably and may either substitute or, critically, for some prepare for action (Beres, 1961). How many young people activate sadistic fantasy and in what context remains uncertain (Crepault and Couture, 1980). Once a fantasy builds to a point where inner stress is unbearable, action may follow (Schiesinger and Revitch, 1980). Early expression of fantasy development is clearly seen in children's play, and in adolescence thinking patterns emerge from and are influenced by earlier life experiences. As a child matures, his or her use of language increases with the fantasy which is usually both positive and seems to promote the child's learning through repetitive thinking and rehearsal of actions.

In violent and sadistic children particularly in the latency period, they start to demonstrate repetitive acting out of the core aggressive fantasy, persistent themes emerging in their own play or in play with others. Secondary attempts at mastery and control over others appear in set situations when the repetition can often become a direct expression of an original assault either against or witnessed by the younger child. A high degree of egocentricity evolves in both fantasy and play and gradually other children, family and significant adults merge to become extensions of the child's inner world.

Adult sadists often report an absence of positive fantasies in their early life, whether never present or lost in very early negative experiences is unclear, but what emerges is the overwhelming importance of the secret reality of the fantasies to the individual in adolescence. The early aggressive behaviours serve to displace anger on to the victim but clinically, as fantasies elaborate, the displaced aggression, whether still in play or against an individual, occurs with diminishing fear or anxiety about adult disapproval. Each subsequent act serves to allow increasingly intense emotions to be incorporated into their imaginations, in turn allowing the intensity of violent thoughts to escalate.

During adolescence the nature of the first sexual experience which is followed by orgasm may be crucial in determining sexual deviation and the sexual component to subsequent sadistic acts. Early general difficulties in social relationships are epitomised after puberty by an inability to make any sort of appropriate approach to their preferred sex. In contrast through the pattern of fantasy in which the young person controls their inner world he or she becomes the success they would like to be but are unable to control in the real world. Fantasy of successful control and domination of the world becomes the key which unlocks the increasing probability of its own recurrence by the relief which it gives from a previous sense of failure. The stage is thus set for the violent sadistic act.

A key issue emerging from our own work with 40 child and adolescent murderers and 121 child and adolescent sex offenders centres on long-standing cumulative risk factors reaching a crescendo as they enter the physical stage of puberty. Critically over a short period of weeks their social interactions prior to the sadistic act deteriorate, when issues of trust, emerging patterns of verbal and physical aggression, feelings of hostility and paranoid reactions towards peers and adults reach a climax. Even when the child has gained a sense of power and pleasure from organised behavioural try-outs accompanied by sadistic fantasies, they still at the eleventh hour expect an adult intervention positive or negative to occur. If the cues presented to the outside world of both adults and peers goes unheeded, their rage explodes on to a fragile victim in a chaotic, disorganised sadistic act.

Intervention

As a clinician I will leave to others the debate on the rights and wrongs of how young people are currently dealt with by the criminal justice system, in their career routes through secure care, young offender institutions and adult custody (Bullock *et al*, 1994; Little, 1990) save to say that attributing all blame and criticism to any one part of the system is an easy but often counter-productive route to follow.

Realistically, therapy with young people who have committed sadistic acts of violence, in particular murder, has to be tailored to the demands of the external environment and has to be approached cautiously. Motivational dynamics are complex and the monitoring of ongoing level of risk critical, especially if the young person remains within the community and with their family. The emergence of a sense of guilt involves appreciation for negative outcomes resulting from an act of omission (often a key agenda where two or more youngsters have been involved in a sadistic act) or commission. A sense of shame is associated with negative feelings on the basis of a self-perception of being unworthy or bad (often a characteristically poorly-defended feelings state the youngster has wrongly held about him/herself for much of their existence). Thus, given the frequent distortion of perception of self and others, the emergence of a true sense of guilt and shame can and often is a slow, difficult, painful and angry process.

Detention itself can provide allowance of time for further neurodevelopmental, cognitive and emotional growth, allowing the adolescent to gain better control of his or her emotional and aggressive impulses. Irrespective of the available, if any, treatment model provided by the care or custody institution, the parallel process of education, vocation, avocation, consistent role models and continued family contact are of critical importance. This parallel process is best facilitated in a milieu characterised by warmth and harmony, with clear organisation, practicality and high expectations allowing for the establishment of positive staff-adolescent, staff-staff and adolescent-adolescent relations (Harris, Cole and Vipond, 1987).

The majority initially dissociate themselves from the reality of their act but gradually experience a similar progression of reactions and feelings akin to a grief reaction (Hambridge, 1990). Their grief is initially about their own loss of freedom and enforced separation from family and, lastly, they grieve about their victim. The effect on the young person's family can be as devastating as the victim's family (Macleod, 1982). Against the inevitable waxing and waning of outside pressure the child has to move safely through the process of disbelief, denial, loss, grief, anger/blame and - now increasingly recognised - post-traumatic stress disorder, arising from the participation in the sadistic act, either directly or observing the action of their partners in the act, or arising from the past personal abuse.

Our own service has found in working with the sadistic children and adolescents referred to us over twelve years, that a combination of cognitive behavioural psychotherapy and non-verbal therapies have most to offer those who have committed sadistic acts. Qualities such as previous frequent and severe aggression, low intelligence and a poor capacity for insight weigh against a positive safe outcome. The clinician has to remain alert to the possibility of emerging formal mental illness, in particular depression (Stewart, Myers and Burnet, 1990).

In understanding the role of violence in the youngster's life, it is necessary to understand the depth of their sensitivity and reaction to a perceived threat, seeing threat and ridicule in many day to day events. A related theme is saving face. As the youngster starts to discuss their murderous act, they have to fact past loss, trauma and abuse, disclosing fears of being vulnerable, that therapy may bring about change they do not like and above all cannot control.

Burgess, Hartman and Hare (1990) described the use of drawing, painting and sculpture with juveniles in accessing memory of sadistic acts allowing further insights into the motivational dynamics. Since 1990 I have been fortunate to be able to work in conjunction with an art therapist (Aulich, 1994) making easier the task of enabling the young people to face the most sadistic elements of their own acts and past abuse, particularly in those cases where the spoken word has become such a painful and destructive reminder of how systems have dealt with them. The drawing series has given a potentially non-invasive way of providing information and critically has allowed the youngsters to make contact with gaps in their own emotional state. Both can then help direct intervention that will diminish rather than escalate future risk.

In our own series of cases a range of motivational dynamics have become apparent—victim provocation, the victim as a physical threat and role reversal of victim and offender with often gross size distortion. Victim and offender will often merge and the drawings show a remarkable variation in use of detail and colour, some critically showing clear attribution of blame and emotional expression.

The exposing of the distortions via non-verbal images can represent the first therapeutic effort to separate out causal constraints, that another person is the cause, from being responsible for one's own rage. This can help the young person come to terms with their own behaviour and their sense of needing to seek revenge on vulnerable people.

Addressing victim empathy, saying sorry, reattributing blame does lead to expression of anger and distress within sessions often sexualised in both form and content. When the emotion this engenders spills outside sessions, it leads to disruptive behaviour within the institution. This is both difficult for the child and carers and can in turn lead to becoming both collusively rejecting and dismissive of the therapists. However, disclosure and understanding is essential if safe resolution is to be achieved. In the stage of investment the youngster can assume far more responsibility for the content of sessions, honesty is enhanced, acting out diminishes and, critically, the youngster starts consciously to link their sadistic behaviour to conflict, loss and trauma in the past whilst coping with their feelings in the present.

Conclusion

Kazdin (1995) in a review of conduct disorder points to the multiple opportunities to reduce influences that can contribute to violence, in particular social practices that permit, may facilitate or tacitly condone violence and aggression. No one influence accounts for or causes violence. If a risk factor model is adapted with respect to policy, practice and research, it will help to order what can at times become professionals' rhetoric rather than action, to understand and then act upon influences that may have a small impact (e.g. the debate re the effect of media violence on children) but can still have great importance in terms of ultimate social outcome.

34

Multiple influences may combine to increase the likelihood of violent outcome or may, as importantly, interact to influence outcome. The purpose of reducing risk factors in any group of potentially violent and sadistic children and adolescents is not to remove the problem in its entirety but to ensure a positive palpable impact. The expressed fear is that such action on the one hand requires infinite unavailable manpower and funding resources and that, on the other hand, interventions required may clash with the rights of the individual or more likely the perception and interpretation of such rights. The real risk is that in the cut and thrust of the debate, our energy to carry out the day to day work with violent, sadistic or even troubled and troublesome youth is diminished.

If I am to listen to the opinion of another person it must be expressed positively. Of things problematical, I have enough in myself (Goethe).

Dr Susan Bailey is consultant adolescent forensic psychiatrist at the Gardener Unit, Manchester

REFERENCES

American Academy of Child and Adolescent Psychiatry, Committee on Rights and Legal Matters. *Position Statement on Firearm Safety* (1991). Summer AACAP Newsletter.

Attick, R.D. (1970), *Victorian Studies in Scarlet*. New York: W.W.Norton

Aulich, L. (1994). *Fear and Loathing; Art Therapy. Sex Offenders and Gender in Art Therapy with Offenders* (Fd. Liebman, M). Jessica Kingsley. London.

Bailey, S.M. (1996). 'Adolescents Who Murder'. *Journal of Adolescence* 19, 19-39.

Bailey, S.M. (1993). *Criminal Justice Matters* 6-7.

Bailey, S. (1994). 'Critical Pathways of Child and Adolescent Murderers'. *Chronicle of the International Association of Juvenile and Family Court Magistrates,* 1(3), 5-12.

Bender, L. (1959). 'Children and Adolescents who have Killed'. *American Journal of Psychiatry* 116: 510-513.

Bender, L., Curran, F.J. (1940). 'Children and Adolescents who Kill'. *Criminal Psychopathology:* 297-322.

Beres, D. (1961). 'Perception, Imagination and Reality'. *International Journal of Psychoanalysis* 41: 327-334.

Bowlby, J. (1953). *Child Care and the Growth of Love*. London: Hogarth.

Brittain, R.P. (1970). 'The Sadistic Murderer'. *Medicine, Science and the Law,* 10, 198-207.

Bullock, R., Little, M., Millham, S. (1994). *The Part Played by Career, Individual Circumstance and Treatment Interventions in the Outcomes of Leavers from Youth Treatment Centres.* Dartington Social Research Unit.

Burgess, A.W., Hartman, C., Howe, J.C.W. (1990). *Journal of Psychosocial Nursing.* Vol 28, No 1, 26-35.

Busch, K.G., Zagar, R., Hughes, J.R., Arbut, J., Bussell,R.E. 'Adolescents who Kill' (1990). *Journal of Clinical Psychology* 46: 472-84.

Cornell, D.G., Benedek, E.P., Benedek, B.A. (1987). 'Juvenile Homicide: prior adjustment and a proposed typology'. *American Journal of Orthopsychiatry* 57: 383-93.

Crepault, C., Couture, M. (1980). 'Men's Erotic Fantasies'. *Archives of Sexual Behaviour.* 9: 565-81.

Dolan, M., Holloway, J., Bailey, S. 'Psychosocial Characteristics of a Series of 121 Child and Adolescent Sex Offenders'. In press. *Medicine, Science and the Law.*

Easson, M.B., Steinhilber (1961). 'Murderous Aggression by Children and Adolescents'. *Arch. Gen. Psychiatry* 4: 27-35.

Glover, E. (1960). *The Roots of Crime.* New York International Universities Press.

Hambridge, J.A. (1990). 'The Grief Process in those Admitted to Regional Secure Units following Homicide'. *Journal of Forensic Sciences* 35, 5, 1149-1154.

Harris, D.P., Cole, J.E., Vipond, E.M. (1987). 'Residential Treatment of Disturbed Delinquents. Description of Centre and Identification of Therapeutic Factors'. *Canadian Journal of Psychiatry* 32: 579-583.

Hayes, J.R., Solway, K.S., Schreiner, D (1978). 'Intellectual Characteristics of Juvenile Murderers versus Status Offenders'. *Psychol Rep* 43: 80-2.

Heath, L. 'Effects of Media Violence on Children' (1986). *Arch General Psychiatry,* Vol 46.

Hellsten, P., Katila, O. (1965). 'Murder and Other Homicide by Children under Fifteen in Finland'. *Psychiatr Q Suppl.* 39: 54-74.

Hollin, C.R., (1990). *Cognitive Behavioural Intervention with Young Offenders.* New York. Pergamon Press.

Kazdin, A.E. (1995). *Conduct Disorders in Childhood and Adolescence.* 2nd Edition. Sage publications. London.

Kohut, H (1972). 'Thoughts on Narcissism and Narcissistic Rage'. *Psychoanal Study Child* 27: 360-399.

Kraft-Ebbing, R. (1986). *The Psychopathia Sexualis.* Revised Edition (1959). London: Panther.

Labelle, A., Bradford, J.M., Bourget, D., Jones, B., Carmichael, M. (1991). 'Adolescent Murderers'. *Canadian Journal of Psychiatry,* Vol 36. 583-587.

Lewis, D.O., Moy, E., Jackson, L.D., Aaronson, R., Restifo, N., Sena, S., Simos, A. (1985). 'Biopsychological Characteristics of Children who later Murder. A Prospective Study'. *American Journal of Psychiatry* 142: 1161-1167.

Lewis, D.O., Pincus, J.H., Bard, B. (1988). 'Neuropsychiatric, Psychoeducational and Family Characteristics of 14 Juveniles

Condemned to Death in the United States'. *American Journal of Psychiatry.* 145: 584-9.

Liebert, J.A. (1985). 'Contributions of Psychiatric Consultation in the Investigation of Serial Murder'. *Interpersonal Journal of Offender Therapy and Comparative Criminology* 29: 187-200.

Little, M. (1990). *Young Men in Prison,* Dartmouth, Aldershot.

MacCulloch, M.J., Snowden P.R., Wood, P.J.W., Mills, H.E. (1983). 'Sadistic Fantasy, Sadistic Behaviour and Offending'. *British Journal of Psychiatry* 143, 20-29.

Macleod, R.J. (1982). 'A Child is Charged with Homicide. His Family Responds'. *British Journal of Psychiatry.* 141, 199-201.

McCarthy, J.B. (1978). 'Narcissism and the Self in Homicidal Adolescents'. *American Journal of Psychoanalysis* 38: 19-29.

McNally, R.B. (1995). 'Homicidal Youth in England and Wales 1982-1992: Profile and Policy'. *Psychology, Crime and Law,* 1, 333-342.

Miller, O., Looney, J. (1974). 'The Prediction of Adolescent Homicide: Episodic Dyscontrol and Dehumanisation'. *American Journal of Psychoanalysis* 34: 187-98. Myers, W.C., Kemph, J.P. (1990). 'DSM-III-R Classification of Homicidal Youth—help or hindrance?' *Journal of Clinical Psychiatry* 5: 239-42.

Newson, E. (1994). 'Video Violence and the Protection of Children'. Vol 16: 4, 190-5.

Pfeffer, C.R. (1980). 'Psychiatric Hospital Treatment of Assaultative Homicidal Children'. *American Journal of Psychotherapy* 34: 197-207.

Ressler, R.K., Burgess, A.W., Douglas, J.E. (1988). *Sexual Homicide Patterns and Motives.* New York. Lexington Books.

Satten, J., Menninger, K.A., Rosen, I. (1960). 'Murder without Apparent Motive: A study in personality disorganisation'. *American Journal of Psychiatry* 117: 48-53.

Schlesinger, L.B., Revitch, E (1980). 'The Criminal Fantasy Technique. A Comparison of Sex Offenders and Substance Abusers'. *Journal of Clinical Psychology* 37: 210-218.

Singer, J.L. (1966). *Day Dreaming.* New York: Random House

Spitzer, R.L., Feister, S., Gray, M., Pfohl, B. (1991). 'Results of a Survey of Forensic Psychiatrists on the Validity of the Sadistic Personality Disorder Diagnosis'. *American Journal of Psychiatry* 148:7, 875-879.

Stewart, J.T., Myers, W.C., Burket, R.C. (1990). 'A Review of One Pharmacotherapy of Aggression in Children and Adolescents'. *Journal of American Academic Child and Adolescent Psychiatry* 29: 269-277.

Walsh-Brennan, K.S. (1974). 'Psychopathology of Homicidal Children'. *R.Soc. Health - Journal.* Vol 94(6) 274-277.

Wilson, P. (1973). *Children Who Kill.* London: Michael Joseph.

CHAPTER 4

The Sleep of Legal Reason

Allan Levy QC

The spectacularly awful death of two year old James Bulger, for which two ten year olds were held responsible, brought fully into the public domain the whole question of how the legal system in England and Wales should deal with such a case.[1] Immense media coverage brought the topic into almost every home in the land. The media also, of course, from time to time reminds us that it is not only an English or British problem.

Two examples will suffice. In November 1993, in a Paris suburb three boys, aged eight, nine and ten years respectively, regularly played with a group of tramps on a stretch of waste ground near their homes south-east of Paris. Two of the tramps had a fight after their shelter burned down. One of the men was knocked to the ground. Spurred on by the other tramp, the three boys then punched and kicked the man on the ground and hit him with sticks, and killed him.

Once they realised that he was dead they stripped him naked and dumped his body in a shallow well and covered it with wooden planks. The boys were soon caught and accused by the local examining magistrate of the equivalent of manslaughter. The magistrate concluded apparently that the second tramp was largely to blame for the first man's death. As the boys were under 13, the age of criminal responsibility in France, the case against them did not proceed. They were, as I understand it, put by the examining magistrate into the care of social workers and ultimately two of the boys returned home and one remained in council care.

The predominant reaction of the commentators in the French media, comparing the matter with the Bulger case, was not to demand more severe treatment of the French boys, but to question the wisdom of submitting Jon Venables and Robert Thompson to a full blown criminal trial. In addition it has been said that the consensus among dozens of French experts who commented on the Bulger case was that the punishment of the British boys was less humane than that offered by the French system, and that it was a response to society's need for vengeance. At least one interesting comment by a leading French child psychiatrist was noted in the English media: he said that the French

38

system tended too far in the other direction from the British one: 'It is dangerous to make such crime ordinary. The child no longer knows what is good and what is evil.'

The other example of a case is from the United States of America. It was reported in the media in November 1995 that a judge in Chicago found two boys of eleven and twelve guilty of killing a five year old boy by dropping him from the fourteenth floor window of a Chicago building because he had got them into trouble at school after refusing to steal lollipops for them. The boys, who were aged 10 and 11 respectively when the crime was committed, were sentenced to at least five years in state custody. Originally placed in a detention centre run by social services, they were then transferred to a juvenile penitentiary because they were said to be 'unrepentant' and 'dangerous to others'.

The Bulger case triggered, and continues to provoke, a wide-ranging debate about the nature of our legal system here and how it deals with children who kill. Inevitably many began to ask about how other countries deal with the problems that arise. It was not really surprising to learn that not a great deal of information about other systems was available in this country.

Fundamental Questions

I have referred in the title to the 'sleep of legal reason'. It reflects, of course, a reaction to the criminal justice system in this country and in particular to the way it dealt with the Bulger case. The case raises fundamental questions: should, for example, the children be subject to the *criminal* justice process at all? Should the age of criminal responsibility be raised from ten years in England,[2] a level which is significantly out of line with many other countries? It is necessary to refer to England because, of course, the age in Scotland is eight years.

I should make clear that I am not advocating that nothing should be done in respect of a child who kills. We could have in place a civil as opposed to a criminal process which could, after an appropriate finding in relation to the child, enable a court to decide on the correct course to be followed.[3] The options would include detention (in e.g. secure accommodation) or other restriction of liberty where the risk factor necessitated it. Rehabilitation and prevention should unhesitatingly replace any ethos of retribution.

Trial

Should children under 14, for instance, be subject to the full panoply of an English criminal trial in a Crown Court in public, at the mercy, in many senses, of the media? Are they capable of understanding the adversarial process, of giving detailed and necessary instructions to their lawyers, both solicitors and barristers? Can they properly participate with any sense of understanding in the decisions in respect of whether to give or call evidence? The trial of ten to fourteen year olds in the adult criminal courts may well be described as unedifying, unnecessary and unacceptable.

As to sentence, should there be a mandatory one—detention during Her Majesty's pleasure—for children and young persons between the ages of ten and 18 under the present system? The sentence was introduced in the Children Act 1908 which abolished the death penalty for children. The Act itself was a significant reforming statute. The government introduced the measure as being one to 'rescue' and not punish children, 'to shut the prison door and open the door of hope.' The same sentence was re-enacted in 1933 and 1965 and on both occasions it was made clear during the course of the respective Bills through Parliament that the sentence of detention during Her Majesty's pleasure was not to be confused with the sentence of life imprisonment imposed on adult murderers.

Individualisation should be the key factor. This is reflected in a number of international conventions.[4] Discretion giving freedom of action is surely crucial. The present sentence, which it can be argued was originally intended to be primarily rehabilitative and preventive, has been viewed by the government in the last decade as equivalent to the mandatory life sentence imposed on adults. It is argued that there is a complete discretion. This is said to include a right to detain beyond the tariff and the preventive period, if release is deemed unacceptable to the public—a new and vague concept.

I have referred to the trial and disposal aspects. The prior investigation and interrogation phases of the criminal process are also important. They are the subject of analysis and comment elsewhere in the later papers by Mike Grewcock and Mark Ashford.

Childhood Denied

One of the themes common to many aspects of our youth justice system is that of 'childhood denied'. This is in stark terms the treatment of children as if they were adults. It can be demonstrated in four areas.

40

First, the trial of children who are alleged to have killed takes place in the adult criminal courts.[5] The basis for it is, in a legal context, inconsistent. The fact of childhood, being under 18 and having the incomplete development of a child, is recognised in many areas of the law, particularly the civil aspects. In the criminal law recognition of childhood is essentially reflected in the doctrine *doli incapax* being applied between the ages of ten and 14. The prosecution has to prove in a criminal case not only that the allegation is made out, but also that the child knew what was being done was seriously wrong. No concession, however, is made in the mode of trial.

The doctrine of *doli incapax* provides the second example. Recently in a startling judgment the Divisional Court purported to abolish it.[6] A key element in their reasoning was that it was out of line with the general law—in other words, why should children have this special consideration? Fortunately, the House of Lords fairly promptly reversed the decision,[7] although the basis of their reasoning was that the lower court should not behave as if it were Parliament and usurp the function of changing such a fundamental principle.

The third indicator is the proposed building and running of secure training centres. These are children's prisons for twelve to fourteen year olds.[8] Their existence will flout international law and also by analogy the principles introduced in the much heralded Children Act of 1989. It is interesting that when the government, having ratified the United Nations Convention on the Rights of the Child,[9] had to report progress to the UN Committee in Geneva recently, the Committee was not only severely critical of secure training centres, but also commented strongly on indeterminate sentences for children and young people.[10]

Fourthly, the plight of the child witnesses in criminal cases has to be considered.[11] This is an issue separate from the general topic under consideration. An allusion to it, however, is not irrelevant because it is another clear example of treating children as if they were adults with the unfortunate consequences that follow.

Age of Criminal Responsibility

It is necessary to return to the age of criminal responsibility because it is central to the question of how allegations of killing by children are dealt with. There has been growing discussion over the age and the fact that in England, Wales and Northern Ireland it is ten years and in Scotland eight, both significantly lower ages than in many other countries. The trend in other countries has been to raise the age: in Canada from seven to twelve; in Israel from nine to thirteen; in Norway from 14 to 15; in Cuba from twelve to sixteen; and in Romania from 14 to 18. In France the age is thirteen; in Germany, Austria, Italy and many of the eastern European countries it is 14; in Scandinavian countries it is 15; in Spain, Portugal and Poland it is 16; and in Belgium and Luxembourg it is 18.

The Children and Young Persons Act 1969[12] set the minimum age for prosecution in England and Wales at 14. This did not, however, include homicide although the intention was probably to encompass it eventually. The provision was never implemented and has been repealed by the Criminal Justice Act 1991. The then Labour government's reasoning was that children up to 14 should be taken out of the criminal justice system, and where appropriate be made subject to care and control. In the international context, the United Nations Committee on the Rights of the Child, which has considerable authority in that the Convention has been ratified by over 170 countries, has pointed out that the age of twelve is certainly too low. When replying to the recent report of the United Kingdom, the Committee proposed that serious consideration should be given to raising the age throughout the United Kingdom. [13]

The official commentary to the United Nations Standard Minimum Rules for the Administration of Juvenile Justice—the Beijing Rules[14]— notes the wide differences in the age of criminal responsibility and observes:

> The modern approach would be to consider whether a child can live up to the moral and psychological components of criminal responsibility; that is whether a child, by virtue of his or her individual discernment and understanding, can be held responsible for essentially anti-social behaviour. If the age of criminal responsibility is fixed too low or if there is no lower age limit at all, the notion of responsibility would become meaningless. In general, there is a close relationship between the notion of responsibility in delinquent or criminal behaviour and other social rights and responsibilities (such as marital status, civil majority etc.).

The conclusions of the Report of the Gulbenkian Commission on Children and Violence, published recently, are also very relevant:[15]

> We have emphasised that acts of criminal violence are by definition acts of individual choice. Children who act violently, like those who act violently to children, are immediately 'responsible' for their actions. If we wish to move as we do towards a society in which everyone takes responsibility for reducing violence, it is not helpful to cloud or confuse the issue of individual responsibility. But the general acceptance of the concept of individual responsibility for violence does not mean that juvenile offenders should be tried as adults. The process must be one that they can understand and respect. Nor does it mean that once regarded as responsible, young

people should face retribution. It is for these reasons that the Commission proposes raising the age of criminal responsibility.

The recommendation of the Commission is to raise it to at least 14 throughout the United Kingdom in the light of United Nations instruments and European experience.

Generally, there are two different approaches across Europe to determine the appropriate age of criminal responsibility. It may be decided on the basis of capacity to form the necessary intent or to know that what is being done is criminally wrong. Alternatively, as a matter of policy, it may be decided that, irrespective of individual capacity, children below a certain age should not be prosecuted in the criminal courts.

Treatment

What is the appropriate treatment for children who commit homicide or other serious crimes? Contradictions in the law in this country have already been noted. In particular, while recognising that children need special protection, the tendency is to sacrifice that in favour of trial as an adult when serious crimes are being considered. Similarly, in respect of the present disposal in the courts of children who kill, there are unhappy features. The recent emphasis on retribution and punishment is a disquieting feature which clearly breaches international obligations voluntarily undertaken by the government.

Some of the issues that have to be grappled with are:

(i) what are the principles and procedures which should be the foundation for sentencing?
(ii) what is the purpose of detention? and
(iii) what are the appropriate criteria and procedures for deciding upon release?

At present in the United Kingdom children face an indeterminate sentence if convicted of murder—detention at Her Majesty's pleasure. [16] Surely it is better to build into the system complete or extensive discretion which can cater for the particular facts of the homicide and the individual characteristics of the child or young person. The purpose would be rehabilitative and preventive and any question of a minimum term would be dealt with on a case by case basis. There should be reviews annually subject to, in an appropriate case, a short non-review period. The Home Secretary should not have any role. It should be a judicial process and not be, or be at risk of being seen as, a political

43

exercise. There could, for instance, be a multi-disciplinary review body acting judicially.

Ultimately, it is for those in the legislature to awake and enact the reasoned legislation that is urgently required.

Allan Levy QC is a specialist in child law; a practising barrister, author and broadcaster; and a member of the Council of Justice and of the Medico-Legal Society.

ENDNOTES

1. *R v Thompson and Venables,* Preston Crown Court, 1-24 November 1993
2. Originally at common law it was seven; in 1933 it was raised to eight and in 1963 to ten
3. e.g. an amended form of care proceedings under the Children Act 1989
4. e.g. UN Convention on the Rights of the Child, Article 40
5. The Crown Court
6. *C v DPP* [1994] 3 WLR 888, DC
7. *C v DPP* [1995] 2 WLR 383, HL
8. See Criminal Justice and Public Order Act 1994, sections 1 to 15; Schedules 1 and 2
9. Treaty Series No 44 of 1992 (Cm 1976)
10. See Concluding Observations of the Committee, January 1995; CRC/C/15/Add. 34, page 7
11. See e.g. *Report of the Advisory Group on Video Evidence* ('Pigot Committee'), Home Office, 1989; 'Witness to Cruelty', A Levy QC, *The Guardian,* 26 April 1994
12. Section 4
13. See endnote 10 *ante*
14. 1985, para. 4.1
15. *Children and Violence,* Report of the Gulbenkian Foundation Commission, 1995, page 176
16. Section 53 (1), Children and Young Persons Act 1933.

CHAPTER 5

Some Issues for the Statutory Agencies

Dr Norman Tutt

Having been a Director of Social Services and having also worked in the Department of Health, I have been involved both in the placement of children who have killed and in the wider considerations involved.

To set the context, we have to understand two things. First, children are more likely to be victims of homicide than to be offenders. Secondly, children who kill are not a clearly defined, different and discrete group. There is a whole range of reasons why people—children or not—kill. This is exemplified by looking at just four cases in which I have been directly involved. One was a young man of 15 who committed a burglary with his own father and, in the process of the burglary, they killed a 70 year old occupant of the house. They ran what is called a 'cut-throat defence' in that one said 'He did it' and the other said 'He did it.' In the end the court found them both guilty of murder.

The second case was a 15-year-old who had been in care for a number of years and behaved like a likeable rogue. He had a long history of minor, petty offences but was a quite intelligent lad. He was walking with his girlfriend when somebody passed some comments that he did not like. He went home, got a bread-knife, came back and stabbed the victim through the heart.

The third case (the Maxwell Confait case) was of three juveniles who were charged with arson and, after the remains of the building were examined, a body was found in it. They were all charged with murder. The fourth case was of two juveniles aged 14 and 15 who were charged with a very serious rape and the woman ultimately died from the injuries she sustained.

I defy anyone to find a common thread in those four cases. There is no simple, homogenous reason why children kill: there are a whole range of very different reasons, and that is one of the problems when we come to look at how best we can help those children.

Children as Homicide Victims

If we look at the age of homicide victims in this country, some very telling figures emerge.

Offences currently recorded as homicide by age of victim: England and Wales 1992

Age range	Number per million population
Under 1	46
1 - 4	9
5 - 15	3
16 - 29	16
30 - 49	17
50 - 69	9
70+	7
All ages	12

In 1992 the number of victims of homicide per million of the population in England and Wales was about 12. By far the highest incidence of homicide victims occurs for children under one year old: 46 children of this age per million are likely to be victims of homicide. The next largest group is young males, reflecting an entirely different issue—the tendency of young men to fight, kill and maim each other in certain circumstances.

It is also important to note the relationship between the suspect and the victim:

Relationship of suspect to victim, in recorded cases of homicide, 1991

Age of victim	1-4	5-15	16-18
Daughter or son	35	10	1
Other known	8	8	19
Stranger	0	13	16
TOTAL	**42**	**31**	**36**

If we look at the homicides where the victim was under the age of 18, we can see that a high proportion were the son or daughter of the person who committed the murder. Parents are more likely to kill their children than children are likely to kill their parents—not

46

surprisingly because children are smaller, weaker and have less opportunity to kill than the parent, who is bigger, tougher, stronger and has the means to do it.

The figures show that the older the victim, the more likely they are to be murdered by a stranger. There is no great mystery about this. It reflects the different levels of dependency as people grow older. Very young children are very dependent, they are confined to their home, and the person who is most likely to kill them is the person who is confined to that home with them. By the time you are 16 to 18, you are out on the streets and often exposed to enormous dangers, particularly if you do not come from a stable family background.

Children Who Kill: The Statistics

Turning specifically to children who kill, there several offences which can involve children killing another person. Although the offences vary, the outcome is that somebody has died. These offences include murder, manslaughter, infanticide, causing death by dangerous (formerly reckless) driving, and causing death by aggravated vehicle taking.

There are therefore a number of ways in which young people may kill another person. In each of these instances there are clear needs which that the young person has, and which the law has to deal with in relation to that young person. The table (reproduced at the end of this chapter) shows that at least some young people who caused the death of another person received a police caution and did not even get to court, as the police and the Crown Prosecution Service decided that they could be dealt with in other ways. One can surmise that one was a young woman of between 14 and 16 who killed her illegitimate child, and everyone thought it reasonable that she be dealt with in a therapeutic way. The other was a young man who caused death while driving a stolen vehicle. He received a police caution; but I would argue that he would also need a great deal of help because his adjustment to the fact that he has killed somebody is just as important as for someone who is charged with manslaughter and processed through the courts. You can see that the range of children who kill is very wide, and we need to think more widely around the subject than just concentrating on one or two spectacular cases.

Moving on to murder cases specifically, the numbers are very small but show very wide variations. In answer to a Parliamentary question on 20 December 1994, the Home Office Minister David

47

Maclean MP gave the following figures for the number of people under the age of 18 sentenced under section 53(1) Children and Young Persons Act 1933—i.e. they had committed murder:

Year	s53(1)	Year	s53(1)
1974	7	1984	22
1975	6	1985	18
1976	7	1986	16
1977	10	1987	19
1978	9	1988	22
1979	26	1989	15
1980	20	1990	10
1981	15	1991	12
1982	30	1992	11
1983	16	1993	24

The figure rose from seven in 1982 to 22 in 1984; but it then fell back to 15 in 1989 and eleven in 1992; then in 1993 it went up to 24. So over a 20 year period the number went from seven to 24 with very wide variations in between. For example, between 1981 to 1982 there was a 100 per cent increase in the number of murders committed by young people, from 15 to 30; but the next year the number went back down to 16. So we are looking at a very individualised form of behaviour which seems to be separate from major social trends. Overall trends in juvenile crime are much clearer year on year; but here we see very wild annual fluctuations. Because it is such a small problem, inevitably the figures shoot up and down, affected by only a few cases in a year.

In contrast, if we look at the number of young people sentenced under section 53(2) of the 1933 Act, which covers a much wider range of offences including manslaughter, arson and robbery— offences which if committed by an adult would carry a maximum penalty of 14 years' imprisonment or more—there is a much more consistent overall trend, which seems to be upwards.

Year	s53(2)	Year	s53(2)
1974	20	1984	99
1975	14	1985	154
1976	43	1986	156
1977	45	1987	154
1978	56	1988	177
1979	53	1989	114
1980	65	1990	125
1981	73	1991	102
1982	84	1992	93
1983	69	1993	315

Four Key Considerations

Children who commit murder go through the same processes as any other young offender *except* when they go to court. They have been arrested by the police, interrogated by the police and remanded to the local authority. There are four considerations which immediately leap to your mind as a Director of Social Services when you get that dreaded phone call from one of your staff who says 'The police have just arrested a boy and they think he's committed a murder.' First: how do I, as the person statutorily responsible, ensure the child's welfare in this situation? Something which the press seems never to have understood is that we have in this country a separation of powers in which different people in different roles have different responsibilities. The police clearly have a responsibility to interrogate and charge the young person; the Director of Social Services' statutory responsibility is to regard the child's welfare as paramount and to ensure their welfare. That will immediately create difficulties, conflicts and tensions because you have to say: 'Is this child's welfare best served by being left in a police cell while the police carry out investigations? What sort of body samples might the police wish to take which I might consider to be contrary to his or her welfare?'

The second consideration is: what should I be doing at this stage to ensure the protection of the public? Curiously enough in my experience, when dealing with children who murder, the protection of the public is not a major issue because I do not really believe that these children are going to go out and immediately commit another murder. The child's placement is not crucial to the protection of the public. However, it would be very unwise for any public official to say that, because you would be berated as ignoring the protection of the public. I think most people have therefore found themselves washed along, with the protection of the public subsuming the child's welfare.

The third consideration is: what are the national political consequences of this event? In the cases discussed by Gitta Sereny (see Chapter 2) there were major national consequences. People have talked about these cases as somehow symbolically showing the state of decay we have reached in Britain. They have talked about the Liverpool case in huge grandiose terms: television programmes have discussed whether it is symbolic of the moral decline of the Western world. More overtly party political issues also arise. If you are working in a local authority run by a different political party from central government, you are very conscious of that, and that not only are you going to be criticised widely in the local press, which you might live with, but questions will be asked in Parliament about why this was allowed to happen.

Fourth, there are a range of local political issues, by which I mean pressures from the local community. In one of the cases in which I was involved, a case of causing death by dangerous driving where a boy of 14 from a local estate had run down and killed two university lecturers, the boy had in my view to be protected from the local community because of the uproar and agitation this created.

Pre-Trial Processes

The local authority will probably be required to provide an 'appropriate adult' to sit in with the police while they interrogate the young person, possibly even if the parents are there as well. This person may become heavily involved in a case. As a Director you have to think: 'Who are the best people in my department to sit in with the police, who will be accepted by the police but who will if necessary challenge the police if they believe that the child's welfare is not being best met?'

There is then the issue of legal representation. At what point should I, as somebody responsible for the child's welfare, decide that this is now best served if they have a solicitor who goes in and says to the child: 'Say nothing more, because you have a right to silence'? Are the child's best interests served by saying to him or her: 'Go on, you tell the police what they want to know'? They may well not be.

You then have to make a remand placement, to keep the child where the police may still want frequent access to him or her. We always worked on the assumption that we should get the child out of police cells as soon as possible, because a young person is probably not best helped by being in police cells; but where do you place them so that the police can have access and take evidence?

You then have to prepare the other children in the placement to which the young person who has committed the offence is going to go. We have children living in local authority residential care who may suddenly find themselves sharing that facility with a child who is facing a charge of murder. What does that tell those young people about themselves? There is therefore a whole set of issues about preparing the children in the placement.

You may also have concerns about other children in the family. Some of the children who commit these offences have clearly been subject to abuse in their own families, and you may be setting up a separate investigation in relation to the other children. Alternatively, you may find yourself having to relocate the family because of the local pressure: in one instance we had to offer the family and children alternative accommodation and move them out to a secret address because the local hostility was so great.

You must then have a review of the files. Organizations go back to the files and say: 'Do we know this case? Does the health service know this case? Does education know this case?' And you suddenly find with horror that you have all known the case for some time. You have to examine what you have done to these children in the past and whether or not it was effective. Last but not least, you have to set up some way of dealing with the huge media response with which you are going to be faced.

The child or young person will probably be remanded for several months in local authority care before they actually come to court. There is a range of issues that need to be considered before a court appearance. First, is the child or young person going to make a guilty or not guilty plea? This is critical because if a young person is exercising the right to make a not guilty plea, then the form of assessment you can carry out will be very limited. In the Maxwell Confait case, three young men who were charged with the murder of Maxwell Confait always denied that they had done it. They admitted the arson of the house but said that they had broken in, found a dead body in the house and then fired the house. However, they were found guilty of murder and served a number of years. Throughout these years, one young man in particular denied murder, and I have on file report after report from psychiatrists who said: 'We will not be able to treat this boy until he admits his offence.' In the end the Court of Appeal decided that he had not committed the offence. Now you can see the dangers here. If the young person is pleading not guilty, it is very tempting to start talking to them about the offence and almost persuading them that they must be guilty and that, if only they told you that they were guilty, then you would be able to assist.

There is a huge halo effect over assessments. If you know that the young person is charged with murder, that event is so overwhelming that you relate all your evidence towards it, regardless of whether there is any connection or not. In the commentaries in the media about the case in Liverpool, people ranged widely about what they thought had caused this. They would say: 'There has been unemployment and economic decline in Liverpool for a long time. What can you expect?' People often put up explanations which have no causal link to the event. The challenge in any assessment is to try to explain 'Why did this take place on this occasion?' It has to be borne in mind that the purpose of the assessment is a court hearing and treatment must await the hearing: we cannot start treating somebody for their offence if they have not yet been found guilty of that offence.

The Trial Process

There are some critical issues in relation to the trial process. First, there is the preparation of the child. What is reasonable preparation of the child for the event of going to court? Do you take the child to see the court, explain to them who is in the court, what people will be saying and what their roles are? This is very difficult: how do you prepare a child for the fact that they are going to sit in a court for many days on end, not understanding what is going on, and then say to them: 'But the decision of the court will affect you for the rest of your life.'

Preparation of the staff is extremely important as well because they will be going backwards and forwards with the child. By this time they will probably have been in contact with the child for up to a year. They will have a set of relationships with the child. They have to live with the fact that if the child is found guilty, even if by this time they might be convinced that he or she is not guilty, that is not their concern.

There is a further issue of what we regard as appropriate behaviour. One of the things that fascinated me about the Liverpool case was the way in which the media constantly criticised the boys' behaviour in court whatever they did. One minute they would fidget about, just like 10 or 11 year olds in a long, boring session—but this was seen as a clear sign of the fact that they took it all very easily. If the boys cried, then it was not seen as remorse: some other feeling was attributed to them. It was very difficult to see how these two young people ought to behave in court in order that they would not get a very negative image of them built up.

Another area is the preparation of the family. How do you prepare the family for the court and trial process, for the enormous exposure of their own failings that might arise during that process, and for the horror to which they will have to adjust, that it was their child that did these dreadful things to somebody else?

What do you do about the preparation of children in care with whom the children going to court have lived with for some time and may or may not be returning to live with them. Those children all have access to the news media. Imagine yourself in a small unit of probably eight or 10 children, you are watching the six o'clock news that is telling you about these two demons who have committed a dreadful offence, and they walk through the door and come in for their tea at your table. Somehow that has to be coped with in the establishment.

And how do you prepare for the enormous invasion by the media that I believe is now totally out of control? The way in which we have to respond to the demands of the media becomes quite unrealistic for departments that have an incident like this perhaps once every ten years. Suddenly you have this huge demand for interviews and formal responses and you have staff being offered large amounts of money to reveal information about the child: all of this has somehow to be coped with.

I have tried to discuss the complexities which children who kill pose for statutory agencies.

Dr. Norman Tutt is Executive Director of Social Information Systems. He was Chair of the Justice working party on Children and Homicide

Offenders by age group and sex, cautioned, prosecuted and convicted for offences resulting in death of the victim 1992

Offence		Cautioned		Prosecuted		Convicted	
		10-13	14-16	10-13	14-16	10-13	14-16
Murder	M	-	-	-	13	-	2
	F	-	-	-	5	-	2
Manslaughter	M	-	-	2	4	-	3
	F	-	-	1	-	1	1
Infanticide	M	-	-	-	-	-	-
	F	-	1	-	-	-	-
Causing death by reckless driving	M	-	-	1	2	-	5
	F	-	-	-	-	-	-
Causing death by aggravated vehicle taking	M	-	1	-	4	-	4
	F	-	-	-	1	-	1
TOTAL		-	2	4	29	1	18

CHAPTER 6

A System Which Neglects the Child

Mike Grewcock

Many thousands of words have been written about the killing of James Bulger and the awful prospect that such an offence could be committed by two ten year old boys. However, even amongst the more serious media commentaries, little has been said about the response of the criminal justice system to such events in England and Wales, and even less about the wider implications for criminal justice policy.[1]

This is a system which fails the accused. It places a child as young as ten in an adversarial framework designed for adults, and judges that child essentially by the same standards. The principles of protection and care underpinning the Children Act 1989 and the UN Convention on the Rights of the Child operate in inverse proportion to the seriousness of the offence. This increases the potential for miscarriages of justice and militates against addressing the welfare needs of the accused until an unacceptably late stage.

Here, I want to examine how the system operates from the point of arrest until the actual trial. This part of the process can take months and is primarily focused on obtaining evidence against the accused. Meanwhile, an accused child will probably be separated from his or her parents and isolated in a secure unit or a prison service establishment.

The General Framework

The age of criminal responsibility in England and Wales in ten. No child under this age can be arrested or detained. This minimum is very low by international standards. Of the 36 Council of Europe countries, only seven—Cyprus, Ireland, Liechtenstein, Malta, Switzerland and Northern Ireland—are lower. Countries with comparable social and economic conditions and legal and political institutions typically set the minimum limit at 15 or 16.[2]

However, some special protections do exist for children and young people aged ten to 17. The doctrine of *doli incapax* requires that when an accused is aged ten but under 14, the prosecution must show that the child understood that what he or she did was seriously wrong as opposed to naughty or mischievous.[3] The practical implications of this are discussed below.

The Criminal Justice Act 1991 renamed the juvenile court the youth court and included all children and young people aged 10 to 17 within its jurisdiction, although during the police investigation of an offence and for the purposes of bail 17 year-olds are regarded as adults.[4]

Most cases against 10 to 17 year olds are dealt with by police cautioning or closed youth court hearings. The main exception, which includes children charged with homicide offences, is the procedure for those charged with an offence which is likely to attract a sentence of long term detention under section 53 of the Children and Young Persons Act 1933.

Section 53(1) applies to a person aged ten to 17 charged with murder. Section 53(2) applies to offences (including manslaughter) for which an adult could receive a maximum sentence of 14 years or more; an offence of indecent assault under section 14 of the Sexual Offences Act 1956; and causing death by dangerous driving or causing death by careless driving while under the influence of drink or drugs (contrary to the Road Traffic Act 1988).

A charge for which a section 53 sentence is a possibility will be heard on indictment before an adult Crown Court and jury. The doctrine of *doli incapax* applies but otherwise the procedures are the same as those for an adult. The gravity of the charge therefore exposes a potentially vulnerable and damaged child to a set of procedures with which many adults find it difficult to cope.

The Investigation of the Offence

The police are responsible for the investigation of an offence within the guidelines largely determined by the Police and Criminal Evidence Act 1984 (PACE) and its associated Codes of Practice. Strictly speaking, the police are responsible for gathering evidence and laying the initial charge, whereas the Crown Prosecution Service undertakes the prosecution following an independent assessment of the evidence.

However, many defence solicitors share the view of McConville *et al* that despite the presumption of innocence that operates as 'the golden thread of English law', the nature and aim of the police investigation is the construction of the prosecution case.[5] Ed Cape comments that a police interview, '. . . rather than being an investigation to establish the truth . . . is a mechanism for justifying and helping to prove that the police's belief that the suspect is guilty is correct'.[6]

56

From the point of arrest, a child suspected of an offence as serious as murder can expect to be placed in a potentially hostile and bewildering environment, cut off from the outside world, with the central focus from authority being placed on the incidents leading to the death rather than background causes.

Limits to Detention

Under section 41 of PACE, an arrested person can be detained without charge for a maximum of 24 hours. This can be extended to 36 hours by a police superintendent or to 96 hours by a magistrates' court if the person is under arrest for a serious arrestable offence (which obviously includes homicides).

While a child is in police detention, PACE Code C para. 8.8 stipulates that she or he shall not be placed in a police cell unless no other secure accommodation is available and the custody officer (who is responsible for the child's welfare while in detention) considers that it is not practical to supervise the child if she or he is not placed in a cell or the custody officer considers that a cell provides more comfortable accommodation than other secure accommodation in the police station. The child may not be placed in a cell with a detained adult. The reason for placing a juvenile in a cell must be recorded (para. 8.12). In practice, a child detained for several hours will normally be keep in a police cell.

Free Legal Advice and the Appropriate Adult

Once detained in a police station, the child has the right to free legal advice (section 58 PACE). This is provided either by a solicitor of choice or an independent duty solicitor.

If the child is under 17, an appropriate adult must be present prior to the commencement of an interview. The police must take such steps as are practicable to identify and notify the person or authority responsible for the child's welfare (section 57 PACE). If that individual is unable to attend the police station, a social worker or another responsible adult aged 18 or over who is not a police officer nor employed by the police must be present.

The function of the appropriate adult is not clearly defined for all steps of the investigation, and tensions between the solicitor and the adult can sometimes arise. PACE Code C, para 11.16, states:

Where the appropriate adult is present at an interview, he shall be informed that he is not expected to act simply as an observer; and also that the purposes of his presence are, first, to advise the person being questioned and to observe whether or not the interview is being conducted properly and fairly, and secondly, to facilitate communication with the person being interviewed.

This guidance could be interpreted to mean that the parent encourages the child to 'own up' or explain the full story even if this would clearly be against the child's interests as a defendant. When the charge is as serious as murder, the legal and emotional stakes can be high for both child and parent. Clear legal advice is required for both the child and the parent before the interview starts.

The Police Interview

A police interview room is an intimidating environment. Normally, it is small with a door resembling a bank vault. In addition to at least one police officer (probably two or more), the child is in the company of the appropriate adult and possibly a solicitor. The seating arrangements and the procedures connected with the taping of interviews add an air of unfamiliar formality.

The interview in the police station is probably the single most important feature of the police investigation. Admissions made during the course of interviews are often the only compelling evidence against an accused. The recent miscarriage of justice cases illustrate the extent to which false confessions can be the basis for wrongful conviction.

There must be a serious doubt whether a child aged ten (who may be even more immature intellectually) understands the consequences of a false confession or the distinction between precise and limited admissions and an explanation based partly on fact and partly on information the child thinks the adults present (police and parents) want to hear.

The risk that children will make unnecessary and damaging confessions has been increased by recent changes to the law regarding the right to silence. This is a common law right sitting hand in hand with the notion that a defendant is innocent until proven guilty and that it is the prosecution's responsibility to prove guilt beyond reasonable doubt.

Under section 34 of the Criminal Justice and Public Order Act 1994, a jury may draw such conclusions as appear proper from the failure of an accused to answer questions during interview. This does not remove the right to silence but does require the solicitor to give considered advice about the advisability of not answering questions. It is arguable that in the absence of other evidence, solicitors should advise clients to remain silent as, without admissions, there is little in the way of a *prima facie* case. If the child is under 14, the doctrine of *doli incapax* should be used to prevent questions being answered as the initial responsibility rests with the prosecution to show that the child understood the 'seriously wrong' nature of the offence.

As a result of the 1994 Act, a new caution was formulated which is read to the accused at the commencement of an interview:

> You do not have to say anything. But it may harm your defence if you do not mention when questioned something which you later rely on in court. Anything you do say may be given in evidence.

Interpreting what this actually means will not be easy until case law provides firm guidance. In the meantime, solicitors must rely on their judgment in giving advice. Whether or not parents, let alone ten year old children, can appreciate this, is open to question. What is certain is that a child suspected of killing someone will be placed under considerable pressure to talk.

The following extracts from Gitta Sereny's account of the investigation into the killing of James Bulger illustrates the tensions that can exist during an interview:

> During the 33 minutes of Jon's second interrogation that day, he had become increasingly distressed, bursting into tears every few moments and beseeching his mother with that repeated "I never touched him" to believe him. And Susan Venables (Jon's mother) tried desperately to help him: "Calm down, first," she said.
>
> "No, I can't, I never touched him . . . we just went home and I . . .I left Robert on his own until he came back to Walton Village."
>
> "Tell me the truth now, please Jon," his mother urged.
>
> "I never killed him, Mum. Mum, we took him and we left him at the canal, that's all (he now admitted for the first time taking James) . . . I never killed him, Mum."
>
> "I believe you," Sue assured him.
>
> "You think I done it," he cried. "I'm telling youse . . . " He starts almost to hyperventilate. "Don't," she tries to quiet him, "we don't, Jon. Come on."

"I want to go home. I've already told youse what I know. Ooh . . . you're going to put me in jail . . . I never Mum," he wails until his "I never, I never" no longer sounds like words but one long cry.

"I know you wouldn't hurt a baby," his mother said . . .

"As they listened to the increasing tension in Jon's voice, they (the investigating officers) knew they had to do something. "By the end of that second session," Tanner (one of the officers) said, "it was clear to us that the boy had a desperate need to confess, and the mother's reassurances were stopping him."

"They had taken Susan Venables to another room and explained to her that she wasn't doing Jon any good by helping him suppress what he was trying to get out." [7]

Jon Venables subsequently made an admission to his parents in his cell in the presence of a police officer. The admission was repeated in interview shortly after. No comment is made here on the role of the solicitor who is noticeably absent from Sereny's account. However, the extract does highlight the highly charged atmosphere brought to the investigation by the age of the accused and the nature of the offence.

The solicitor's role and duty to the defendant remains the same regardless of the client's age or severity of the allegation. PACE Code C, Note 6D, states:

The solicitor's only role in the police station is to protect and advance the legal rights of his client. On occasions this may require the solicitor to give advice which has the effect of his client avoiding giving evidence which strengthens a prosecution case.

Jon Venables could have been advised not to answer any questions and his mother should not have been expected to facilitate a confession. Rather than be subjected to an interrogation, a ten year old child could be more fairly dealt with through a form of investigatory civil proceedings not overshadowed by the prospect of an indefinite prison sentence at Her Majesty's pleasure, and which could also aim to address the often manifest social and behavioural problems of the accused.

The Decision to Charge and Bail

The decision to charge rests with the custody officer (section 37 PACE). For less serious categories of juvenile offending, a formal police caution is a viable option but is virtually inconceivable for murder or manslaughter.[8] In considering whether to caution, the custody officer must take into account the public interest criteria in the Code for Crown Prosecutors discussed below.

Once the charge has been laid, a decision must be reached in relation to bail. Section 38(1) of PACE requires that the custody officer authorises the person's release either with or without bail unless certain conditions apply, including:

- the custody officer has reasonable grounds for believing that the person arrested will fail to appear in court to answer bail;

- in the case of a person arrested for an imprisonable offence, the custody officer has reasonable grounds for believing that the detention of the person arrested is necessary to prevent his committing an offence;

- the custody officer has reasonable grounds for believing that the detention of the person arrested is necessary to prevent him from interfering with the administration of justice or with the investigation of offenders or of a particular offence; or

- the custody officer has reasonable grounds for believing that the detention of the person arrested is necessary for his own protection.

The last condition is probably the most relevant for a child aged ten. It is complemented by section 38(1)(b)(ii) which allows refusal of bail if the custody officer has reasonable grounds for believing that the juvenile ought to be detained in his own interests. This becomes a serious consideration if through media coverage or other means, the identity of the accused becomes known. But in principle, there is no reason why a child charged even with the most serious of offences should not be returned to his or her family or to another safe address.

If police bail is refused, the child must be presented to the youth court as soon as is practicable. This will normally mean by the next morning unless it is a Sunday, Christmas Day or Good Friday. If a child is to be detained overnight, section 38(6) requires that he or she be placed with the local authority unless it is impracticable (e.g. there is a blizzard rather than the local authority are not answering their phone) or, if the child is twelve or more, no secure accommodation is available and keeping him or her in other local authority accommodation would not be enough to protect the public from serious harm from the child.

Remands into Custody

It is extremely unlikely that a child charged with murder or manslaughter would be granted bail by a court. When considering an application for bail, the court is bound by the Bail Act 1976. Section 4(1) creates a presumption in favour of bail but Schedule 1 lists five grounds for the refusal of bail if the accused is charged with an imprisonable offence. Schedule 1, part 1, para. 2 states:

> The defendant need not be granted bail if the court is satisfied that there are substantial grounds for believing that the defendant, if released on bail (whether subject to conditions or not) would —
> (a) fail to surrender to custody, or
> (b) commit an offence while on bail, or
> (c) interfere with witnesses or otherwise obstruct the course of justice, whether in relation to himself or any other person.

Paragraph 9 requires that, when considering these conditions, the court should have regard to the following factors:

(a) the nature and seriousness of the offence and the probable method of dealing with the offender for it;
(b) the character, antecedents, associations and community ties of the accused;
(c) his record of having answered bail in the past; and
(d) the strength of the evidence against him.

Paragraph 3 allows bail to be refused if the court is satisfied that it would protect the accused and, in the case of a juvenile, 'for his own welfare'.

There is no consistent practice for the placement of young people aged ten to 17 who are refused bail, Remands into Prison Service custody are limited to boys who have reached 15 years, and girls aged 17. The Criminal Justice Act 1991 contains provisions for the removal of all 15 and 16 year old remands from prison custody and gives magistrates the power to remand directly into local authority secure care. However, these provision have not yet been implemented which means that a boy aged 15 can be remanded to an adult prison, to a remand centre or to the local authority who may choose to apply to the court for permission to place the boy in secure residential care.[9]

Boys aged ten to 14 and girls aged ten to 16 (inclusive) who are refused bail are remanded to the local authority and placed at the discretion of the local authority. A child charged with an offence likely to attract a section 53 sentence will normally be placed in a secure unit with the permission of the court, although this will not necessarily be within the local authority's own area. If the child is under 14, the Secretary of State for Health must approve an application for secure placement. There are presently 25 secure units in England (one is shortly due to open in Wales) holding children who are in care, on remand or serving section 53 sentences. The units are run by individual local authorities and monitored by the Department of Health according to guidance derived from the Children Act 1989. The ethos of these units is fundamentally more 'child centred' than anything to be found in the prison service.[10]

The Decision to Prosecute

The Crown Prosecution Service is responsible for bringing the prosecution. In deciding whether to do so, it considers both the sufficiency of the evidence and the 'public interest'. The revised Code for Crown Prosecutors, published in June 1994 at a time when the approach of the criminal justice system to young people was becoming more draconian, removed some of the special consideration that the age of the child may have required when making the decision.[11]

Before bringing the prosecution, Crown prosecutors must be satisfied that there is enough evidence to provide a 'realistic prospect of conviction' against each defendant on each charge (Code 5.1). This is an objective test which means that a jury, properly directed in accordance with the law, is more likely than not to convict the defendant as charged (Code 5.2). Crown prosecutors must also be satisfied that the evidence can be used and is reliable (Code 5.3).

If the evidential test is satisfied, the 'public interest' test makes a prosecution for murder or manslaughter almost automatic. Code 6.2 requires that a prosecution will occur in cases of any seriousness unless public interest factors clearly outweigh those tending in favour. Factors in favour of prosecution include:

- a conviction is likely to result in a significant sentence;
- a weapon was used or violence was threatened during the commission of the offence; and
- the victim of the offence was vulnerable, has been put in considerable fear, or suffered personal attack, damage or disturbance (Code 6.4).

Most of the individual factors against prosecution have to be set against the seriousness of the offence (Code 6.5). This is explicit in relation to youth offenders:

Crown Prosecutors must consider the interests of a youth when deciding whether it is in the public interest to prosecute. The stigma of a conviction can cause very serious harm to the prospects of a youth offender or a young adult. Young offenders can sometimes be dealt with without going to court. But Crown Prosecutors should not avoid prosecuting simply because of the defendant's age. The seriousness of the offence or the offender's past behaviour may make prosecution necessary. (Code 6.8).

The Role of the Media

The decision to prosecute does not take place in a vacuum. The perception of 'public interest' is often shaped by the media as part of a broader ideological agenda.

A free media can play an important role in highlighting miscarriages of justice and focusing public attention on the rather closed world of the criminal justice system. However, it can also play a very negative role if it sensationalises the facts of a particular case, gives a false or exaggerated picture of the scale and nature of criminal offending, or unnecessarily intrudes in the lives of victims and defendants.

The courts have powers to prevent the identity of a teenage defendant being disclosed. This is automatic in the youth court although an application must be made by the defendant's counsel in the Crown Court (sections 39 and 49 Children and Young Persons Act 1933). However, there is always the possibility that extensive media coverage prior to trial could prejudice the defendant whether or not his her name has been disclosed. Counsel for the two boys charged with murdering James Bulger unsuccessfully applied to stay the proceedings prior to their trial on the grounds that media coverage had prejudiced their position. Two hundred and forty-nine newspaper extracts were presented to the court.

The most worrying aspect of the media response to the Bulger case is the way it has shaped the subsequent debate on young people and crime. Murders carried out by children are, thankfully, very rare. The last recorded case of a ten year old convicted of murder was in 1748.[13] In 1994, 16 young people aged ten to 17 were convicted of murder and sentenced under section 53(1) of the Children and Young Persons Act 1933.[14] However, the Bulger case has been widely used as a metaphor for promoting an image of violent, out of control young people and for justifying measures against persistent, lower level offenders typically involved in car theft and burglary. The shadow of this case hung over the proposals for secure training centres for twelve to 14 year olds introduced in the Criminal Justice and Public Order Act 1994.[15]

On 3 March 1993, shortly after the then Home Secretary, Kenneth Clarke, proposed the secure training centres, *The Times* cautioned:

> One horrific child murder does not make a crime wave . . . . Even allowing for the fall in the population's total number of children, juvenile crime seems to be on the decrease. According to Home Office research, the number of known male offenders aged ten to 17 has fallen by 32 percent since 1985. Among ten to 13 years olds, the fall is 43 percent . . . .

> If rehabilitation is the aim, evidence suggests that locking up young people is the least useful form of punishment . . . Any suggestion that these new schools might "solve" juvenile crime is misguided . . . .

In strictly legal terms, the issue of secure training centres is not connected to children who kill. The latter are covered by legislation passed in 1933. However, the way in which the media and both the main political parties have mixed the two issues gives further cause to find alternative ways of responding to violent and serious crime by young people.

The Welfare of the Child

Section 44 Children and Young Persons Act 1933 requires every court dealing with a child or young person to have regard for that person's welfare. However, the emphasis on due process which drives the criminal justice system in England and Wales means that this cannot happen in any meaningful way. A child charged with murder cannot have his or her medical, behavioural, educational and social needs addressed until after the trial. To the extent that there is intervention in the period running up to the trial, it is aimed at either discharging the prosecution's burden in relation to *doli incapax* or assisting the preparation of the defence case.

Children who commit violent offences have invariably been the victims of violence and abuse themselves. Recent research published by the Prince's Trust found that 72 per cent of teenagers convicted of such offences had been physically or emotionally abused and 91 percent had suffered abuse or serious loss.[12] This does not minimise the impact of their offending but it is a strong argument for taking a radically different approach to such young people in trouble—an approach which removes them from the criminal justice system.

Mike Grewcock is a solicitor at Moss and Co. and was formerly the Legal Policy Officer at the Howard League for Penal Reform

ENDNOTES

1. Two notable exceptions are Allan Levy, 'The end of childhood', *The Guardian*, 29 November 1994; and Blake Morrison, 'James Bulger's Killers: a child's right to justice in an adult world', *The Independent on Sunday*, 29 May 1994.
2. For a full comparison, refer to Hansard, House of Lords, 27 February 1995, col. WA82.
3. *C (a minor) v Director of Public Prosecutions* [1994] 3 Weekly Law Reports 888 and (1995) 2 Weekly Law Reports 383. See also Howard League for Penal Reform, *Child Offenders: UK and International Practice*, 1995; and Penal Affairs Consortium, *The Doctrine of Doli Incapax*, November 1995.
4. Children and Young Persons Act 1933, ss 31 and 34 as amended by the Criminal Justice Act 1991, Sch.8, para.1(1).
5. McConville M, Sanders A, and Leng R, *The Case for the Prosecution: Police Suspects and the Construction of Criminality*, Routledge, London 1991.
6. Cape E, with Luqmani J, *Defending Suspects at Police Stations*, Legal Action Group, London 1995, p. 206.
7. Gitta Sereny, *The Case of Mary Bell*, Pimlico edition, London 1995, pp. 321-322.
8. Cautions are subject to the revised National Standards on Cautioning in Home Office Circular 18/94.
9. For a full discussion of this issue, see Howard League for Penal Reform, *Banged Up, Beaten Up, Cutting Up*, London 1995; Howard League for Penal Reform, Troubleshooter Report, London 1995; and ACOP and NACRO, *A Crisis in Custody*, London 1995.
10. Howard League, *Banged Up, Beaten Up, Cutting Up*, op.cit, pp.69-95.
11. For a full discussion of these changes, see Ashworth A. and Fionda J. 'Prosecution, Accountability and Public Interest', [1994] *Criminal Law Review* 894.
12. Boswell G., *Violent Victims*, The Prince's Trust, March 1995.
13. Edward Pilkington, 'Killing the age of innocence', *The Guardian*, 30 May 1994.
14. Home Office, Criminal Statistics England and Wales, HMSO, London 1994.
15. See *Secure Training Centres: repeating past failures*, Howard League briefing paper, September 1995.

CHAPTER 7

The Trial Process in England and Wales

Mark Ashford

The law of England and Wales contains two definitions of a 'child'. One is contained in the Children Act 1989, this country's principal piece of welfare and family legislation, which defines a child as anybody under the age of 18 (the age of majority in this country). There is also a very specific criminal justice definition, which is anybody aged between ten and 13. For the purposes of this talk, I will address the whole age range between ten and 17.

In this country the age of criminal responsibility is ten, which is one of the lowest ages in Europe: most other European countries have considerably higher ages of criminal responsibility. We have an ancient presumption that between the ages of ten and 13 the law presumes that a child is incapable of committing a crime, and it is up to the prosecution to convince the court beyond reasonable doubt that the child not only committed the crime but also knew that what they were doing was seriously wrong. This presumption goes under the Latin name *doli incapax* or 'incapable of doing harm'. The presumption was abolished last year for about eight months by the Divisional Court and was reinstated by the House of Lords; and it is now being reviewed by the Government.

The criminal justice system makes virtually no concessions towards the age of the suspected or accused person. In the police station the only specific account that is taken of age is that somebody under the age of 17 must have an 'appropriate adult' present during the interview and during any other procedures which take place at the police station. An appropriate adult can be a parent, a social worker or anybody else who is described as a responsible adult not employed by or connected with the police force. There is no specific training for these people. The requirement for the presence of an appropriate adult is the only safeguard provided especially for children.

There is a philosophy in this country that if you are young there will be efforts made to divert you from the criminal justice system. There is a series of reviews before people are charged by the police. The

Crown Prosecution Service has a code of practice which emphasises the need to consider that criminal prosecution may not be the best way forward and that the public interest would be better served by diversion to another agency, usually social services. In the case of very serious crimes it would be virtually inconceivable for the police or Crown Prosecution Service to consider dropping a prosecution if a child has actually killed somebody. The system would go through to some kind of court proceedings.

The Trial Process

Anyone under the age of 18 who is charged with a crime of homicide must be tried in the Crown Court. We have a two tier system. We have a system of magistrates' courts and, if you are under the age of 18, you would normally be dealt with by a special magistrates' court called the youth court. In a homicide case, however, once the court has determined that there is sufficient evidence for a trial, then you will automatically be sent to the Crown Court for trial, whether you are ten or 17.

Our system is adversarial. For people who come from the Roman law tradition on the continent, it is worth emphasising quite how adversarial it is. In the Middle Ages in this country we had a system of trial by combat. The idea was that God would make the innocent person win. So two people would fight it out with swords and the winner was the innocent one. We have dropped the swords, but we now argue with words, and that adversarial approach affects the whole system

It affects the way the police work. Although the police often claim that in interviews they are looking for the truth, in fact they are trying to construct a case for the prosecution. So you end up with young people faced with the full might of the state against them, not investigating why it happened but collecting evidence for the prosecution.

In court you have a lawyer or lawyers (in a murder case you would almost always have two lawyers for the prosecution) who are there to put the prosecution case forward—not to put forward information that might help the young person but to prosecute and to put forward information adverse to them. Then you have one or two lawyers representing the child who have to put forward material that is favourable to the defendant. The judge in theory sits there purely as a referee and, with limited exceptions, does not get involved in the presentation of evidence.

There are twelve jury members, who are lay people with no specific training at all who decide issues of fact. The judge makes no decisions of fact but only makes decisions on the law. The judge decides what weapons the lawyers may use in front of the jury. In the jury's absence the judge will decide, for example, if a particular piece of evidence or a particular statement made by the defendant will be heard by the jury. Then the jury decide, on the information which they hear in court, whether the person is innocent or guilty. As with an adult, the burden of proof is beyond reasonable doubt: the jury must be sure of guilt. The basic principle in this country since the Middle Ages is that defendants have the right to have their innocence or guilt determined by their peers, people of their own standing and status. The minimum age of a jury member is 18, so by definition the jury members will not be peers of a child defendant.

The proceedings in the Crown Court are intimidating, for an adult or for a child. The judge will wear a wig and a gown. All the lawyers involved wear gowns and wigs as well, and there will be other people in court as well. It is physically very intimidating. A child defendant in the Crown Court is not usually put in the dock (a special raised box in which a defendant stands): they are allowed to sit in one of the rows of seats and would normally be expected to sit with a parent or social worker.

The press and the general public are allowed into the Crown Court but the judge would normally (and certainly prior to any conviction) make an order that the press are not allowed to report any information which would lead to the identification of any child defendant. However, journalists can still report all the gory details of the case.

There is a very serious concern in our system as to whether the child can understand the proceedings. It is difficult enough in the youth court trying to explain the proceedings to defendants who are 15 or 16, who may have special educational needs or who may be illiterate because they have hardly ever been to school. In the extreme example of the murder of Jamie Bulger, a two year old, by two young people who were ten at the time of the killing and eleven when they came to court and whose names were actually published, there are very real concerns about whether those two children understood what was going on in court.

Several years ago a survey of some 30 juvenile court defendants in Ontario asked them 'who is on your side in court?' Only three mentioned their lawyer. Seven or eight mentioned the judge. In general there was a very worrying lack of communication between the defendants and their lawyers and an almost total incomprehension of what was going on in court. If that was true of a specialist court for young people, what on earth is it like in the Crown Court which makes virtually no concessions to the age of the defendant?

The only concession is the *doli incapax* presumption that someone between the ages of ten and 13 can only be convicted if it is proved beyond reasonable doubt that they knew what they were doing was seriously wrong. In the case of Jon Venables and Robert Thompson (defendants in the Jamie Bulger case), that was largely proved by the calling of psychiatrists and child psychologists. There were three called for the prosecution and two called for the defence.

The jury has to take a decision on the facts. They have to decide whether there was a killing, whether the defendant caused the killing, whether the defendant intended to kill and, if not, whether there was some level of culpability in relation to the killing. In general the law starts off from the point of view of an adult: would an adult have realised that his conduct was likely to lead to death? There is a worrying trend throughout our legal system for the law to impose adult standards of understanding and responsibility on children, both in terms of culpability and in terms of defences. For example, in the defence of duress—e.g. 'Yes, I did it but I was forced to do it through fear caused by someone else who threatened to kill or seriously injure me if I didn't do it'—the question of whether it was reasonable to give into the threats largely amounts to whether it would be reasonable for an adult to give into them.

In the youth court, when very young children are forced into committing crimes by older boys but are not threatened with death or serious personal injury, the law says 'Sorry, you're guilty'. It is very difficult in a trial process to argue 'This child did it, but it is unrealistic to tell him that he should have stood up to threats when he is twelve and being threatened by a near-adult adolescent.' I find that a very worrying development.

When the jury makes a decision as to the facts, it has three options. One is to find that the defendant is not guilty, in which case that is the end of the proceedings as far as the criminal law is concerned. In such a case it is quite possible that, although there has been a killing, the child will receive no counselling of any description unless social services are specifically approached and asked to help the child get over the experience. Secondly, the jury might decide that the defendant committed the act but, because of mental disorder, should not be held criminally responsible, in which case the defendant would be diverted to the mental health system. Thirdly, the jury might decide that the defendant committed the act, had the relevant criminal responsibility and (if aged between ten and 13) knew that what he or she was doing was seriously wrong, in which case it would return a verdict of guilty. That is the end of the jury's role in the case: they have no role in the sentencing decision, which is primarily up to the judge.

70

Sentencing

The judge will then often seek psychiatric reports on the defendant and would normally request a pre-sentence report prepared by a social worker or a probation officer which discusses the defendant's background and attitude to the offence, and which makes proposals about the sentence. However, for these very serious offences there is a very limited range of penalties available. If a child or young person is convicted of murder, the judge has absolutely no discretion: the only penalty the judge can impose is detention during Her Majesty's pleasure under section 53 Children and Young Persons Act 1933, which is the children's equivalent of a mandatory life sentence. There are four other offences which could be described as homicide—manslaughter, which is killing which is not premeditated murder; infanticide, in which the law takes account of the particular mental state of a mother who kills her child shortly after childbirth; and two offences of killing people while driving cars—causing death by dangerous driving, and causing death by careless driving while under the influence of drugs or alcohol. Where a defendant aged ten to 17 is found guilty of manslaughter or infanticide, the court can order detention at Her Majesty's pleasure or a determinate sentence of detention under section 53 of the Children and Young Persons Act 1933. In the case of killing while driving a motor car, a custodial sentence can only be imposed if the young person is aged 14 or over at the time of conviction. For any of these offences other than murder, non-custodial sentences are available; but it would be very rare in our system for a Crown Court to consider a non-custodial sentence for homicide.

It is open to children, as well as adults, to appeal against both conviction and sentence from the Crown Court to the Court of Appeal. Here again, there is no concession to the age of the appellant and the same principles would apply as to adults.

Once sentence has been passed, the system becomes more welfare orientated. Anyone sentenced to be detained under section 53 Children and Young Persons Act 1933 is detained as directed by the Home Office. Depending on age, that could be in a young offender institution (a prison for people aged from 15 to 21) or in a secure child care establishment run by a local authority social services department. In the latter case the young person would normally be detained at one of the country's four large secure units which largely deal with children who have been placed there by the criminal justice system: the secure care system also takes young people who are there for care reasons but whose behaviour cannot be controlled anywhere else.

It is also possible, if it is considered that a therapeutic environment is important, to transfer a child or young person sentenced under section 53 to a youth treatment centre run by the Department of Health. There is only one of these left in the country; the other was closed down recently. If the young person is still in the system by the time they reach the age of 21, they will be transferred to an adult prison.

The other issue is how long they will serve. (This was a particular cause of controversy in the Jamie Bulger murder case when Jon Venables and Robert Thompson were given the mandatory sentence of detention during Her Majesty's pleasure.) The trial judge makes a recommendation to the Home Secretary as to the minimum period the child should serve in custody. This period is called the 'tariff' and is the punishment element of the sentence. When this punishment element has been served, the decision as to release is taken on the basis of protection of the public. If the person is still a danger to the public, they will remain in custody and could eventually spend the whole of their life in custody.

In the Bulger case the trial judge recommended that the tariff be set at eight years; the Lord Chief Justice recommended that it should be ten years; but the Home Secretary then fixed the tariff at 15 years, so that those two eleven year olds will spend a minimum of five years in adult prisons. I understand that an application has been made to the European Court of Human Rights arguing that a politician's involvement in deciding how long someone should serve is contrary to the European Convention and that there should be a judicial system involving the trial judge, or the trial judge and the Parole Board.

There are concerns that the system involves far too much political influence. In answer to questions from a pressure group, the Home Office said that they received 26,000 letters regarding the tariff in the case of Jon Venables and Robert Thompson. On further questioning it turned out that most of these were from a particular newspaper which had been running a campaign and had invited its readers to cut out and send in a coupon already addressed to the Home Office, saying that they wanted these two eleven year olds to spend the rest of their lives in custody. It is very worrying that decisions like this about individual's liberty are being determined by ill-informed public opinion.

Mark Ashford is a solicitor with Taylor, Nichol Solicitors, specialising in work with young people and the youth court.

CHAPTER 8

The Scottish System

Andrew Normand

In Scotland children who commit serious crimes, such as murder, are dealt with by a separate Scottish legal system. Scotland's juvenile justice system is separate and distinctive. It is not based exclusively on either a welfare model or a punishment model, but includes elements of both. It is governed principally by two Scottish statutes of the British Parliament, Scotland having no separate legislature of its own. The statues are the Social Work (Scotland) Act 1968, and the Criminal Procedure (Scotland) Act 1975—to be replaced in 1996 by a new consolidation Act, the Criminal Procedure Act 1995. (I shall refer to the Acts subsequently as the '1968 Act' and the '1995 Act'.) The 1968 Act set up the welfare-based system of children's panels and children's hearings which is a unique feature of the Scottish arrangements for dealing with children who offend, or are offended against or otherwise in need of compulsory measures of care. However, in the Scottish system cases involving children alleged to have committed crimes as serious as homicide are normally processed through the criminal justice system by criminal justice agencies (at least until the stage of final disposal), rather than being dealt with by the welfare-based children's hearing system. Such cases are rare.

Definition of 'Children'

What is meant by a 'child' for purposes of proceedings relating to crime in Scotland? Looking first at the upper age limit—in Scotland 'child' is normally defined for such proceedings as a person who has not attained the age of 16 years. (The relevant definition is contained in section 30(1) of the 1968 Act, as amended). It is possible for a person between 16 and 18 to be classified as a child under that Act for purposes of proceedings relating to crime, if that person is the subject of a supervision requirement of a 'children's hearing' under Part III of the 1968 Act or if his case has been referred to a children's hearing under the provisions of Part V of that Act, which deals with absconders and children moving between England and Scotland. Generally, though, 16 and 17 year old offenders in Scotland are not classified as 'children'. Turning to the lower age limit, in Scots law it is conclusively presumed that no child under the age of eight years can be guilty of an offence (1975 Act, sections 170 and 369). Therefore no formal criminal proceedings are competent against a child under eight.

Discovery/Detection and Reporting

The discovery or detection of a child culprit alleged to have committed a serious crime, such as homicide, is likely to be made by the police. (There are eight regional police forces in Scotland.) Under the Scottish system the police do not themselves make decisions about the commencement of formal proceedings against alleged offenders. The normal rule (contained in the Police (Scotland) Act 1967, section 17) is that the police report alleged offenders to the independent public prosecutor—who is known as the Procurator Fiscal—to consider whether criminal proceedings should be instituted. (There is a national public prosecution service in Scotland with 49 local Procurators Fiscal. They are government lawyers, accountable directly to the senior Scottish Law Officer—the Lord Advocate, who is the head of the Scottish prosecution system.)

Special rules apply to the reporting by the police of alleged offenders who are children. In such cases police officers making reports on children to the appropriate prosecutor in terms of section 17(1)(b) of the Police (Scotland) Act 1967 are also required to make a report to the appropriate Reporter to the Children's Panel (section 38(2) of the 1968 Act). The Reporter to the Children's Panel is responsible for 'welfare'-based proceedings in respect of children. (Currently reporters are officials of a regional local government authority, but with effect from 1 April 1996 reporters will become locally-based officers of a national children's reporter service.)

The procedure for the reporting by the police of alleged child offenders is further governed by a direction issued to all Chief Constables in Scotland by the Lord Advocate (in the exercise of the Lord Advocate's power under section 9 of the 1975 Act). The current direction was issued in 1987, after consultation with reporters and Chief Constables. It operates in such a way as to ensure that the great majority of alleged child offenders are reported to reporters for such further action as they consider appropriate as regards the welfare of the child and the child's need for measures of protection. Comparatively few children are now reported to Procurators Fiscal for consideration of prosecution. However, the most important category of alleged child offenders who continue to require to be reported by the police to the Procurator Fiscal for consideration of criminal proceedings is that of children alleged to have committed serious offences. Serious offences are defined in the direction as offences which require to be or are normally prosecuted on indictment in Scotland—that is before a judge and a jury in the two divisions of courts in Scotland in which jury trial proceedings are competent (the High Court or the Sheriff Court). Homicide cases, of course, fall within this category.

Detention and Arrest

The general law relating to detention and arrest in Scotland applies to children as to any other suspected persons. There are, however, certain modifications to the preliminary procedures at this stage. Where a person who has been arrested and is in custody in a police station or other premises, or who has been detained under section 2 Criminal Justice (Scotland) Act 1980 in such a place, appears to a constable to be a child, the constable is obliged to send intimation without delay to his parent or guardian of the fact and place of his custody or detention. (This contrasts with the corresponding procedure for adults, which permits the police to delay intimations of arrest or detention when necessary in the interests of the investigation or the prevention of crime or the apprehension of offenders.) The parent has a right of access to the child, unless there is reasonable cause to suspect that the parent has been involved in the alleged offence—in which case the police may, but are not obliged to, permit him access to the child. Any access may be restricted to the extent necessary for the furtherance of the investigation or the well being of the child. (The relevant provisions are contained in section 3(3) Criminal Justice (Scotland) Act 1980.)

The seriousness of the offence for which the child has been arrested is a factor in determining whether or not the child is further detained or released pending a decision about proceedings. The normal obligation on the police to liberate arrested children is subject to a number of qualifications, one of which relates to the seriousness of the crime. The senior police officer at a police station is bound to liberate an arrested child unless, for example, the charge is of 'homicide or other grave crime' (1975 Act, section 296(1) as amended by Bail etc. (Scotland) Act 1980, section 9(a)). If liberated, the child or his parent may require to provide a written undertaking that the child will attend at any hearing of the charge. Where an arrested child is not liberated he must be detained in a place of safety other than a police station, unless the police officer concerned certifies that such detention is impracticable, or unsafe because of the child's unruly character, or inadvisable because of his state of health or mental or bodily condition. The appropriate certificate must be produced to the court when the child appears there (1975 Act section 196(2)). A 'place of safety' is 'any residential or other establishment provided by a local authority, a police station, or any hospital, surgery or other suitable place, the occupier of which is willing temporarily to receive a child'. (1968 Act section 94(1); 1975 Act, section 462(1)). Where a child is to be detained in a local authority residential establishment, he may not be placed in secure accommodation at that establishment unless the Director of Social Work and the person in charge of the establishment are satisfied that this is in his best interests and that other statutory criteria relating to absconding or danger to self or others apply (Secure Accommodation (Scotland) Regulations 1983, regulation 13(b)).

A child accused of a serious crime such as murder is likely to be detained, rather than being released. If initial criminal proceedings are to be commenced against him, the child must be brought before a judge on the first court day after arrest (section 321(3) of the 1975 Act). If it is decided not to proceed with the charge by criminal prosecution, the child may continue to be detained in a place of safety for up to seven days while the reporter decides whether he wishes to take further action (section 296(3) and (4) of the 1975 Act).

Deciding on Further Action

Let us now turn to consideration of the procedures for deciding what further action is taken in relation to the child alleged to have committed a serious crime such as homicide. The statutory rule is that 'No child shall be prosecuted for any offence except on the instructions of the Lord Advocate . . . ' (section 31(1) of the 1968 Act). This provision has been judicially interpreted as not requiring the authorisation of the Lord Advocate for each individual case in which a child is prosecuted; general instructions are sufficient (*McGuire v Dean* 1973 JC 20). However, the prosecution of *any* case in Scotland involving a *serious* crime requires the ultimate authority of the Lord Advocate or one of his Deputes (known as Crown Counsel).

There are effectively two stages to the process. The first is the decision whether to commence initial criminal proceedings against the child. The second is the decision whether to proceed with the formal trial of the child. The decision to proceed to formal trial does not follow automatically in every case from the decision to commence initial criminal proceedings. These decisions are taken essentially by the prosecuting authorities in serious cases in Scotland. But there is an element of consultation with the welfare-based system.

The decision to commence initial criminal proceedings is taken by the appropriate Procurator Fiscal with the approval of Crown Counsel and after consultation with the appropriate reporter to the children's panel. Procurator Fiscal Service regulations approved by the Lord Advocate direct Procurators Fiscal that no proceedings may be commenced against a child under 13 years of age without the express authority of the Lord Advocate. For children aged 13 and above no proceedings for a serious crime may be undertaken without the instructions of Crown Counsel. In cases where such instructions are given, the procedure involves the appearance of the child in private before a professional legally-qualified judge (sheriff) and the committal of the child either to detention or to be released on bail conditions (1975 Act, sections 20 and 22). No evidence is presented to the judge, simply the petition document setting out in brief terms the details of the crime allegedly committed by the accused child.

The order of the sheriff at the petition hearing also formally authorises the full investigation of the crime and checking of evidence by the Procurator Fiscal. This is thereafter undertaken by the Procurator Fiscal and his staff, with further assistance, if necessary from the police, who are subject to the direction of the Procurator Fiscal in relation to the investigation of crime (Police (Scotland) Act 1967, section 17).

After investigation and preparation of the case, the Procurator Fiscal submits the case papers for Crown Counsel's consideration and instructions as to whether the accused child should be formally indicted for trial before a judge and jury. In a case of murder or culpable homicide the trial would be in the High Court of Justiciary. (Indictment proceedings for less serious crimes may be in the appropriate local Sheriff Court.)

If the accused child is detained in custody or circumstances amounting to custody, the investigation and preparation of the case and decision about continuing formal criminal proceedings by indicting the accused child for trial must be carried out speedily as the indictment must be served no more than 80 days after the sheriff's committal and the trial commenced no more than 110 days after that committal. If the child has been liberated on bail, the trial must be commenced within one year of the child's first appearance before the sheriff (1975 Act, section 101).

The essential elements in decisions about whether criminal prosecutions should be undertaken in Scotland are whether there is sufficient evidence to support such proceedings (which usually means whether there is credible, corroborated evidence that a crime has been committed by an identified person) and whether prosecution is appropriate in the public interest. The policy followed by the public prosecutor in Scotland in dealing with children accused of committing serious crimes takes account of the provisions of the UN Convention on the Rights of the Child that the best interests of the child shall be a primary consideration and that every effort should be made to deal with such cases expeditiously and, where possible, to keep the child at liberty. A direction in regulations governing Procurators Fiscal, issued on the authority of the Lord Advocate, requires the Procurator Fiscal to discuss such cases with the appropriate reporter to the children's panel and to report the reporter's views to Crown Counsel. It is Crown Counsel who make the decision about further proceedings against a child culprit alleged to have committed a serious crime such as murder.

Although there is consultation with reporters, in most cases involving serious crimes—and in almost all homicide cases - the decision is taken to proceed with formal prosecution. Explaining his policy on this in addressing the Association of Children's Reporters at a conference in 1994, Lord Advocate Rodger said: `The best interests of the child are not the sole criterion in the decision which must also take into account such matters as the need for the protection of the public from immediate or likely harm and the possible deterrent effect of prosecution. This effect may derive not simply from a punitive disposal but also from the public examination of the facts in court proceedings which may signal the community's abhorrence of the most serious crimes. In addition one must also remember that victims or their relatives may feel outraged if the perpetrators of a heinous offence are not dealt with openly and formally in the courts of the land.' He went on to mention the Bulger case in England as an extreme example of the kind of thing he had in mind.[1]

Bail and Remand

Children accused of serious offences may be released on bail in accordance with the normal bail provisions in Scottish criminal procedure. However, bail is not normally available in cases of murder (in terms of section 26(1) of the 1975 Act) and is less likely to be granted for other very serious offences. Where a court remands or commits for trial a child who is not liberated on bail, the child is normally not committed to prison but to the local authority in whose area the court sits in order for the local authority to detain the child in a place of safety. It is for the local authority to specify the place of detention, not the court. A child over 14 years of age may be committed to prison if the court certifies that he is of so unruly a character that he cannot safely be committed to the local authority or of so depraved a character that he is not a fit person to be detained in a place of safety. (1975 Act, section 24). A child committed to a local authority for detention in a place of safety may only be placed in secure accommodation in a residential establishment if conditions relating to unruliness, mentioned previously, apply. Procurator Fiscal Service regulations direct that Procurators Fiscal should not seek to have a child certified by the court as unruly without good reason; that consideration must be given to whether such a certification is in the best interests of the child, with reference to article 37(b) of the UN Convention on the Rights of the Child; and that where possible it is always preferable for a child to be committed to a place of safety. Each local authority will have provided the courts and Procurators Fiscal in their area with a list of all the accommodation which they have available for children. Procurators Fiscal are directed that they should consult the local authority officer whose name has been supplied on whether there is secure accommodation available as an alternative to recommending an unruly certificate.

16 and 17 Year Olds

As previously explained, 'children' for purposes of the juvenile justice system in Scotland are essentially those aged under 16. The Scottish prosecution service recognizes that the United Nations Convention on the Rights of the Child applies to persons under the age of 18 years. Procurator Fiscal Service regulations require Procurators Fiscal to bear in mind that the best interests of the child is a primary consideration when dealing with accused persons who are under 18 years of age and in identifying where the public interest lies in any decision made or action taken in respect of such persons. However, while minor offences committed by young offenders aged 16 and 17 may be dealt with by an alternative to prosecution, serious offences committed by young persons of that age are considered suitable for prosecution in the public interest and crimes as serious as murder would invariably be dealt with by formal criminal proceedings. Although there has been some debate in Scotland recently about including 16 and 17 year olds within the jurisdiction of the children's hearing system, proposals for such an extension of that jurisdiction have not suggested any change so far as cases of serious crime are concerned.[2]

Media

As mentioned above, initial court procedure for a serious crime involves appearance in private before a judge. No press are present. The usual practice is for the name of the accused person and the nature of the charge to be provided to the press. But, in the case of an accused person under 16 there is a restriction on revealing the name, address or school, or including any particulars calculated to lead to the identification of any such person in any published or broadcast report of any court proceedings (section 169 of the 1975 Act).

Alternative Procedure

While serious offences committed by children are likely to result in formal criminal proceedings, as outlined above, the prosecuting authorities from time to time decide against formal prosecution and instead refer the case to the reporter to determine whether children's hearing proceedings should be commenced to consider compulsory measures of care. It is exceptional for a case of homicide to be so referred. This was, however, done last year in a culpable homicide case in Glasgow involving three boys aged eleven to 13, alleged to have been responsible for the death of another boy who died as a result of a fire started by the three accused.

Lord Advocate Rodger has stated: 'I should stress that I have no desire whatsoever to propel all serious cases into court, but I do consider that complex issues arise and precisely for that reason I welcome the flexibility which the court may exercise in determining the appropriate approach'.[1] The Lord Advocate was referring there to the availability to the court of welfare-related disposal options and the potential involvement of children's hearings in the sentencing stage of criminal proceedings.

As has been seen, children who commit serious crimes in Scotland, particularly homicide, are likely to be directed into the formal criminal justice process, rather than the children's hearing welfare-based process. The number of such cases is, however, very small. In 1993 one person aged under 16 was accused of an offence recorded as homicide, and there were in total only 147 disposals of children under 16 in criminal proceedings in Scotland—not all of these being for serious crimes.[3] In the ten year period between 1985 and 1994 there were only 43 persons aged under 16 accused in cases recorded as homicide.[4]

Selection of the criminal proceedings route for dealing with cases of serious crimes allegedly committed by children does not totally preclude the involvement of the welfare-based process at a later stage. The children's hearing system may have a role in the eventual disposal of such cases.

As with the pre-hearing stage, the hearing and disposal stage of the process is also governed primarily by two statutes - the Social Work (Scotland) Act 1968 and the Criminal Procedure (Scotland) Act 1975 (this will be replaced in 1996 by the Criminal Procedure (Scotland) Act 1995).[5]

Notification of Prosecution

When a child offender is to be prosecuted, two groups of people must be notified. Firstly, the parent or guardian of the child must be notified and is required to attend court unless the court is satisfied that this is unreasonable (section 39 of the 1975 Act). Secondly, the Chief Constable is required to notify the local authority in whose area the court sits; the authority is then to investigate and present a report to the court concerning the child's circumstances in order to assist the court in dealing with the case (section 40 of the 1975 Act.)

Court Process

A child prosecuted for a homicide offence (murder or culpable homicide) in Scotland will be tried in the High Court of Justiciary before a judge and jury. Judges of the High Court of Justiciary are senior, professional, full-time judges appointed by the Queen on the advice of government ministers. They are responsible for ensuring compliance with the rules of criminal procedure, for deciding any questions of law which arise during the course of a trial, and for imposing sentence. The responsibility for deciding whether the accused person is guilty rests with the jury of 15 lay persons selected at random from a jury list prepared from the electoral register. The age limits for jurors are 18 and 65. High Court judges do not have any special training in dealing with children; nor, of course, do jurors. The standard of proof is 'proof beyond reasonable doubt' and there is a general requirement for corroboration in Scottish criminal cases, without which the evidence is insufficient to allow a conviction.

The law requires arrangements to be made for separating children from adults while waiting at courts (section 38 of the 1975 Act). However, no special arrangements are required to be made in relation to the court room in which a child is tried in the High Court and members of the public and members of the press may be present. The court has a general responsibility in dealing with a child who is brought before it as an offender to have regard to the welfare of the child (section 172 of the 1975 Act). The process is adversarial, with the Crown being represented by Crown Counsel (a Law Officer or one of the Lord Advocate's deputes, known as Advocate Deputes) and the accused being represented by counsel (an advocate or solicitor-advocate), funded by legal aid.

No opening statements are made in Scottish criminal trials which normally commence immediately with the leading of evidence from witnesses. Most evidence is led directly from witnesses, rather than by using documents, including statements. Witnesses are examined, cross-examined, and (if necessary) re-examined. The accused person is entitled to give evidence in his own defence, but not obliged to do so. At the end of the trial if the evidence is sufficient to allow a jury to convict, Crown Counsel and defence counsel address the jury, the judge directs the jury on the relevant law (but normally says relatively little about the facts) and the jury discusses the evidence in private and reaches a verdict. There are three verdicts in Scottish criminal trials—guilty, not guilty, and not proven. Both not guilty and not proven are acquittal verdicts which render the accused person immune from any further prosecution on the charge of which he has been acquitted. A simple majority is sufficient for a conviction (i.e. eight jurors who are satisfied that the accused is guilty).

Press Reporting

The law imposes restrictions on the reporting of proceedings involving persons under 16. No newspaper, radio or television report of any proceedings in a court may reveal the name, address or school, or include any particulars calculated to lead to the identification of any person under the age of 16 concerned in the proceedings. This includes the person against or in respect of whom the proceedings are taken. No picture may be published of any such person in a context relevant to the proceedings (1975 Act, section 169). That restriction is subject to the qualification that the court may direct that the requirements of the statutory provision shall be dispensed with to such extent as the court may specify, if the court is satisfied that it is in the public interest so to do. This happened in a recent Glasgow case involving a 14 year old girl convicted along with a number of youths of murder in a case relating to concerted attacks on homosexuals in a city park. The restriction was lifted apparently because of public concern about the circumstances of the case.

Disposal

Where a child is convicted of murder, the sentence is a mandatory custodial sentence. Any person under the age of 18 who is convicted of murder must be sentenced to be detained without limit of time and shall be liable to be detained in such place and under such conditions as the Secretary of State of Scotland may direct (1975 Act, section 205(2)). The precise number of children so sentenced in recent years is not clear from published homicide and criminal proceedings statistics, but so far as I can ascertain there have probably only been four or five cases of children being convicted of murder in the past five years or so, with most of the accused being aged 15. Release from custody in due course in such cases in a matter for the Secretary of State, on the recommendation of the Parole Board. Such release is on licence.

At the disposal stage in proceedings for a serious crime, other than murder but including culpable homicide, the court in Scotland may make use of welfare-related disposal arrangements and in some circumstances must do so. The children's hearing system may have a role in providing advice or in taking over responsibility for final disposal of the child. If a child, who is not already subject to a supervision requirement imposed by a children's hearing, pleads guilty or is found guilty of a serious offence, the court may refer him to the reporter to the relevant children's panel to arrange for the disposal of the case by a children's hearing (under section 173 of the 1975 Act), unless the sentence is fixed by law, i.e. in the case of murder. Alternatively, the court may request a reporter to arrange a hearing for the purpose of obtaining their advice as to the treatment of the child. If remitted for advice only, the child is returned to the court for sentence, but the court may after considering the advice remit the child back to the hearing for disposal.

Where a child is already the subject of a supervision requirement, the High Court of Justiciary may remit the case to the children's hearing for advice, but is not obliged to do so. In cases of a slightly lower level of seriousness prosecuted before a jury in the Sheriff Court, the Sheriff must remit the case if the child is under supervision. After receiving such advice the court may dispose of the case itself or remit the case to the reporter for disposal by a hearing. Thirty-three of the 147 children with a charge proved against them in criminal proceedings in Scotland in 1993 were dealt with in this way. ('Criminal Proceedings in Scottish Courts, 1993').

Disposals which are adopted for adult offenders may also be used for children convicted of serious offences. A child may, for example, be dealt with by absolute discharge, admonition, probation order, community service order or fine. Alternatively, where the court is of the opinion that a child convicted on indictment (i.e. of a serious crime) cannot appropriately be dealt with by any other method, it may sentence him to be detained for a specified period and the child is liable to be detained in such place and on such conditions as the Secretary of State may direct (1975 Act, section 206). Scottish homicide statistics record five sentences of detention of a child for culpable homicide in the 19 year period 1985-94.

It has been held that detention 'without limit of time' is a competent sentence in terms of the requirement that the sentence must be for a specified period. That decision was reached in a 1990 Glasgow case in which a boy of 12 was convicted of the culpable homicide of a three-year-old child, the original charge for trial having been murder (*RJK v HMA* 1991 SCCR 703). The convicted child was found to have assaulted the three year old boy by seizing hold of him by the head and neck, struggling with him, striking his head repeatedly against stones in a burn (stream) and thereafter leaving him, whereby he drowned. The trial judge was held to be correct in deciding that the most appropriate course was to impose detention without limit of time in order that the convicted child's condition might be monitored and his release date decided on the basis of the facts as they would later appear rather than on speculation at the time of sentencing, and that the sentence imposed was both in the interest of the child and in the public interest. Where a child is sentenced to detention without limit of time he may be released on licence by the Secretary of State on the recommendation of the Parole Board. Children sentenced to fixed terms of detention are released on licence after one half or two thirds of the sentence, depending on the length of the sentence, and may be released earlier by the Secretary of State on the advice of the Parole Board.

The Children's Hearing System

As has been seen, few cases of children accused of committing serious crimes are directed into the children's hearing system at the outset and it is even more rare for homicide cases to be dealt with in this way. However, there are some such cases and, as noted, the system has a role in some cases in the disposal process. The procedure is primarily laid down by Part III of the 1968 Act, as amended.

Except in the case of a remit or request by a court, a child comes before a children's hearing because the reporter to the children's panel considers that child to be in need of compulsory measures of care. In the case of offender referrals (section 32(2)(g)), the offence is the ground of referral. A children's hearing differs from a court in a number of important respects including its composition and the way it makes its decisions. Each 'hearing' comprises three members of the children's panel, at least one of whom must be male and one female. (The panel is a group of selected and trained lay persons who volunteer their services to take part in children's hearings). A hearing is private and more informal.

Unlike a jury in court proceedings or a judge (unless there is an appeal), a hearing has to give reasons for its decisions. It must gather as much information as possible about the child and his circumstances, from written reports from such sources as the child's social workers, school, educational psychologists and psychiatrists, aided by a full discussion at the hearing. Both the child and his parent may be accompanied at the hearing by a representative, who may be legally qualified. However, legal aid is not available. A hearing may therefore take place without the presence of any legally qualified person. In cases where there is or may be a conflict between the interests of the child and those of a parent, the chairman of a hearing may appoint a 'safeguarder' to safeguard the interests of the child. Although informal, procedure at a hearing must abide by the framework laid down in the 1968 Act. In particular, the grounds of referral must be accepted by the child and his parents, both of whom are required to attend.

Hearings are concerned with deciding the measures of care best suited to each child, but cannot decide matters of fact. If the child cannot understand the grounds of referral or if the child and parents do not accept them, the grounds must go to the Sheriff Court for proof. At the proof, the reporter will lead evidence in support of the grounds of referral. The child and parents are entitled to legal representation and may be eligible for legal aid.

If the grounds of referral are found proved, the case is referred back to the hearing for it to be dealt with as if the grounds had been accepted. However, if the Sheriff holds that the grounds of referral are not established he will discharge the referral and the matter will end.

Disposal by the Children's Hearing

The hearing must decide what course is in the best interests of the child (section 43(1) of the 1968 Act). It may decide that no compulsory measures of care are required, and discharge the referral from the reporter; or it may decide that the child is in need of compulsory measures of care, and make a supervision requirement that he submits to supervision conditions imposed by them, or that the child is to reside in a specified residential establishment.

Other Procedural Matters

The 1968 Act also makes provision for such matters as restriction of publication of proceedings, appeal against the decision of a hearing and also review of a supervision order - an important feature of the 1968 Act procedure being the continuing supervision of a child who has been dealt with by a children's hearing.

Detention of 16 and 17 Year Olds

Although 'children' for purposes of the UN Convention, young persons aged 16 and 17 are only exceptionally 'children' for purposes of Scottish criminal procedure and they are dealt with for serious crimes by the formal criminal justice system. In most years the 16 to 20 age group accounts for the largest number of persons accused of cases recorded as homicide in Scotland ('Homicide in Scotland 1985-1994'). Reference has already been made to the sentencing procedure for persons under 18 convicted of murder. Detention of young offenders of 16 and 17 convicted of other serious crimes may be imposed if the court is of the opinion that no other method of dealing with the person is appropriate, after taking account of information about the offender's circumstances, character and physical and mental condition. Detention is in a young offender's institution. Although statutory 'children' (mainly those under supervision) may be remitted to a children's hearing, this course is unlikely to be followed in the case of serious crimes.

Victims and Victims' Families

Victims and victims' families do not have a formal role in the process in Scotland and there has been criticism from time to time of the system's suggested lack of consideration for them. Support agencies do exist to assist them, however, the most important of which is Victim Support. The Crown Office and Procurator Fiscal Service recently commissioned research on victims' information needs and is currently considering the report of that research.

Among other smaller and more local agencies and groups for providing support to victims and victims' families (in the case particularly of homicides), it is of interest to note that one such group in Glasgow was set up by the parents of a teenage girl who was murdered by a 15-year-old female schoolmate.

I do not know of any evidence that victims or their families are generally critical of the use of the criminal justice process to deal with such cases, rather than the welfare-based system, and indeed there are occasional indications of approval of the existing prosecution-based approach. In a recent case involving a 14-year-old girl as one of the accused, the sister of the murder victim was reported in the press as saying: 'we are grateful to the Crown and jury for ensuring that justice was done.' (*Daily Record*, 4 October 1995). I am also aware that the parents in the case of the schoolgirl murdered by a schoolmate, to which I have referred, were bitterly critical of what they regarded as excessively sympathetic portrayal of the position of the convicted 'child' by some of the press. Generally speaking, the media do not appear to challenge the appropriateness of the use of the criminal justice system for such cases and there is no evidence, of which I am aware, of any groundswell of public opinion against the current approach to dealing with such cases.

Andrew Normand is Regional Procurator Fiscal for Glasgow and Strathkelvin, Scotland

ENDNOTES

1. Address by Lord Rodger of Earlsferry to the conference of the Association of Children's Reporters on 'The Child and the Young Offender: the interface between the children's hearing and the criminal justice system', 23 March 1994.
2. See *Offenders Aged 16 to 18*, Report of a Working Party appointed by the Scottish Association for the Study of Delinquency, November 1993.
3. 'Homicide in Scotland 1985-1994', *Scottish Office Statistical Bulletin* CrJ/1995/5, October 1995; 'Criminal Proceedings in Scottish Courts, 1993', *Scottish Office Statistical Bulletin* CrJ/1994/6, November 1994.
4. 'Homicide in Scotland 1985-1994', *supra*.
5. The principal textbook which covers the relevant procedure is *Renton and Brown's Criminal Procedure according to the Law of Scotland* G. H. Gordon ed, W. Green and Son Ltd, Fifth Edition, Edinburgh, 1983. The leading text on sentencing is *Sentencing: Law and Practice in Scotland*, C.G.B. Nicholson, W. Green and Son Ltd, Second Edition, Edinburgh, 1992.

CHAPTER 9

The System in Northern Ireland

Roger Bailey

In Northern Ireland government responsibilities for young offenders are divided between the Department of Health and Social Services and the Northern Ireland Office. Within the Northern Ireland Office the responsibility rests with the Criminal Justice Services Division, which also has responsibility for the training schools system.

The legislation regarding the treatment of children and young people who offend and are brought before the courts in Northern Ireland is contained in the Children and Young Persons Act (Northern Ireland) 1968 and the Treatment of Offenders Act (Northern Ireland) 1968. References in parentheses throughout this paper are to sections of the Children and Young Persons Act (Northern Ireland) 1968. There are proposals to update this Act, but these have yet to be completed.

The Secretary of State for Northern Ireland is responsible for:

a) introducing law reforms to Parliament
b) the penal system and treatment of offenders, e.g. he has the power to refer convictions of some criminals to the Court of Appeal for reconsideration, to release prisoners on licence or to grant special remission or grant pardons
c) special functions under the emergency laws

A person under ten years of age cannot commit a criminal offence in the eyes of the law: a child of that age is said to be *doli incapax* ('incapable of wickedness') (s69). Children under ten may, however, be subject to care proceedings. Under exceptional circumstances they may be detained within a secure care facility within a training centre.

The law divides juveniles into two categories. A child is a person of at least ten years but under 14 years. A young person is someone aged at least 14 but under 17 (s180). People in these age categories are capable in law of committing criminal offences.

Special considerations apply to juveniles in pre-trial proceedings:

- When a juvenile is arrested, such steps as may be practicable must be taken to inform his parent or guardian (s52(2)).
- A juvenile detained in a police station, or being brought to or from court, or waiting before or after a court appearance should not be allowed to associate with adults who are charged with an offence. If the juvenile is a girl, she must be placed under the care of a woman (s49).

Juveniles charged with murder or manslaughter who are remanded in custody by the court are sent to training centres. Young people (14 to 16 years) may be detained instead in a young offenders centre where the court certifies that the defendant is so unruly that he could not be safely detained in a training centre or is of so depraved a character that he is not fit to be so detained.

The person who initiates proceedings against a juvenile must notify, as soon as possible, the probation office and Health and Social Services Board of the relevant district of Northern Ireland. The notification should include details of the time of the upcoming court appearance and the nature of the charge or complaint.

Both children and young persons appear before the juvenile court, a special court of summary jurisdiction. The process is a criminal one. There is a juvenile court in each petty sessions district in Northern Ireland. In the case of homicide or manslaughter the juvenile court covers pre-trial committal proceedings. The public are excluded from these courts. Other differences between juvenile and adult trials are:

- The juvenile court is held at a different time and if possible in a different part of the building from the adult court, in order to prevent the juvenile coming into contact with adult offenders (s56).
- Special efforts are made to ensure the privacy of criminal proceedings against juveniles. There are reporting restrictions on press coverage in that reports must not reveal the name, address or school of the child or young person, or any particulars which may make him identifiable. These restrictions also apply to children or young persons who may be called as witnesses. Only certain accredited press representatives are allowed into court. Upon a finding of guilt the child's name may then be revealed, though normally it would not be.
- The parent or guardian of the child may be required to attend throughout the proceedings. Further, on a finding of guilt, the court must inform the parent or guardian of how it intends to deal with the juvenile and must give the parent or guardian the

opportunity of making representations in relation to the proposed order.

- The terms 'conviction' or 'sentence' are not used in the juvenile court (s70): the terms 'finding' and 'disposal' are used.
- Upon a finding of guilt the juvenile court must obtain a wide array of information on matters such as the juvenile's general conduct, home surroundings, school record and medical history. The court may also request specific medical, psychiatric or psychological reports before making its order in the case.
- Lay assessors also sit with the county court judge in appeals from juvenile courts.

Juveniles charged with an indictable offence have the same right to trial by jury as the adult offender. Juveniles charged with murder or manslaughter cannot be tried by a juvenile court. However, trial within the Crown Court follows the same special conditions in dealing with juveniles as the juvenile court. The case is heard by a judge and jury. Where a Crown Court finds a juvenile guilty of an offence, they may send him back to be dealt with as appropriate by the juvenile court. This will depend upon the gravity of the case.

Which Agencies are Involved and What are Their Roles?

The Northern Ireland Office Criminal Justice Services Division maintains responsibility for placement of the young person within the training school system to be held prior to any hearing, during trial, and following any disposal. The training centres in which juveniles may be held are inspected and approved by the Social Services Inspectorate.

The Royal Ulster Constabulary. Police are involved in special arrangements for detention in police stations, informing parents and social services when a juvenile is apprehended and bringing the young person to court.

Director of Public Prosecutions (DPP). The DPP is a barrister or solicitor who has practised in Northern Ireland for not less than ten years. His chief function is to bring prosecutions for indictable criminal offences and less serious offences which he feels should be dealt with by him e.g. under the emergency legislation. The Director of Public Prosecutions makes the decision as to whether or not to proceed to a formal hearing on the basis of the adequacy of the available evidence in

90

the case. The DPP represents the Crown in all criminal cases in the Crown Court.

The juvenile court consists of a resident magistrate (all resident magistrates must have been a barrister or solicitor of at least seven years standing) who acts as chairman, and two lay members, at least one of whom must be a woman. The lay members are selected for cases by the Lord Chancellor's Committee in accordance with directions issued by the Lord Chancellor. In the case of a juvenile charged with murder or manslaughter, the juvenile court conducts the committal and may be involved in the disposal aspects of the case.

The Health and Social Services Board will normally produce a home surroundings report which, together with school record and medical history, will be made available to the court by a social worker of the relevant Health and Social Services Board. Advice may be provided regarding the care and placement of the child.

A probation officer may be called upon by the courts to provide similar information in a social enquiry report, including information relating to disposal options and the suitability of the client for community based programmes.

A psychiatrist may be consulted regarding the mental state of the juvenile, fitness to plead, or other mental health questions which may arise.

Psychologists provide a service to all training schools and to the Probation Board for Northern Ireland. They may be consulted regarding the juvenile's placement, intellectual, emotional and social development, ability to comprehend proceedings, capacity to comprehend the nature and seriousness of the offence and factors surrounding and related to the offence behaviour itself.

Responsibility regarding the placement of the child rests with the resident magistrate or judge during the trial. In serious cases the child may be detained within a secure training centre.

The Trial Process

A young person charged with an offence of murder or manslaughter will be tried by a Crown Court judge and a jury. There is no difference from an adult trial in the process for testing the evidence. However, the special conditions regarding the management of the trial, reporting restrictions etc which apply to juvenile courts will also apply to such a trial.

The child or young person will be represented by a lawyer who will protect the child's interests. A child may be accompanied during the hearing by a social worker appointed by an Area Health Board. The special conditions relating to juvenile trials may be monitored by the Social Services Inspectorate.

Disposals are governed by a number of specific rules:

Young persons (aged 14-16 years)
The power of the court to order detention in a young offenders centre (juvenile prison) or imprisonment in respect of young persons is curtailed by s72(3) Children and Young Persons Act (Northern Ireland) 1968, which stipulates that such an order may only be made if the court certifies that the offender is of such unruly or depraved a character that no other method of dealing with him is appropriate. If the offence is one for which an adult could be sentenced to 14 years' imprisonment (or five years in the case of scheduled offences), the young person may be detained in such place and for such time as the Secretary of State may direct (see s73(2) Children and Young Persons Act (Northern Ireland) 1968 and s10(1) Northern Ireland (Emergency Provisions) Act 1978). A young person aged 14 to 16 years may thus be detained in a prison, a young offenders centre or a training centre: in most cases they would initially go to a training centre.

There are four training centres throughout Northern Ireland. The aim of these institutions is to help the juvenile to readjust to society and to grow accustomed to attending school. Provision is made to assist the young person in dealing with family, educational and emotional problems which may have contributed to offending behaviour. These centres are staffed by social workers, and are subject to regular inspections by the Social Services Inspectorate.

A young person may not be sentenced to life imprisonment: the court is required instead to order detention at the pleasure of the Secretary of State (s73(1) Children and Young Persons Act (Northern Ireland) 1968).

Children (10-13 years)
The provisions mentioned above in relation to detention at the pleasure of the Secretary of State apply also to children. For obvious reasons, the courts' powers to use the more severe custodial measures in relation to children are very limited. The court may order detention only when a

child is found guilty on indictment of an offence for which an adult may be sentenced to a least 14 years' imprisonment and the court feels that no other method of dealing with the child is suitable.

The child will be detained in such place (which may be a young offenders centre) and under such conditions as the Secretary of State may direct. Once again, a life sentence is replaced by detention at the pleasure of the Secretary of State. Thus the Secretary of State directs which training centre the child is sent to. This may (and in a case of murder or manslaughter almost certainly will) include the choice of a secure setting.

Length of detention

The length of detention is determined by review by the Secretary of State. In making such a review the opinions of the managers of the training centre, together with others who have responsibility for the care and treatment of the young person, will be sought. There is no provision for remission as it is not a determinate sentence.

Within Northern Ireland procedures are in process to bring in provisions similar to the Criminal Justice Act 1991 which applies in England and Wales. This will be applied to both adult and juvenile offenders. Custody is only to be ordered when the offence passes the 'seriousness' and 'protection of public from harm' criteria which will essentially make custodial disposals more difficult. There will be more encouragement of courts to consider pre-sentence reports in all cases. This should ensure greater consistency in the ways in which cases are conducted and in sentencing.

Roger Bailey is a forensic psychologist at the Adolescent Psychology and Research Unit, Belfast

CHAPTER 10

The System in the Republic of Ireland

Tom O'Malley

In describing the Irish juvenile justice system, much of what I am going to say may appear rather like legal history to an English audience, because the Irish system is like going back to your system as it was before 1939. Strange as it may seem, we still operate the Children Act of 1908.

That is a highly unsatisfactory situation. On the other hand, it must be recalled that the Children Act 1908 was a very progressive piece of legislation in its day. It provided for a wide range of dispositions which could still be adapted to contemporary conditions. Our biggest problem is not the antiquity of the legislation, which is about to be cured, but the lack of resources made available to give proper effect to the range of sentencing provisions included in the Act.

Until recently in Ireland the Children Act 1908 governed not just juvenile justice but also the whole issue of taking children into care through civil proceedings in respect of deprived children. However in 1991 a major child care Act was introduced which replaced most of the 1908 Act as far as civil proceedings are concerned. It was modelled to some extent, though not exclusively, on your own recent legislation in that field such as the Children Act 1989 in England and Wales. There is now juvenile justice legislation in preparation, which is likely to be completed some time in 1996 and in force shortly after that.

Perhaps one of the reasons why we have such antiquated legislation is that until relatively recently serious crime was not a significant problem in Ireland. For example, in 1960 the average daily population of our prisons was 360. It is now about 2,300. Until the drug problem hit the streets in the late 1960s, and progressively throughout the 1970s and 1980s, crime was not really a major problem and so it was possible to make do with older legislation. Not only do we have the Children Act 1908. We also maintain loyally the Probation of Offenders Act 1907, although this is now being abolished in all the jurisdictions to which it originally applied.

Even today the number of young people who commit serious offences is very small indeed. A report published recently on homicide in Ireland between 1972 and 1991 showed that no person under the age of 13 had committed any form of homicide in that 20 year period. I am not aware of any case earlier than that since the formation of the state in 1922: there may have been but I cannot think of any. Nor can I think of anyone convicted of murder under the age of 17. Some have been convicted of manslaughter, but they amount to only a very small percentage of all homicide offenders. The overall number of homicides in any one year in Ireland is anyway very small, averaging about 20 to 23. If we look at children who have committed very serious crimes other than homicide, that is becoming a live issue with us in the context of sexual offending. A number of young people each year are accused and convicted of rape.

A debate has been going on for many years about whether juvenile justice should be governed by a justice model or a welfare model: in other words, should the focus be on giving the child due process of law in the same way as an adult, or should we focus instead on looking at the best interests of the child? Like many others in the common law world, our system is a mixture of both elements. The justice model applies more or less up to the moment of conviction and then to some extent the welfare model takes over after the conviction stage.

A child who is accused of a serious crime is entitled to all the rights to which an adult would be entitled if accused of a similar offence. In Ireland those rights are quite significant in that we have a written constitution enacted in 1937 which incorporates a Bill of Rights and allows for the judicial review of legislation. If Parliament passes an Act that is in some way unconstitutional, then the courts are entitled to strike down that law as being in violation of the constitution. The constitution provides that everybody accused of an offence is entitled to due process of law —everybody has a right to personal liberty and cannot be deprived of it save in accordance with law—and to a host of other rights as well. In addition we have ratified the European Convention on Human Rights and the United Nations Convention on the Rights of the Child. The latter Convention is vitally important, in that Articles 37 and 40 set out very specific standards and rules that are to be followed in connection with the trial of people under the age of 18 and also the values that should govern the sentencing of children and young persons who have been convicted of offences. As a result of that constitutional background and our international human rights obligations, we have no option but to ensure that all children are given the same trial rights as adults would have.

Age of Criminal Responsibility

At what age can children become criminally liable? Here the antiquity of our laws makes itself evident because we now have the lowest age of criminal responsibility in Europe, which is seven years. That was the common law and the Roman law age of criminal responsibility and, whereas most other countries have intervened by statute at various times to increase the age—to ten in England and to higher ages in many European countries, up to 15 in some cases—we have still remained firmly anchored at seven. However, that is due to change. There have been several reports written over the past 20 years recommending a change. The juvenile justice legislation which is being drafted will change it, probably to ten years.

There was a major report on child care published in 1970 in Ireland called the 'Task Force Report on Child Care', which dealt with the entire range of issues relating to children in care or in need of care. Most of it was given over to civil proceedings but, in relation to juvenile justice, it was interesting that the Task Force was split on the age of criminal responsibility. The majority opted to stay at seven years. That might sound surprising because it was a very child-centred committee. The reason was the old 'justice versus welfare' conflict. They believed that if there was a high age of criminal responsibility, there would have to be some form of intervention by the state if children below that age committed crimes and that form of intervention might be more intrusive than criminal proceedings would be. That is the old argument against the welfare model of juvenile justice—the idea of a child going into a shop, stealing £5 worth of goods and, if you adopt a welfare model, you may send the child away to a residential home for three years for his or her own good, whereas if treated as an adult offender they would probably get a small fine or a probation order. It was out of fear of undue interventionism that the majority of the committee decided to recommend that the age of criminal responsibility stay at seven years. The minority went to the opposite extreme and recommended that it should be raised to 15 years. It now looks as though we are going to have a compromise at ten years, or possibly 12.

The reason why we can now raise the age, as opposed to when the Task Force report was published, is that the new child care legislation of 1991, which deals with civil proceedings for the care of children, is a very modern piece of legislation. It concentrates very much on caring for children in the community and in their family rather than putting them into institutions. Therefore, it is now safer to allow for more intervention at an earlier stage because that intervention is no longer as intrusive as it may have been in the past.

Criminal Procedure

Children accused of criminal offences are, like adults, entitled to a presumption of innocence: it has now been held that this is a constitutional imperative. The burden of proof rests very firmly on the prosecution throughout. They are entitled to legal aid: that again is a constitutional right which applies both to children and adults. It has been decided by the Supreme Court that if someone is charged with a serious offence and they do not have the means to employ legal counsel and advice, they have a constitutional right to legal aid. We have a rather controversial provision that if evidence is obtained in breach of an accused person's constitutional rights, that evidence must be excluded from the trial, even if that leads to an acquittal.

Which court can try a young person? The Summary Jurisdiction Act of 1984 still applies with some modifications. Our court of summary jurisdiction is called the district court. It is roughly the equivalent of a magistrates' court in England, but all our district courts are staffed by professional judges, lawyers who must have at least ten years' experience as a solicitor or barrister. They therefore have somewhat more extensive jurisdiction than the English magistrates' court: they can try virtually any offence other than homicide. If the judge is satisfied, by virtue either of the nature of the offence or of the nature of the offender, that the child can be tried in a summary fashion, he can proceed to do that; but he cannot do so in the case of a homicide offence, which would have to be tried on indictment before a jury. Nowadays if the case was one of rape, no district judge would take that on. He would exercise his discretion to send it forward to the High Court. There used to be a presumption in Ireland, as in England, that a boy under 14 was incapable of committing rape. That legal presumption was abolished in Ireland in 1991, two years before it was changed in England.

The rules in relation to publicity are not hard and fast. For sentencing purposes a child is somebody under the age of 15: in no circumstances will the media ever report, nor would it be lawful for them to report, the name of a child accused or convicted of an offence under the age of 15. It would be rare for that to happen until the child reaches the age of 17: even where a child has reached the age of 16 and is convicted of a very serious offence, it is very seldom done and they certainly would not name him or her as a defendant until the moment of conviction.

Custodial Trends and Facilities

We have a shortage of custodial facilities for people who have been convicted of serious offences. It may seem that one of the biggest social changes that has taken place in the Republic of Ireland in the last 30 years or so has been an increase in the level of imprisonment, which has increased over sixfold between 1960 and the present day. We now have about 2,300 people in prison on an average day, with a total population of three and a half million people in the country.

In many ways, however, the biggest social change that has taken place is a reduction in custody if you look at custody in its broadest sense. For example, in 1960 and for many years before that we had about 20,000 people in psychiatric hospitals throughout the country. Psychiatric hospitals tended to be used not just to treat the mentally ill but, very undesirably, as a convenient means of effectively disposing of people who could not otherwise be cared for. That population has now been drastically reduced to a population today of about 6-7,000.

The country was also dotted with industrial schools and reformatory schools. In 1960, although the number was beginning to decline, there were 3-4,000 children in industrial schools and reformatory schools, which meant that quite a high proportion of young people were in institutional care. That number has also drastically declined. So we have had to face the problem of deinstitutionalisation rather than of institutionalisation, and one of our problems nowadays is to find adequate institutions in which to incarcerate serious offenders.

When a young person has been convicted of a crime, the welfare approach comes into effect after a fashion. For the most part every effort is made to keep the young person out of custody and there is a fairly full range of options available. It may seem rather strange that we still maintain the Children Act 1908; but if you go back and read that legislation, it is interesting to see the wide range of options it provided, community-based for the most part with some custodial options as well. Even today, if there were proper resources available, you could have a viable juvenile justice system even with the Act of 1908.

One of the main options that we introduced in recent years, less than a decade after it was introduced in England and Wales, was community service, which is available as an option for offenders of at least 16 years of age. The maximum number of hours' service that can be served is 240. People have recommended for some time that the nature of community service should be extended, so that it could effectively be sentencing somebody to go to school. Very often the crimes committed by youngsters are secondary, in that they simply reflect the problems that they have.

Moving on to serious offences for which measures like probation and community service would not be an option, this is where the problem tends to manifest itself. Our definitions for sentencing purposes of a child as somebody under the age of 15 years and a young person as somebody between the ages of 15 and 17 are based on the old Children Act as amended in Ireland in the 1940s when the age limits were increased. The sentence for murder in Ireland is a mandatory one of life imprisonment when it is committed by an adult, which for criminal justice purposes means somebody over the age of 17 although our normal age of majority is 18. According to a Supreme Court judgment in the early 1970s, a child or young person convicted of murder would be committed to a suitable place of detention, to remain there until released by the Minister for Justice. Under our constitution which guarantees the separation of powers, sentencing must be exclusively by a judge. The judge would be effectively giving the young person detention for life as a potential sentence, but he could be released at any time that the Minister for Justice so decided. However, we have not, as far as I know, had any case in the past 35 to 40 years of a child under the age of 15 being convicted of murder, and the numbers convicted of homicide between the ages of 15 and 17 are very small.

The next issue is dealing with people who commit serious offences other than murder, for example rape, manslaughter or serious robbery. We still maintain, despite constant political promises to abolish it, the distinction between imprisonment and penal servitude although in practice there is no difference in the rules between the two. A child under 15 cannot be sentenced to either imprisonment or penal servitude under any circumstances. A person between the ages of 15 and 17 cannot be sentenced to penal servitude under any circumstances; nor can he be sentenced to imprisonment, but with an exception in section 102 of the Children Act 1908, whereby if there is evidence before the sentencing judge that the young person is so unruly and depraved that he or she cannot be kept elsewhere then he can be sent to prison. If young people are sent to prison, then they must be kept apart from adult prisoners: there must be separate facilities for them.

There has been a good deal of case law on that over the years. First, it has been held by the High Court and the Supreme Court that a judge should not lightly come to the decision that a young person is unruly or depraved. They are supposed to hear evidence on the matter and make that decision just as they would any other decision based on evidence, sworn evidence wherever possible. Secondly, the authorities are supposed to take seriously the question of providing separate facilities for the young people in question. However, this is a highly unsatisfactory aspect of our criminal justice system. I worked briefly on a case where two young girls who were just over 15 were sent to prison on the grounds of unruliness and depravity. They were sent to the only female prison which we have in the country, which is in Dublin and has a population of 40 to 50 at any one time. They were in there with the adult women prisoners. We sought a High Court order to declare that this was unlawful. The judge was sympathetic but put the case back for hearing until such time as he would see what the prison authorities would do. A few weeks later the prison authorities came back and said that the problem was solved and that they were now being held separately. We know that this was only formally true: in fact the two young girls were being held in solitary confinement. For effectively 23 hours a day they were locked up in their cells, and that was the 'separate facilities'. That is a highly unsatisfactory situation. Young women suffer in particular because it is effectively prison or nothing once they reach the age of 15: we do not have any other custodial facilities for young women aged 15 or more.

For young males on the other hand, the situation is somewhat better in that once they have reached the age of 16 they can be sent to the former borstal institution known as St. Patrick's. I am afraid that in reality it is very much the same as a prison. It is located in the same grounds as Mountjoy prison and young men can be sent there between the ages of 17 and 21, though they can be sent there at 16 if there are no other facilities for them. The theory is that it is supposed to be a place for education, training, treatment and rehabilitation, and the judge is only supposed to send young people to St. Patrick's if they are suitable for detention as opposed to imprisonment. So young males who commit very serious crimes are likely to be sent to St. Patrick's institution if they are aged 16 years or older. If they are so unruly or depraved that they cannot be held there or anywhere else, they will be sent to prison. With young women on the other hand, as soon as they reach the age of 15, prison is the only place for them. Although they are only supposed to be sent there on the grounds of unruliness or depravity, there is always a strong temptation for judges to make that ruling just to find somewhere to put them.

We do have schools which in former times would have been known as reformatory schools, mainly based nowadays in Dublin. They tend to be quite small, very expensive and have only a very small number of places available in them, but they are the only places available to which anyone under the age of 15 can be sent. If you are sent to one of these schools, you are kept there until you reach a certain age (which varies with the nature of the establishment) irrespective of your age when you were sent in. In practice it seldom works out like that because the schools are under so much pressure to take in new offenders that they have to try to release people when they consider it safe to do so.

Early release from prison and the former borstal institution is entirely a matter of executive discretion. Everybody serving a sentence of imprisonment in Ireland is entitled to one-quarter remission: we hope that that will be raised to one-third. In addition to that, however, the Minister for Justice has powers to grant early release to an offender at any time, which has given rise to a lot of criticism about a 'revolving door' system. But unfortunately the adult prison system is under as much pressure as the juvenile detention system. Consequently very few prisoners serve their full sentences. Unfortunately we do not have a formal parole system. What we do have is a long sentence review group, which consists of civil servants chaired by a former judge, which looks at the cases of men who have served at least seven years. Beyond that the initiative to grant early release lies entirely with the prison authorities and with the Minister for Justice. That they have been doing quite readily—but nowadays they are reluctant to grant early release in the case of sex offenders and offenders who have a disposition towards violence.

Tom O'Malley is Senior Lecturer in Law at University College, Galway

CHAPTER 11

Placement in Institutions

Rob Hutchinson

I am going to talk about children who kill and those who have committed very serious offences and the role that local authorities have in relation to these young people. This extends from our role when the young person is arrested, the decision where the young person is remanded and what are the main objectives and options when the young person is on remand. I would also like to describe some of the effects of young persons being referred to local authorities for their sentence and some research we have carried out into the effectiveness of our secure accommodation and young people's attitude to this as well as to the Prison Service's young offender institutions.

The Arrest

Most of the young people who commit murder or very serious offences have not been known to us before. Neither Jim nor Mick, both of whom were under 16 when they were charged with attempted murder—Jim against his parents and Mick on an eight year old boy—were known to the social services department before. Liz and Jane *were* known to us. Liz had absconded from care and when she put a screwdriver into a policeman's eye, ruining his eyesight and his career, she was 15, pregnant and had venereal disease. Jane had also been in care but was 17 years old when she stabbed her boyfriend to death, having herself been abused throughout her childhood and adolescence.

In none of these cases was there other than an immediate arrest, and the first requirement was for a member of the youth justice service to act as an 'appropriate adult' during the interview. In Jane's case, she became hysterical and irrational, having delusions of blood-stained walls in the cells, and needed assistance immediately. As with many cases involving less serious offences, the custody sergeant ruled the roost with limited objectives, and psychiatric diagnosis was very difficult to obtain. Police are naturally very sensitive to the possibility of an admission of guilt being affected by inappropriate intervention, though there are serious issues involved if it is thought that the balance of a defendant's mind might be affected. Usually a senior officer such as an Inspector or a Superintendent will help resolve this type of problem but it needs perseverance and determination on occasions by youth justice staff to influence this type of situation.

Initial Placement Decision

Even where this is a first-time offender, the initial reaction by the police is often to say that only prison custody is appropriate, even when a local authority secure accommodation bed is available. With a first offender, not only is a young offender institution remand damaging in the extreme, but even secure accommodation is often traumatic. Although secure accommodation is preferable because of its more caring regime, it is not only the protection of the public that makes it a preferable option but also the need to protect young persons themselves from suicide bids. Both Jim—who attempted to kill his parents by setting light to his home—and Jane—who killed her boyfriend—were considered serious suicide risks and were kept in secure accommodation on remand primarily for this reason.

Occasionally the placement can be negotiated to be back in the community. Recently a first time offender set light, as a prank, to a vagrant's coat when he was sleeping in a park. The man later died from his burns, and the court agreed to the young person being placed away from the area with a relative and his mother who moved with him.

The Press

One major factor is managing the process during the initial period of sensationalism and dealing with the press as skilfully as possible. Frenzied attention to every move increases the pressure on all concerned in the criminal justice process to do something which would be regarded as suitably punitive.

The Remand

The young person who commits extreme acts such as murder is unlikely to be the same young person who steals cars or commits burglary. The shock and disruption to the young person's life cannot be overstated, and since the legal processes are lengthy and slow moving, the average time for a murder case to progress to sentence is often nine months to a year.

A balance has to be achieved between ensuring that life must go on as naturally as possible, for example education, career planning and family contacts, and a proper appreciation of the seriousness of the alleged offence and an acknowledgement of the likely outcome.

To achieve a positive continuation of the young person's life, liaison with a range of key players is necessary first to assess properly the young person and secondly to ensure that whatever the plan is, it is understood and agreed by all concerned. This means that teachers, solicitors and barristers, police, residential workers and family all need to be involved. This also applies to the Home Office who have comparatively recently assumed responsibility for section 53 offenders. They should be informed that a case in which they are involved will be coming up, partly out of courtesy but also to inform them fully of developments in case it becomes our intention to recommend that the young person serves his or her sentence in our secure accommodation.

Pre-Sentence Assessment

Pre-sentence assessment is potentially wide-ranging and includes:

- psychological/psychiatric assessment
- education assessment and provision
- possible bereavement counselling (as in Jane's case)
- anger management
- personal counselling/support
- family therapy.

Although much of the work is undertaken at the request of either prosecution or defence, it begins the process of acknowledging the crime and working with the young person, which will then form the basis of longer term treatment or therapy. There is a comprehensive and regular reviewing process which brings together all these strands and it is self-evident that a transfer to a custodial placement will increase the potential for further trauma and therefore a poorer prognosis for the future.

Hampshire has its own secure accommodation for boys and girls and the local management of assessment, as well as the fact that young people are able to maintain close contact with their families, are undoubtedly the key factors during the pre-sentence remand if full rehabilitation is to be achieved.

Post Sentence

If there is a conviction for murder or a very serious offence, the most likely disposal is via a section 53 order. The first part of this sentence is a three months assessment followed by a decision to place the young person in a custodial environment such as a young offender institution or secure accommodation. This may be for a matter of years.

In Liz's case, with the agreement at that time of the Department of Health, we offered not only the assessment period of three months in our secure accommodation but also the sentence. During this time she gave birth to her baby and with the support of her family, the social worker and the baby's foster parent she maintained contact with her baby, so that at the end of her sentence she moved to a flat in a children's home to see if she could properly care for her baby. Unfortunately this did not succeed but—although the baby was eventually adopted—she stayed at the children's home for a period and eventually moved into her accommodation. Some four years on, she has a new family and has had no criminal convictions.

Jim was a serious suicide risk for a considerable time after setting fire to his parent's home. Secure accommodation was a much safer placement than a young offender institution, where young people have managed to commit suicide on occasions. Jim's attitude to his parents was ambivalent, and their deaths were assessed by the psychiatrist to be the resolution to his dilemma. The forensic psychiatrist felt he needed a secure environment in which to receive therapy and in which he could feel safe and present no risk to the community. However, for various reasons both a youth treatment centre, an establishment administered by the Department of Health for the treatment of severely disturbed young people, and a custodial establishment were considered unsuitable. Instead the court agreed to make a section 7(7) care order which allowed him to be placed initially in Hampshire's secure accommodation and later in an open children's home.

Whilst in both placements he received continuing education, family therapy with a child psychiatrist, individual psychotherapy and individual support from a key worker to help him with personal interests and hobbies. The management of the risk, primarily to himself but also to the community, was overseen by an independent assessor, who had no involvement with him or the department, and a range of agencies were involved and committed to the plan. Four years after his discharge home, Jim has committed no further offences.

The Other Options

I have dwelt on secure accommodation as a preferred option because, in the main, it is local to the young person's home, and it has a child orientated regime designed to rehabilitate. The youth treatment centres referred to earlier have a similar approach though they are few in number and as such are usually a considerable distance from the young people's homes. In practice they have been the usual placement for serious offenders but they also work with children who have significant welfare needs as opposed to criminal records.

Young offender institutions are in effect juvenile prisons and are run by the prison service. They do not pretend to be child orientated and the prison officers do not have the skills to offer the same treatment or rehabilitation that the Department of Health or local authority secure accommodation offer.

The government has just passed legislation which creates secure training centres for twelve to 14 year old offenders who persistently offend. Only five are proposed and despite the protests of all those involved in the youth justice process, the Home Secretary has persisted in his plans to offer a sharp shock to these very young children. Whilst undoubtedly there are young people of this age who need to be protected against themselves and the community, creating these universities of crime for up to a year without any corresponding emphasis on their rehabilitation in the community guarantees failure.

Research

Hampshire has conducted a degree of research into its own secure accommodation and it is interesting to read some of the comments of young people about what happens in young offender institutions. Let me read you two extracts from comments by boys in our secure unit.

The first was a 15 year old, five feet four inches, who looked very young. He was sent to Glen House secure accommodation direct from police custody. He was asked why he had been sent there:

"I had this friend, he was my best mate, he still is, I nearly killed him. The police say it's attempted murder".

"Why was that?"

"I was out with a gang, we were doing a mixture of drugs and we were drinking as well. A boy I didn't know very well told me my best mate was slagging me off. I felt really angry. I went round all the pubs looking for him. I was out of my head. I found him, I pushed him, he pushed me back. Next minute he was on the ground and I was banging his head on the ground again and again. I don't know what happened next. He was in a coma. He nearly died."

"How did it make you feel?"

"I feel really terrible about it."

"What do you think will happen to you?"

"I'll go to Feltham. I'm really scared. I think they'll do things to me. I'm not really hard and I'm quite small. This bloke told me all about sex stuff things that they do."

Another boy of 16 said of prison service custody:

"It was terrible. I was scared all the time. There were all these really hard blokes who'd hurt you if you didn't do what they said. The screws didn't care. I was sick, I was so scared".

This particular young person said that he was going to become hard before the others got him. One has to ask if there is going to be that kind of environment, and looking at rehabilitation which has to be the key issue as well as punishment, is there a way of moving forward better in secure accommodation?

The Future

What we need is flexible provision for these serious young offenders: they need to maintain their local contacts, be exposed to the effects of their crime, to an appropriate form of reparation, and to whatever specific therapy they require. They are usually one-off offenders, but that does not mean they do not need significant rehabilitation when they return home. Local authorities which are properly resourced are the ideal agency to do this, and the outcomes as far as Hampshire is concerned give some cause for optimism.

Rob Hutchinson is Deputy Director of Social Services for Hampshire.

CHAPTER 12

Long Term Statistical Outcomes

Rob Allen

This paper will for the most part discuss what is known about the long term outcomes of children who kill in England and Wales and a little about Scotland. I am most grateful to the Home Office Research and Planning Unit, the Prison Service and the Scottish Office who have furnished me with a variety of statistical information.

The response that is made to children who kill varies. In England and Wales there is a mandatory sentence of detention at Her Majesty's pleasure for all those under 18 who are convicted for murder. But for manslaughter any sentence is possible. Pat Cawson writing in 1979 in her important work 'Children Referred to Closed Units', said that '. . . between 1969 and 1977 only one child under 14 was found guilty of murder and five of manslaughter. Only one of the latter was convicted under section 53 and the others were dealt with by the more *usual* course of juvenile law through care or supervision orders.' The climate seems to have hardened since the 1970s. Between 1982 and 1994 there were 104 juveniles (i.e. those under 17 until 1992, those under 18 in 1993 and 1994) sentenced for manslaughter. While the overwhelming majority were detained under section 53 for long terms (78), others were sentenced to shorter periods of custody (11) and 15 were not detained at all including one case which was dealt with by way of a conditional discharge.

Sentences for manslaughter passed on juveniles 1982-1994

Section 53 (2) detention	78
Borstal, youth custody, detention centre,	
Young offender institution	11
Supervision order	7
Care order	5
Hospital order	2
Conditional discharge	1
Total	104

A similar picture is found in Scotland:

Persons under 18 convicted of culpable homicide in Scotland 1985-1994

	Sentences
Imprisonment/young offender institution (<4 yrs:20; 4-10 yrs 14; >10 yrs 4)	38
Detention	6
Probation	2
Remit to reporter/hearing	3
Community service order	1
Admonition	1
Hospital order	1

Other homicide crime in Scotland

Imprisonment up to 4 years	7
Probation	6
Imprisonment 4-10 years	1
Community service	1
Detention	1

It is also possible that youngsters who kill are not involved in criminal proceedings at all. This must be the case in relation to those under the age of criminal responsibility.

For those children who are detained their experience will vary in terms of the length of detention, the place of detention and the quality of life they experience. We know something about juveniles under 18 who are sentenced to be detained at Her Majesty's pleasure and to detention for life.

Numbers of, and mean time served by life sentence prisoners released 1981-1994

	No	Mean time
Detention at Her Majesty's pleasure	101	10.61
Detention for life	22	10.21
Custody for life	132	12.60
Life imprisonment	871	12.01

There were 101 people serving the sentence of detention at Her Majesty's pleasure who were released from prison establishments during the period 1981 to 1994. They were all under 18 at the time of sentence. The mean time served by those released during these years was 10.6 years. That period is measured from the date of sentence and does not therefore include remand time which in many cases can be the best part of a year.

This average figure masks some large variations. The four people released in 1984 had served an average of 7.4 years, while the seven released in 1993 had on average served 14.6 years. In addition there were 22 people released between 1981 and 1994 having served a sentence of detention of life—that is a discretionary life sentence imposed when they were under 18. This group will include those convicted of rape, robbery or any of the other life sentence offences as well as homicide. On average, they had served 10.2 years. The two released in 1982 had served an average of less than seven years while the one released last year had served almost 16. The average length served by offenders in all age groups serving all of the different kinds of life sentence available in England and Wales during this period was about twelve years. What we can say therefore is that young people serving mandatory life sentences tend to serve shorter, but not that much shorter, periods in custody.

How well did they do when they were released? We do have some figures about reconviction and recall to custody which can give us some indication. During the period 1972 to 1993, a 21 year period, a total of 1,575 people in England and Wales were released from prison on life licence. Of these 113 or 7 per cent were under 18 when they received their life sentence. Not all of these were convicted of homicide. In fact only 92 of the 113 (81 per cent) had such a conviction, 71 for murder and 21 for manslaughter. The remainder had received life sentences for other grave crimes.

By the end of 1993, 27 of the 113 had been reconvicted of what the Home Office calls a 'standard list offence'—a list which covers almost all of the main sorts of crime. Five of these convictions were for grave offence categories which include serious wounding, rape, buggery, robbery, aggravated burglary or arson. 20 of the 113 had been recalled or given a further life sentence.

Reconviction and recalls 1972-1993 England and Wales

Life sentence prisoners aged under 18 when sentenced	113
Number of these prisoners who had original conviction for homicide	92

Number of life sentence prisoners under 18 when sentenced who were reconvicted by the end of 1993	27
Number of reconvictions which were grave offences	5
Number of prisoners recalled or given further life sentences	20

We also know the *rate* at which these people were recalled or reconvicted within a particular period following their release. Since this analysis follows up criminal histories until the end of 1993, it is only possible to calculate two year rates for those released up to 1991 and five year rates for those released up to 1988. The base figure of people we are talking about is therefore lower than the 113 referred to before: it is 94 for the two year analysis and 73 for the five year analysis.

On this analysis 7 per cent of all those given a life sentence when under 18 had been reconvicted within two years of release. One of these was for a grave offence. The offence groups for the reconviction offences were violence against the person (2), burglary (2), theft (1), fraud and forgery (1), other offences (1). Of the seven who were reconvicted only five were homicide lifers. On the five year follow-up, 16 had been reconvicted or 22 per cent of the sample but none for a grave offence.

Percentage of life sentence prisoners sentenced when under 18 who are reconvicted within two years and five years

Number released 1972-1991	94
Number reconvicted within two years	7=7 per cent
Number released 1972-1988	73
Number reconvicted within five years	16=22 per cent

Life licensees (sentenced at all ages) who were reconvicted

| Within two years | 10 per cent |
| Within five years | 21 per cent |

We can compare these sorts of figures with the reconviction and recall rate for life licensees as a whole. These overall rates show that about 10 per cent of life licensees are reconvicted within two years, 21 per cent within five years. Rather fewer youngsters seem to be reconvicted within two years and slightly more after five years; but I do not think we should read too much into that.

What the reconviction rates for lifers as a whole have always shown is that a very small percentage of lifers are reconvicted of a grave crime. In England and Wales lifers released over a 19 year period were reconvicted of a grave crime in fewer than 4 per cent of cases. Juvenile lifers were reconvicted of grave crimes at about the same rate. A total of 24 offences of homicide were committed by lifers released on licence between 1972 and 1991. Two were committed by those who had received their life sentences before the age of 18. According to a United Nations study of life imprisonment published in 1994, recidivism rates among released homicide offenders in Canada and Germany were found to be similar to those in England and Wales.

The most obvious points about this level of reconviction rate is how low it is compared with other offenders and other offences. About 50 per cent of adult male prison discharges between 1972 and 1986 were reconvicted within two years. The reconviction rates for lifers are also very low compared with reconviction rates for young offenders convicted for other grave crimes and detained under section 53(2). Home Office research found that 53 per cent of those who had served their sentences in young offender institutions run by the prison service were reconvicted within two years of release and 40 per cent of those who had served their sentences in local authority community homes as part of the child care system. The vast majority of these further offences are relatively minor—nothing like the gravity of the offence which brought them into security.

Juveniles sentenced for serious offences

% reconvicted within:	Community homes	YOIs
6 months	9.7	17.1
12 months	21.4	35.9
18 months	31.1	46.1
24 months	39.8	53.0

Offenders released from community homes who are reconvicted are less likely to receive custodial sentences—43.9 per cent receive non-custodial sentences compared with 25.4 per cent of those released from young offender institutions.

What are the factors which are likely to affect the reconviction of children who kill? The first factor is likely to be the number of previous convictions which the offender had prior to the conviction for homicide. Home Office figures show that the reconviction rates of those with no previous convictions were less than half of the reconviction rates for those with one or more previous convictions.

The second factor which is likely to be important is the nature of the offence and in particular the relationship between the victim and offender. Statistics show that in homicide cases the victim is known to the offender in almost two thirds of cases. Between 1992 and 1994 the figure where the suspect was under 18 was rather lower. In 51 per cent of cases the victim was acquainted with the suspect and in 49 per cent of cases not. Not surprisingly perhaps, where the suspect was under 18 and acquainted with the victim, the victim was less likely to be a family member and more likely to be a friend or acquaintance than in cases involving older suspects. This is because this age group is less likely to have wives or children. It is also true that when the suspect was *not* acquainted with the victim, the victim was less likely to be a police officer or person encountered in the course of employment.

The third factor likely to impact on how a young person who kills fares will be the nature of the help on offer. In England and Wales the placement of children who kill is generally either in the child care system or the prison system and in many cases will involve placement in both. We know from a study of juveniles sentenced for grave crimes (not murder, but grave crimes which would include manslaughter) that child care secure units delivered far superior regimes to prison service institutions. They provided significantly more and better quality education and training, a greater variety of physical exercise and recreational activity, a higher level of through-care and more help and advice with detainees' problems.

Perhaps not surprisingly, the reconviction rates from the child care establishments were better. In a matched sample of 40 offenders which took account of the main factors likely to discriminate between youngsters placed in prisons and placed in child care establishments, 52.5 per cent of those leaving young offender institutions and 39 per cent of those leaving child care establishments were reconvicted. While more than half of the reconvictions of the *prison* sample were for violent offences, this was true of fewer than a third of the community home discharges. The numbers involved were very small, however, so the differences on both these measures were not statistically significant.

It would, however, be surprising if regimes which provided significantly better help with detainees' problems did not produce better results given what we know about the characteristics of those who are convicted of grave crimes—in particular Gwyneth Boswell's research which found that the total number of section 53 offenders who had experienced abuse and/or loss to a potentially traumatic degree was 91 per cent.

One of the main problems for those facing long sentences, is that many will have to move from child care to prison. It could be argued that much good work is undone by this process and that prison establishments should be enabled and resourced to provide a much higher level of regime.

In conclusion, it might of course be argued that the reason for the very low reconviction rates of those leaving custody following life sentences is an argument for the effectiveness of long and indeterminate sentences in custody. This is unlikely. Long sentences are generally no more effective than short, and the dangers of institutionalisation, of dependency and of isolation have been well catalogued.

It is right to detain young people who have killed, even if they are young, for as long as it is considered that there may be a danger of their committing another serious offence. But all of the indications are that very few of them would do so anyway. The artificial surroundings of a closed establishment, whether secure child care accommodation or in the prison system, are not the best setting for a young person to mature and grow into a responsible independent adult.

Rob Allen is Director of Policy, Research and Development of the National Association for the Care and Resettlement of Offenders.

CHAPTER 13

The Italian Juvenile Penal Process and Children Who Kill

Matilde Azzacconi

This paper has been written in collaboration with Dr. Roberto Janniello, Magistrate at the Juvenile Court of Rome, with Professor Dr. Carla Vecchiotti, Professor of Forensic Medicine at the La Sapienza University of Rome, and with Dr. Giancarlo Cesaroni, psychologist. The statistical data have been gathered at the Central Office for Juvenile Justice of the Ministry of Justice.

Homicide is a crime against the individual and, more specifically, against life. According to its method and seriousness, it is classified as under the following categories—slaughter, wilful murder, attempted wilful murder, infanticide, culpable homicide and manslaughter.

The new Italian juvenile penal process is regulated:

- by Presidential Decree (DPR) No 448, published on September 22, 1988 (New Juvenile Penal Procedural Code);
- by Government Decree (DL) No 272, 1989, Implementation, co-ordination and transitional rules governing the Code of Criminal Procedure;
- by the Gozzini Act No. 354 of 1975 on Penitentiary Acts.

The agencies responsible for the juvenile penal judicial system are the Ministry of Justice; the Office for Juvenile Justice; the Supreme Court; the Public Prosecutor at the Supreme Court; the Court of Appeal; the Public Prosecutor at the Court of Appeal; the Juvenile Court; and the Public Prosecutor at the Juvenile Court.

The state agencies which may take part in the process are the police (state police, judicial police, carabinieri, metropolitan police), public prosecutor, tribunal, child welfare service of the Ministry of Justice, welfare services of local agencies, and children's institutions.

The new Italian juvenile penal process envisages some special and innovative elements. It does not vary on the basis of age but on the basis of *chargeableness*. The child is chargeable only between the ages of 14 and 18. Before the age of 14 a minor is not chargeable because he is regarded as having incapacity to intend and to exercise will and hence cannot be put on trial. Above the age of 14 chargeableness is presumed but must be demonstrated. The process is based on the assumption that the child is not guilty and until evidence is produced the court cannot proceed to make any final decision. The ultimate aim of the process is the psychological and social rehabilitation of the child. The penal process must not interrupt nor interfere with the psychological and social development of the minor.

The physical presence of the minor is required during all the phases of the process. He is assisted by his lawyer (either his own or one appointed by the court), by social workers, his parents or any other significant adult person indicated by the minor himself. The parents or the person who has parental authority over the minor must compulsorily be summoned to court or the process is invalidated.

Measures other than the detention of the child are: house arrest (when the minor has to take care of children below the age of five, or if he or a relative is affected by a serious illness), referral to a community, placement in the care of the welfare services, placement in a community. Such measures are implemented in collaboration with the welfare services, which plan the socio-psychological rehabilitation of the minor. The proceedings can be discontinued at any phase of the process. Upon a request by one of the parties involved (public prosecutor, judge, lawyer, minor) the process may be suspended and 'probation measures' may be adopted. If the probation period ends with positive results, the process is automatically cancelled. The victims of the crime committed by the minor cannot file any civil (economic) claim at any stage of the process, nor can they institute any civil proceedings.

In the case of a punitive sentence the minor does not have to pay the legal expenses, unlike the position in an adult trial. The counsel for the defence appointed by the court is paid by the state.

The judge can acquire information by hearing individuals, teachers, relatives and by gathering documents in order to assess the child's personality and make an adequate decision. The judge may appoint a technical consultant, psychologist or psychiatrist, who must verify the psychological, physiological and environmental conditions of the minor, to help the judge decide on chargeableness and on the sentence. At each stage of the process the judge must explain to the minor what is happening so as to make him aware and increase his sense of responsibility. The judge becomes a neutral party who always assumes the minor is innocent until and unless the evidence to prove the case is produced. During the process, or at the end, civil protective measures can be taken to protect the minor who has committed a crime.

Identikit Picture of the Minor Who Kills

A psychological analysis carried out on minors held in Italian juvenile prisons has shown that, in general, minors who kill have a family history of parents who are physically or emotionally absent, or who do not teach rules. When present, the parents are unstable, overprotective, negatively critical, or destructive. Their inadequate or rigid behaviour produces destructive feelings of anger in the child, who will then turn such destructive feelings either against himself or, later on, against society in anti-social behaviour. When the world reacts negatively to his deviant behaviour, the minor may adopt a lifestyle based on destructiveness which he also uses towards those people who wish to help him.

In short, he is an individual who is immature because during childhood he did not receive from his parents the ability to live a physically and psychologically healthy life, to feel emotions, to think and to act autonomously, and to have the right to love and be loved. Consequently, he cannot exist as an autonomous and balanced human being and may be dangerous to himself and to others.

The deviant minor is characterised by the following psychological characteristics:

- his family relationships are inadequate;
- he has an inadequate identification with either one or both parents, who were incapable of meeting his needs and who were either too authoritarian or too permissive;
- he experienced deprivation and suffered from a lack of maternal care;
- he had a devalued or discounted father figure;
- he received contrasting or incongruous parental messages;
- there was confusion and competition in parental roles;
- he experienced violence within the family itself, where he was also raped or violated or abused in some way;
- he was the family scapegoat, and now he reacts by being violent to others;
- he experiences uncontrollable anger that explodes unexpectedly;

- he experiences thought-splitting, self perception as being socially unacceptable, and is afraid of being rejected by others;
- unawareness and irrational behaviour;
- alternation of passive behaviours (closure to the external world) and aggressive behaviours (assaults on the world);
- he unconsciously searches for personal humiliation;
- he has a sado-masochistic personality;
- he has morbid curiosities;
- he lives in stressful situations and in inadequate or promiscuous cohabitation;
- low socio-cultural level;
- non-acceptance of his own and others' diversity.

Chargeableness

According to the law, once mental maturity has been reached, individuals are endowed with the natural qualities that allow them consciously and freely to regulate their actions. The fact of having these qualities is a necessary condition in order for an individual to be considered 'chargeable'. Article 85 of the Penal Code introduces the notion of chargeableness by stating that: 'Nobody can be punished for a deed envisaged by the law as being a crime if, at the time of the crime, he was not chargeable. A person who has the capacity to intend and to exercise will is chargeable.'

At the beginning of this Article a definition of a 'normal' person is given, namely a person endowed with the faculties that enable him to be free to violate a criminal rule and liable to bear the consequences of such violation. The term 'capacity to intend' indicates the capacity to discern the value of one's actions and of other people's actions with the awareness of the ethical, legal and social consequences that may derive from such actions. It is not necessary for the individual to be capable of judging whether his action is against the law, it is sufficient for him to understand that such action is in contrast with the needs of community life.

The term 'capacity to exercise will' means the capacity a person has to exercise personal responsibility and to resist impulses. This refers to the free will to achieve a goal and to adjust one's behaviour in accordance with the choices made. There are individuals who are capable of discerning what is good from what is bad but who are incapable of determining to act in a way consistent with their judgement (cyclothymia, schizophrenia, obsessive drives).

Chargeableness is therefore a necessary qualification in order for the person who commits an offence to be punishable. The lack of this requirement is a reason for being exempt from punishment: this is confirmed in the Criminal Code which describes as an 'offence' or 'crime' even a deed committed by an individual who is not chargeable. In order for there to be chargeableness, both these characteristics need to be present. If one of the two is missing, the individual is not chargeable.

The law sets forth the cases in which chargeableness is excluded or mitigated:

- for physiological causes: i.e. the individual is a minor;
- for pathological causes: i.e. the individual is affected by insanity (mental derangement, being under the effects of alcohol, drugs, being deaf and dumb).

For minors below the age of 14 it is assumed that they are wholly incapable of intending and of exercising will because the above-mentioned capacities presuppose a certain degree of intellectual maturity which cannot be achieved before that age, as expressly stated in Art. 97 of the Criminal Code: 'An individual who, at the time of the act was not yet 14, is not chargeable'. There is no assumption of capacity or incapacity for minors between 14 and 18 and so it is up to the judge to ascertain whether the conditions of chargeableness exist or not on a case-to-case basis. Art. 98 of the Criminal Code states that: 'An individual who at the time of the act was over 14 but not yet 18 is chargeable if he had the capacity to intend and to exercise will, but the punishment is mitigated.'

In order to establish whether an individual is chargeable in the case envisaged in Art. 98 of the Criminal Code, reference is made exclusively to the maturity of the individual. Incapacity deriving from immaturity (a concept which is different from mental derangement because the minor may be immature even though he is mentally healthy) is global and concerns not only an insufficient development of intellectual skills and of will-power, but also an inadequate development of moral conscience which enables the individual to orientate his conduct according to the fundamental principles governing co-existence in society. Moreover, immaturity is to be evaluated in relation to the type of offence committed because an individual may have capacity for certain offences but may lack capacity for others, depending on the degree of maturity achieved. It is evident that one cannot expect a minor to have the same degree of mental and ethical maturity as is typical of adults.

As concerns the sentence, non-chargeable minors, both those who were not yet 14 at the time of the crime and those who were over 14 but not found to have the capacity to intend and to exercise will, are acquitted without punishment and, in the case in which they are found to be guilty and dangerous, they are either sent to a judicial reformatory or are put on probation (Art. 224 Criminal Code).

If minors between the ages of 14 and 18 are found to be chargeable, they receive a mitigated sentence. If the minor is dangerous, the judge may order that after the execution of the penalty (sentence served) the minor be placed in a judicial reformatory or put on probation (Art. 225 Criminal Code). When there are grounds indicating partial mental disability, the minor is assigned to an establishment for treatment and custody (Art. 219 Criminal Code).

The Process

The public prosecutor is the party who brings the charges. The police collect the evidence as indicated by the public prosecutor and can be summoned to give evidence. The judge makes decisions on precautionary measures, at the end of the preliminary hearing and at the end of the trial proper (during which evidence is taken and witnesses are heard). Social workers assist the child and investigate his personality. The results are submitted to the judge. The judge may appoint as technical consultants a psychiatrist and a psychologist to ensure a thorough understanding of the minor's chargeableness.

In a case in which the minor is arrested by the police, the judge for preliminary investigations may confirm the arrest or decide on precautionary measures (custody in an institution, community, house detention) if so requested by the public prosecutor. Pending the hearing to confirm his arrest, the minor is placed in a temporary detention centre for no more than 48 hours. The judge for preliminary investigations decides to proceed to a trial proper when there is adequate evidence.

When the child's subjective situation is such that the offence was the result of an exceptional event, he can be given 'judicial pardon'. The judge refrains from passing a sentence on the condition that the child does not commit any other crimes in the future. Since 'pardon' presumes that the child is guilty, when the evidence of his guilt is not certain the defence prefers a formal trial so as to demonstrate the child's innocence.

In Italy a penal trial involving minors is divided into two phases. During the first phase—preliminary hearing—the offender is taken by the public prosecutor before the court, consisting of a regular judge and two honorary judges who are expert in psychopedagogical issues. On the basis of the information provided by the parties involved and by the welfare service, the hearing may decide whether he should be 'pardoned', 'put on probation' or declare that 'the deed was irrelevant'.

The second phase of the process is the trial proper, before a tribunal consisting of four judges, two 'regular' and two 'honorary' judges. Both the judge of the preliminary hearing and the judge of the trial proper can take temporary civil protective measures such as assigning the minor to the welfare services or appointing a guardian. All the members of the tribunal are trained professionals. The minor is always assisted by a lawyer, either his own or a counsel appointed by the court from the lists of experts in juvenile law whose fees are paid by the state.

The court may decide to sentence the minor, it may ascertain his responsibility and grant 'pardon' (hence abstaining from punishment), it may interrupt the trial to put the minor on 'probation' for a certain time period and issue a decision of acquittal if the minor behaves well during the probation period. In the case of conviction the adolescent may be sent to an institution for minors where he will serve a sentence, which is however always only one-third of the punishment envisaged for an adult. The minor may ask to be assigned to the welfare service for a period equivalent to the sentence and take part in a welfare readjustment programme or in a rehabilitation programme for drug addicts. If the minor or a family member is severely ill or if he has to take care of a child below the age of five, his sentence is turned into house arrest. For good conduct the sentence is shortened by 45 days for each six months served.

As occurs with adults, minors can also be admitted to a semi-freedom scheme according to which they can go to school or work or carry out their social activities during the day and in the evenings return to the institute of detention for the night. The authorities empowered to take such decisions that are alternatives to imprisonment are the magistrate and the Surveillance Tribunal at the juvenile court.

Mass Media

There are some restrictions on the press in reporting the cases of crimes committed by children. There is also a self-regulation code called the 'Treviso Charter', but the press does not always comply. The process always occurs behind closed doors and the press is not admitted. The interest of the mass media in judicial events involving minors is closely dependent on the importance of the case, on the seriousness of the crime and on the specific characteristics of social alarm. However the names and addresses of the minors must not be reported by the press.

Data Analysis

Documents issued by the Central Office for Juvenile Justice of the Ministry of Justice—Division 1—General Affairs are the source of the following tables.

Minors reported to the Public Prosecutor's Office at the Juvenile Courts broken down by age and type of offence

1992	14 years	14-17 years	Total	%
Crimes against the person	760	7,058	7,818	17.46
Life-threatening crimes	17	300	317	0.71
Slaughter	0	1	1	0.00
Wilful murder	1	49	50	0.11
Attempted murder	8	92	100	0.22
Infanticide	0	1	1	0.00
Culpable homicide	1	18	19	0.04
Manslaughter	7	139	146	0.33

1993	14 years	14-17 years	Total	%
Crimes against the person	779	7,214	7,793	17.85
Life-threatening crimes	10	247	257	0.59
Slaughter	0	1	1	0.00
Wilful murder	1	47	48	0.11
Attempted murder	0	68	68	0.16
Infanticide	0	2	2	0.00
Culpable homicide	2	7	9	0.02
Manslaughter	7	122	129	0.3

1994	14 years	14-17 years	Total	%
Crimes against the person	748	7,082	7,830	17.66
Life-threatening crimes	5	239	244	0.55
Slaughter	0	0	0	0.00
Wilful murder	1	46	47	0.11
Attempted murder	1	67	68	0.15
Infanticide	0	3	3	0.01
Culpable homicide	0	13	13	0.03
Manslaughter	3	110	113	0.25

The data in the above tables concern the minors reported to the Public Prosecutor's Office at the juvenile courts broken down by age and type of crime for the years 1992-94. They refer to crimes against the person (blows, injuries, threats, violence, rape) and life-threatening crimes (slaughter, wilful murder, attempted murder, infanticide, culpable homicide, manslaughter).

What emerges very clearly is that there are many more crimes against the person than life-threatening crimes, which on the whole are decreasing. The 14-17 age bracket is the one in which crimes are most common. Among the life-threatening crimes the most frequent is manslaughter, followed by attempted murder and by wilful murder; then comes manslaughter, whereas infanticides and slaughter are rare.

Given that manslaughter is the most frequent of the life-threatening crimes, it could be said that when minors kill a person they do so either unintentionally or as a result of their irresponsibility, perhaps due to their 'juvenile self-centredness'. This statement may be questioned in view of the fact that, even though the figures are much lower, the second most common crime is attempted murder which does imply the will to kill; however the explanation may be that an adolescent may use this type of crime as a demonstration to prove to his peers what he can do. This assumption could be confirmed by the fact that culpable homicide, which does not indicate premeditation but rather the accidental nature of the crime, is last in the list of crimes considered.

An analysis of the crimes with which minors held at temporary detention centres were charged in the years 1992-94 shows that, as a percentage of the crimes committed by the whole population, adolescents commit a higher proportion of offences against property and of drugs offences than of crimes against the person. Crimes against the person are committed significantly more frequently in the south of the country compared with the north: the lowest rates are those relating to Central Italy.

As concerns the islands, in Sardinia the percentage of crimes against the person and also of other offences attributed to minors is very low. In Sicily the percentage of crimes against the person is very high. The most significant fact is that in the south and in Sicily adolescents kill more than in the rest of Italy.

The following figures for certain Italian cities are for juveniles held in temporary detention centres in 1992-94.

City	Year	Wilful murder	Attempted murder
Palermo	1992	12	23
	1993	3	21
	1994	11	11
Bari	1992	6	12
	1993	6	14
	1994	6	5
Naples	1992	2	17
	1993	9	17
	1994	2	6
Rome	1992	1	20
	1993	0	15
	1994	0	15
Florence	1992	1	2
	1993	0	0
	1994	1	6
Milan	1992	2	4
	1993	2	5
	1994	1	10
Venice	1992	0	0
	1993	2	5
	1994	1	2

All the charges of murder and attempted murder in the above table relate to male offenders with the exception of one charge of murder in

Milan, and one each of attempted murder in Bari and Rome, in 1992; one charge of attempted murder in Naples in 1993; and one charge of attempted murder in Milan in 1994.

It will be seen that wilful murders and attempted murders by juveniles are more numerous in the south of Italy. In terms of the number of murders committed, Palermo comes first, then Bari and Naples. At some distance, with figures that are quite comparable, are Rome, Florence and Milan. The lowest figures in our sample are those for Venice.

It is significant that the largest numbers of murders are committed in towns like Palermo and Bari, and these towns are much less heavily populated than Rome or Milan where the number of murders is much lower. As concerns attempted murders, the largest number in absolute terms is recorded for the centre of the country, that is to say for Rome. This may be explained, as argued earlier, by the fact that adolescents may commit this type of crime as a demonstration. Moreover, we must not forget that Rome is the most populated town in Italy; therefore in percentage terms, the number of crimes of attempted murder is lower.

One last observation: throughout the whole of Italy crimes of murder and attempted murder are mostly committed by Italian male adolescents.

Matilde Azzacconi is a psychologist and transactional analyst who works in Rome in private practice. In 1988 she founded the Association 'Family and Minors' together with a group of other professionals. She has been its President since 1990, and since 1991 has been managing director of the journal 'Family and Minors', which is published by the Association. She previously worked for 15 years in public health organizations and for six years until March 1995 was honorary magistrate at the Juvenile Court of Rome.

CHAPTER 14

Parties to the Proceedings in Germany, France and Spain

Professor Dr. Hans-Heiner Kuhne

There are normally three parties to criminal proceedings—the court, the prosecutors, and the accused with his defence counsel. Witnesses and other evidence are instruments for these main actors to use. The position of these three parties varies, however, in accordance with national procedural criminal law provisions and, as far as juvenile defendants are concerned, with the specific systems for dealing with juvenile criminality.

In Germany there are no criminal proceedings against children aged under 14, which is the age of criminal responsibility. It is the task of the family courts to deal with these problems in a strictly non-criminal sense. Even in the case of children who have killed, they have to decide only whether they should be sent to a home, to a foster family or elsewhere: there is no element of criminal law involved.

While the minimum age of criminal responsibility is 14, the Juvenile Courts Act provides that a decision must be made in the case of juveniles between the ages of 14 and 18 whether in the individual case they are capable of understanding the wrongfulness of their actions. If the judge decides that they do not have this capacity, the case must go to the family court rather than through the criminal process. In theory, a juvenile of nearly 18 years of age could be judged not to be criminally responsible and his case could be sent to the family court even if he has perpetrated a serious crime: the court has complete discretion to make this decision. In practice I do not know of any case involving a juvenile above the age of 16 where a court has decided that the juvenile should be treated as a child.

Court Procedures

Procedurally, we adopt a mixed approach in Germany in relation to juvenile offenders, bringing in welfare aspects but on a basis of ordinary criminal justice provisions. Juveniles who have criminal responsibility are tried according to our penal procedure law. However, the juvenile court has some special features designed better to meet the needs of juveniles in court hearings.

An inquisitorial system operates in Germany, France and Spain. This means *inter alia* that the court co-ordinates and leads the hearing at the trial. The prosecutor and defence counsel are in the position simply of assisting the court. They put forward their perspectives and proposals to the court and the court decides whether to comply with their requests. Evidence is put forward by the court and there are only very limited possibilities for prosecutors and defence counsel to produce their own evidence: in practice this is very rare indeed. So while in legal theory the court is, of the three actors, *primus inter pares*, in fact it is simply *primus*. It is the judge who does all the questioning, directs the hearing and decides on all the requests.

In Germany, the Juvenile Courts Act provides for two options in relation to the composition of courts. One is a professional juvenile judge sitting by himself; the other is one professional judge and two lay judges or 'jurors'. The latter are not jurors in the English-American sense, but hold the position of judges even though they have no legal education. It is a historical accident that we still have lay judges and it is a matter of considerable debate whether we should keep them or have a fully professional judiciary.

There is no judicial pre-trial investigation in Germany. The prosecutors with the help of the police have to collect evidence and present it to the court, and the court then has to decide whether or not to initiate a trial.

The Juvenile Courts Act requires that special juvenile judges and juvenile prosecutors participate in trials of juveniles. This looks good on paper, because it implies that there must be some special training and some special understanding of the problems of juveniles - which indeed was the intention of the law. But in fact this has remained mere theory. Although the law tries to provide for special competency, in reality it is coincidental if someone appointed to this job trains himself on the job to develop such a special perception. The judicial administration does not provide any special training for those appointed to the job. Yet as soon as they become juvenile judges and juvenile prosecutors, everybody thinks that they must have some special competence, which is not the case.

In contrast to adult proceedings, juvenile proceedings are not public. Article 48 of the Juvenile Courts Act prohibits publicity in these hearings to provide some protection for juveniles and prevent them from becoming victims of the media. Because there is no access to juvenile proceedings, the press are not allowed to refer to juvenile proceedings or to the persons involved, even when very serious crimes are tried.

Although we hold to the principle of the presence of the accused for the whole of the trial, a juvenile court can exclude the accused if it deems this advantageous for his or her welfare. However, the court has a duty to inform the accused of what has been said during his absence. It is possible to exclude the parties or legal representatives from the trial, with the exception of defence counsel. This is because quite frequently family members are intertwined with the individual history which led to the perpetration of the offence by the juvenile, and so it might be easier to hear a juvenile's evidence in their absence. The members of the family of the accused can therefore be excluded for the welfare and protection of the child.

There is also a welfare agency which acts as an aide to the juvenile court by collecting evidence relating to the background of the juvenile. Legislation has made it obligatory in juvenile cases for the juvenile court aide to collect information on the social and family background of the accused and to present this information to the court, to enable the court to arrive at a more appropriate sentence for the offender.

The maximum prison sentence for a juvenile is ten years. In the past we had indeterminate sentences within a range of five years, but we decided that these did not work and now we have only determinate sentences in juvenile courts. We also have some welfare-based sanctions, coercive measures of education, very similar to those which a family court judge would have in mind when confronted with juveniles in similar circumstances. These comprise about 88 per cent of all sentences passed on juveniles, whereas just over ten per cent are sentences of imprisonment and many of those are suspended.

The legal situation in France and Spain is similar to that in Germany, although these two countries have a system of judicial pre-trial investigation. In France a presiding judge in a juvenile court can order that proceedings be continued in his office, so that they are held in a more intimate atmosphere in which the accused may find it easier to co-operate; but this is not possible in Germany or Spain. In Spain the exclusion of the public in juvenile cases is not a legal rule, but the court has the right at any time to order exclusion of the public in the juvenile's interests, and this is usually done. As a consequence of this regulation the press is prohibited from publishing material which might identify the juvenile defendant in the media.

New Developments

The only one of the three countries in which legal procedures for dealing with juvenile delinquency are likely to undergo change in the near future is Spain, which has started a Parliamentary discussion on how to improve its procedures.

However, in Germany were are seeing developments in relation to child witnesses, particularly victims in cases of child abuse, which I consider will also affect the position of accused juveniles. As a result of aggressive questioning by defence counsel of young victims in the witness box, some years ago the legislature enacted Article 241A of the penal procedure law. This prevents the prosecutor and defence counsel from directly asking questions of such witnesses. Any question to the child witness has to be passed to the judge who will then put it to the witness. This eliminates the aggressive element from questioning so that the child is better protected and is able, or better able, to communicate. While the other legal actors are present and can assert as much legal influence on the proceedings as they wish, they have lost their potential as a source of psychological disturbance.

However, there are cases which have shown that this provision is still not sufficient. There have been cases in Mainz and Koblenz where up to 20 accused adults, mostly members of the child witness's family, have been sitting in court. As each of the accused in a major trial has at least two defence counsel, there were at least 50 counsel sitting alongside the defendants. (Where a crime carries a penalty of one year's imprisonment or more, courts order an obligatory state-paid defence counsel in addition to the defendant's one or two privately chosen and paid defence counsel). Imagine a young child in the witness box in front of some 20 members of his family who are accused of horribly abusing him and other children, 50 defence counsel in their black gowns, the similarly dressed prosecutors and the judges (in an adult case we have three professional judges and two jurors), totalling more than 77 persons. No-one could possibly expect a child to communicate anything in such a setting.

In a case six months ago, the court with the help of some of the defence counsel decided to adopt a very special procedure. The presiding judge moved into a small room where he and the child remained alone for questioning to take place. Invisible television cameras were installed to enable the rest of the participants to view the scene on a big screen in another room. The rest of the judges, the prosecutors and the defence counsel were electronically connected to the interrogating judge by small electronic devices, so that they could communicate with the judge without the child's being aware of this,

129

and the judge could incorporate their points in his questioning of the child where he deemed it appropriate. This arrangements certainly helped the young witnesses and was applied to children between the ages of four to 15.

However, we do not yet know whether this unusual form of hearing will be approved by the federal court. There is a legal argument as to whether the 'presence' of the parties required by Article 221A of the penal procedure law is satisfied by this kind of electronically mediated presence. It nevertheless demonstrates the serious problems with which juveniles, be they witnesses or accused, are confronted. It is in everyone's interest that no criminal hearing should have the effect of negative intervention on the development of juveniles. Moreover, ensuring adequate conditions for juveniles in criminal hearings is helpful in finding out the truth, which is the aim of a criminal trial.

That is why we need to work hard to develop an appropriate framework for criminal hearings. This need not necessarily involve electronic mediation, but the example demonstrates that possibilities exist if only we think seriously about these problems and try to implement changes which are both helpful and functional.

Professor Dr. Hans-Heiner Kuhne is Professor of Criminal Law, Juvenile Law and Criminology at Trier University, Germany.

CHAPTER 15

The German System

Professor Dr. Reinmar du Bois

In this paper I will emphasise which aspects of the German system I, in my role as a psychiatric expert, consider to be more or less valuable, functional, humane, and in the best interests of the young offender. I shall deal in particular with the precarious balance between educational and juridical considerations.

The German juvenile courts exclude the public: only the parents may attend and they must be heard during the proceedings. If the accused is over 18 the court sessions are open to the public, but the public can still be excluded during parts of a trial if very private matters need to be discussed or if it is assumed that the defendant will be inhibited from expressing himself openly and truthfully. It is my impression that, especially if a psychiatrist is involved in the proceedings, the courts make use of this option quite readily. After the public has been readmitted it must be informed of the basic contents of the evidence given in their absence. The juvenile criminal court can be, and often will be, used for offenders up to the age of 21 (young adults). This decision is at the discretion of the court. The juvenile court's social worker will usually support such a move. If there are several accused in the courtroom and one of them is over 18, the trial must be held in public—i.e. the public interest, which is considered to be an essential of the legal process, prevails.

The German legal system is absolutely rigid about the age of legal responsibility. No child under 14 will be prosecuted. A child over 14 will be prosecuted and eventually brought before a juvenile court, of which there are different types depending on the severity of the crime. The types of courts are the same as those for adults. There is an element of educational philosophy in the Juvenile Courts Act, which is represented in the statutory role of the social worker, in the emphasis on personality and the biographical context of a crime, and in an open disposal system that does not prescribe specified sentences for certain crimes (including the most severe). Nevertheless, the overall character of the German jurisdiction in this age group is more juridical and less educational than in the Scottish system with its 'children's hearing panels', which take over from the judiciary to decide on the measures to be taken after a verdict of guilty has been reached. In Germany the passing of a sentence is inevitably part of the same court proceedings and, especially in cases of serious crime (robbery, manslaughter, attempted manslaughter), the result is routinely a prison sentence of three to six years. This rigidity and lack of pedagogic imagination can only be overcome if an exceptionally ambitious court social worker meets an equally imaginative bench of judges, who take a special interest in these matters, despite the fact that they are of little legal interest and will not be appreciated in regard to their next promotion (not even if they stay in the field of juvenile jurisdiction). Juvenile courts have a low reputation among the legal profession.

In order to alleviate the enormous workload of the professional juvenile courts, several reforms have been introduced. Their common objective is to divert petty criminality away from the courts. A prosecutor can redirect a case to be handled by social agencies. Acting in a similar role a judge can issue a warning. If no further penal measures, but instead a custodial order according to civil law ensues then no formal indictment will be necessary to support this. At the next stage, when an indictment has been framed and a proper court session follows, this will comprise a court social worker, a (single) professional judge and a prosecutor. At the next higher stage a court will consist of two lay magistrates beside the professional judge. Such a court can pass youth prison sentences of up to four years (formerly only two years). All offences exceeding serious bodily harm, from robbery to manslaughter and murder, are dealt with by a district court (Crown Court) manned by two lay magistrates and two or three professional judges.

Judges and prosecutors are transferred or promoted to their respective posts within the justice system, some according to their wishes, others more reluctantly. Some perform very well, others just hope for their next promotion to take them away to other areas of legal work. There is no standardised training or even a diploma course. Most expertise comes with experience, provided a judge or prosecutor stays in this field long enough.

After the reading of the indictment, the youth is questioned about his biography. Especially in the high profile cases involving serious crimes, in which I am involved, this is done in great depth and quite diligently. One of the three judges, usually the one who has studied the case in detail from the files, does most of the questioning before he passes on the right to question to the others, to the defending lawyer and the prosecutor. Even the social worker and the psychiatrist may ask questions. An English colleague whom I once took to a German Crown Court said afterwards that he had never heard a judge talk so much. An

English judge would not manage to say as much during his entire professional career.

The part of the evidence where the biography is evolved is quite distinct and separate from the rest of the evidence which deals with the alleged offence, which has either been admitted by the culprit or has yet to be proven. At the very end of the hearing of evidence, the psychiatrist, in cases where he is involved, and the social worker, who is always a statutory participant in the proceedings, will give their reports. This is an opportunity for more biographical details to be added, in order to complete the impression which the accused has given of himself and to clarify and preclude possible misunderstandings concerning the conduct of the young person in court or during his offending. This is the moment when discussions between the defence lawyer, prosecutor, the judges' bench and the social worker may evolve in order to deepen understanding of the criminal behaviour and to put it into a proper biographical perspective. But as the place where these discussions occur is a court room, and as most people who are present in that room are legal professionals with a very limited understanding of welfare matters, the level and the results of these discussions are all too often rather poor. Many prosecutors and judges are satisfied with the contention that leniency results automatically from the fact that the proceedings occur in the framework of a juvenile court where all sentences are set in a time frame of ten years and that no further educational homework needs to be done.

Range of Disposals

What is the range of actions that can be taken concerning young people who offend? Children under 14 who have committed a severe crime, including manslaughter, will be taken into custodial care. All decisions pertaining to the type of institution or the length of the stay are taken by and at discretion of the social agencies. No other juridical or political authority has any part in this. This also ensures that the children are relatively well protected from the media. The accommodation need not be specially secure. Outside the prisons for young offenders, the amount of 'closed' accommodation is very limited. There has been a constant decline in the number of closed or secure institutions in Germany in the last ten to 15 years and a similar rise in the number of rather expensive new types of intensive care units with a high staff-client ratio (on a one to one basis). The most intensive form of care involves two full or half time nurses who accompany a difficult child every day while he continues to live at home, on the street or in a special care unit, or is moved from one place to another. As far as the under 14 year olds are concerned nobody demands 'security' or public protection, unless it is considered necessary from a welfare standpoint. This system is even applied to young offenders with very disturbed behaviour who are legally responsible, provided a juvenile court resolves that the child should not be sent to one of the young offender prisons, where the age range is roughly from 17 to 24.

This system may have many strengths but the shortcomings should not be overlooked. There is a shortage of secure accommodation for the few 'dangerous' children: by this I mean individuals who are dangerously unpredictable not just in the public imagination but according to psychiatric evidence. Forensic treatment units for this young age group are just as non-existent in Germany as other forms of closed accommodation is extremely sparse. This form of accommodation is still more common in northern parts of Germany and has been virtually abolished in the economically better off areas of southern Germany, where the social services experiment with more individualised forms of intensive care. I regret to admit that in some individual cases a kind of 'tourism' of dangerous child offenders takes place from the south to the north. Only a few adolescent psychiatric units would reluctantly agree to accept a disturbed adolescent who has been sentenced by a court for a criminal offence. Without pressure from the legal system, the German child welfare organizations or the communities would never be prepared to erect closed or secure accommodation. One may of course ask whether the building of new secure accommodation for such a relatively small group of dangerously offending children is justified. Such institutions would have to be centralised, far away from the children's homes. Such special units might attract clients that could and would have otherwise been placed elsewhere, thus avoiding stigmatisation. Other arguments can be used in favour of secure institutions: inexperienced staff in a non-secure institution tend to overestimate the dangerousness of detained children and may reject them. As a consequence these children may move from one institution to the next. Staff may tend to over-react when conflicts occur and may restrict the children's personal freedom more than is necessary.

I once had a 14 year old boy on one of my child psychiatric wards. He had repeatedly lured little girls on to an escalator and flung a blanket over them and tried to suffocate them. This boy was never quite sure, and it was impossible to negotiate with him a common understanding, of what his stay on the psychiatric ward was about: was he there to be locked up like in a prison and by order of a judge or was he rather there just to have a nice time as if nothing had happened? Was he ill or evil or just normal, apart from the fact that he was surrounded

134

by unfriendly people who would not let him do what he liked? But then, why was he on a psychiatric ward? The court had implored me to take this boy as there seemed to be no other suitable place for him, and nobody else dared to take him. One might say that the court was glad to rid themselves of their responsibility. I was assured that no legal responsibility and no additional measures of security were expected of me, but implicitly I now had to bear the full weight of the responsibility of protecting the public from this potentially dangerous boy. This is a task that no psychiatric treatment unit and no child care unit within a welfare system can tolerate at length. It is a task that can only be fulfilled with the support of the legal system in an institution which is either run by the legal system or has other strong attachments to this system.

Detention for life does not exist in Germany, either below 14 under civil law or over 14 under penal law. The time spent in care is decided individually. Under civil law there is an annual conference including the parents and all other relevant persons at which the continuation of a custodial order is discussed. At the end a judge, after hearing the evidence, has to pass the decision. Most children stay in care at least until the end of their schooling or the start of their vocational training.

The maximum penalty under the Juvenile Courts Act for a serious offence is ten years (the minimum being six months). This maximum is hardly ever applied at that age, but may well occur at 16 or 17. Young offenders go to special prison facilities. Their stay in these prisons lasts for two-thirds or seven-twelfths of the overall length of the sentence. Theoretically a discharge after one-third of the time is possible, but this hardly ever occurs. Individuals with very long sentences in the area of seven to ten years may be released at half sentence. Decisions on questions of parole and other liberating measures during the prison sentence are taken by the local courts near the prisons. Some young prisoners eventually live in accommodation outside the prison or go to outside work places during the day and return to their prison cells in the evening.

Conceptual Issues

It is clear from international comparisons that rather diverse and disparate legal systems can achieve tolerable results in the management of young offenders. We may also assume that there is no ideal legal system that can solve the conflicting concerns of emotional maturation on the one hand and of reinforcing law and order on the other hand. I would like to propose a number of criteria that could be applied to different criminal justice systems, that could help to clarify their respective positions and which may reveal how well they perform in some respects and how badly in others.

My first criterion pertains to the stability of moral standards concerning special requirements for children. The criminal justice system is put to test if it is confronted with serious crimes and extreme public attention. How does the system manage to observe and maintain its standards of child welfare under such extreme conditions? How well can the balance between educational and punitive requirements, between individual considerations and general considerations, be safeguarded if a particularly nasty case of criminal behaviour occurs, if the crime is moreover committed by a particularly young person, if it defies easy explanation and evokes strong negative sentiments in the public?

I am not just thinking of the Jamie Bulger case in England but of several other cases in my own country concerning youths who under the influence of right wing extremist ideology have beaten up foreigners with baseball clubs or committed arson on homes in which foreigners live, notably people who have applied for political asylum and people of Turkish nationality. The Turks have been an especially large foreign community in Germany since about 30 years. The most publicised recent incident occurred in Solingen. A whole Turkish family was killed by a fire that was lit by three youths. The criminal proceedings in this case, as in many others, were overshadowed by the growing public concern both nationally and internationally about the re-emergence of fascist sympathies among a part of the young generation. There is a strong sentiment that such tendencies should be condemned and wiped out and that strong and impressive signals should come from the courts to this end.

The problem in the Solingen case as in other cases was, however, that the accused did not fit the public prejudice. Nobody in Germany wants to hear such facts. Nobody wants to realise that in this case, as in many others of dramatic and especially reckless youth behaviour, the reasons should be better understood on an individual basis. As far as collective trends towards racism are concerned these do, of course, pose a major problem to our society but they have to be viewed quite separately from serious criminal acts. The public ignore the fact that long-standing deficient educational attitudes by parents cannot be remedied by impressively harsh reactions of the penal law in spectacular single law suits. The Solingen trial lasted for eight months. To make matters worse, in the Solingen case the evidence remained rather uncertain, yet the court was under enormous pressure to come to a strong verdict. The case was prosecuted by the federal prosecution office, which would normally only prosecute when high treason,

136

terrorism and other affairs of national concern are concerned. The legal proceedings would have been quite different in a normal Juvenile Crown Court, the expertise of the magistrates and judges concerning this type of delinquency would have been higher, and much more common sense would have reigned throughout.

My second criterion concerns the quality of jurisdiction within the lower age group: those ages for which the legal system can only just claim responsibility or (as in other legal systems) even those ages at which a criminal justice system may have no responsibility, although some criminal behaviour has already emerged. How well are different systems prepared to react to the criminal behaviour in this lower age group? How flexible are their reactions? Can and will they react differently in response to individual situations? How suitable or unsuited are the mechanisms by which it is established whether a child should be held responsible no matter whether or not it has passed a legal age barrier? Such an age limit can only be artificial and will be too high in one case and in other cases far too low. How good or how bad an instrument is the *doli incapax* principle or alternatively the German principle of so-called 'legal maturity'? How well do social services and educational staff on the one hand and the judiciary on the other interact and co-operate?

The German age of responsibility of 14 is in many respects a rather high age limit. Fourteen-year-olds are so to speak 'over-mature' and overdue to experience legal reactions to certain illegal actions. Regrettably, the German legal system denies all responsibility below the age of 14 and leaves the task of reinforcing right and wrong—in all its complexity—to the welfare system. Of course a closer co-operation between the welfare system and the criminal justice system can only succeed if the penal law accepts in return that considerations of education and emotional development must prevail in relation to children. The welfare system, however, has to accept that the legal system has a constitutional right to become engaged in the handling of the more serious kinds of deviant criminal behaviour in this age group. And the welfare system must also accept that delinquent acts even below a certain age of legal responsibility should incur and may indeed profit from some kind of public sanctions.

The fundamental difference between juridical and educational reasoning must never be overlooked. Juridical reasoning starts with the definition of a certain crime, educational reasoning starts with the study of personal maturation and only then proceeds to ask why a particular person carries out certain forms of deviant behaviour. I am very doubtful whether the criminal justice system, even if it is concerned with young offenders, will ever want to change its fundamental crime-related nomothetic reasoning and jump over the barrier to join the educationalist.

My third criterion is concerned with the influence of the media and public interest in court proceedings. How can the fundamental right of public participation in the making of justice be preserved and yet a very young person be protected from the adverse effects of the media, which at their worst may cause a lifelong stigmatisation? In the German juvenile courts the public is excluded, but journalists may attend on special application. When reporting about events in the courtroom they are as a rule rather cautious. They are aware that otherwise they would not be readmitted to further juvenile court sessions. Anonymity is assured. Confidentiality for the very young is safeguarded by the fact that these children do not appear in court at all, as they are not legally responsible. The welfare system in charge of these cases is in a far better position to defend the personal affairs of their clients and to ensure confidentiality. I should add that I cannot rule out similarly hysterical reactions in the German tabloids as have occurred in Britain. With the advent of private television channels, the media are getting greedier for sensation, and their methods are getting more and more obtrusive and shameless. I need not remind you of the well known discussion of whether the press is to blame because it manipulates the public or whether the public is to blame as the press only mirrors what everyone thinks and feels.

Adversarial and Inquisitorial Systems

My next criterion concerns different systems of jurisdiction, the adversarial system in Britain and the United States and the inquisitorial system in France, Germany and elsewhere on the continent. Which elements of these two systems are in the best interests of the child during the different stages of the criminal proceedings deserves careful consideration. Up to a certain degree it may be in the best interests of the child if all parties in court act in co-operation; but to a certain degree it may also be of avail to the welfare of the child if the parties stay on opposite sides and pursue separate intentions—bearing in mind that the criminal justice system will always be a separate independent institution in any society and that tensions between education and punishment are inevitable. Perhaps, in the best interests of a child, these differences should not be glossed over. Thus it may be advisable that societal reactions to criminal behaviour in youths should be twofold and take place in two different domains, that justice be done in one domain and that reasonable educational responses be found in another domain.

138

Yet there must be an minimum of mutual acceptance and an understanding of the interdependence of the two domains. The adversarial system may be best suited to determining the facts of a crime and the offender's culpability. The same system, however, may be rather insensitive or even inhumane when it comes to integrating juridical and educational aspects. To compensate for this deficiency the adversarial system may facilitate a procedure which we have seen in Scotland, by which a case is referred to a separate committee (children's hearing panel) which is better equipped to deal with the complex questions of 'disposal' of a legal case into an educational framework. Probably such a body can handle these issues far better than even the most professional juvenile judge within an inquisitorial system, because his bias will always rest on the legal side.

An inquisitorial system may boast of a closer co-operation between the different parties. But nobody should complain if the prosecution still demands more punitive action whilst the defence—usually in unison with the juvenile court social worker—still pleads for a less punitive solution. In my view a defence lawyer usually gives a somewhat clumsy impression if he ventures into the domain of educational issues in order to support his client. In Germany the ultimate solution must be found in court by the judges and the lay magistrates. No representative of the child welfare side has any part in this. Before this, the social worker is obliged to formulate a recommendation in court on whether or not he or she considers an educational reaction to be sufficient. The magic term is 'schadliche Neigung', which means 'criminal inclinations'. If such inclinations must be admitted, which is all too often the case, then little scope is allowed for a disposal other than a prison sentence.

And there is little comfort to be drawn from the fact that special prisons are provided for young people. These are still rather tough institutions which see young offenders on the path to further deviant behaviour, once they have learned to survive the bullying and have adapted to the relentless power struggle. Educational institutions which could serve as a substitute for prisons do not exist in Germany, except for some model institutions designed exclusively for the period on remand before a trial. By having to pass a verdict on the critical issue of 'criminal tendencies' in court the social worker is forced to betray his own professional philosophy. He is forced to cross the front line.

In an adversarial system, especially in the Scottish variety, the dividing line between the criminal aspect and the educational/correctional aspect has been drawn much more clearly. The welfare principle, on the other side of the fence, so to speak, can be defended more convincingly, of course not always more successfully, but certainly with less ambivalence on all sides.

139

My next criterion deals with the older age group from 16 upwards to 18 or even 21. In fact this is the age where the majority of serious criminality takes place. How is the interface between juvenile court proceedings and those for adults designed? How wide is the gap between a legal format paying regard to the developmental needs of young people and the general system displaying no regard to questions of personal development whatsoever? Curiously enough the gap may be especially wide in a system where a special legal construction to protect young people exists if it has only been accepted superficially and is in reality rejected as an alien annexe which does not fit into the overall structure. The fact that Germany's Juvenile Courts Act cannot fully be integrated into the general criminal justice system leads to curious results. It is applied in a mechanistic way, the underlying educational philosophy is often ignored. One may be afraid that this Act may lose even further ground if the political tide turns. On the other hand it has survived troubled waters during the Nazi regime and has been functioning since 1923, thus proving some stability.

Finally, I would like to return to the crucial question of disposal, when the courts have to deal with a particularly serious crime. No matter how well developed a system may be in passing the disposal decision on to educational panels (and the Scottish system excels in this respect) how much of such a system survives when a serious crime has to be handled? Will the judiciary now over-react? Will it switch from leniency to relentless toughness? Will all the people who have previously advocated the welfare principle now take flight? Will no-one accept further responsibility (except the Home Office)? Will the general public suddenly draw absurd images of the viciousness of these children and call them diabolic and evil?

I am still intrigued by the fact that very young children who commit serious crimes are automatically perceived as especially dangerous and especially prone to reoffend. The reverse is true. From the viewpoint of a psychiatrist, it is obvious that these children have suffered the most devastating traumata and that the situation in which they have committed their crime was in many respects unique. From such a viewpoint, these children deserve more rather than less attention by the welfare system, even if they have offended.

Professor Dr. Reinmar du Bois is the Medical Director of the Child and Adolescent Unit at the Olgahospital, Stuttgart

CHAPTER 16

Norway: A Resolutely Welfare-Oriented Approach

Dr. Graham Clifford

In Norway children who have committed serious offences are dealt with by the welfare system and not by the criminal justice system. Norway's approach can only be described as resolutely welfare-oriented. The age of criminal responsibility is 15 and children who commit offences below that age do not appear in court.

There is no juvenile court system. This seems to be bound up with long standing social and political perspectives on children and young people. Norway has traditionally been much influenced by the notion of children becoming adults fairly abruptly at the age of 14 or 15. Children are confirmed then, and that is a major social event as well as a religious event. Abruptly, children are called on to be responsible, to have rights and to have social responsibilities. In accordance with this tradition, Norway for a long time set its age of criminal responsibility at 14, and this has now been adjusted to 15.

When a child below the age of 15 offends, whether seriously or not, the police are enjoined to report the matter to the social services, who have to investigate. The parents are obliged to submit to this investigation, which is so wide ranging that the health services and other official agencies that may have had some contact with the child must co-operate. On that basis a broad picture of the child is built up and that will decide whether any action is taken.

As elsewhere, very serious offences committed by young children under the age of twelve are exceedingly rare—so rare as to cause serious trauma and questioning when they do occur. No-one is ever prepared for them. In a population of four million they occur so rarely that it is very difficult to find any real parallels to a situation we had last year. Other researchers at my Institute, drawing upon historical material, have found a couple of cases from the seventeenth century: it seems apparent from written records that those children were treated with extreme leniency although one of them had murdered his mother.

In my home town of Trondheim in 1994 we had an entirely unprecedented case in which two six-year-old boys killed a five-year-

141

old girl. This incident occurred in unsupervised play in the children's neighbourhood and its effect was entirely traumatic. People were stunned, there was disbelief, there was no understanding of how such a thing could happen.

Under the Norwegian system the police have to find out what has happened. It is expected of them that they will provide a reliable and fully documented account, so far as possible, of the sequence of events. The investigation found that the most probable chain of events was that the girl had been brutally beaten by the two boys with a large stone, but that she had died of hypothermia as a result of being rendered unconscious. Child psychiatric and child protection services looked after the families of all the children involved: the public services were more or less even-handed as far as concern for the families of the perpetrators as well as for the families of the victim was concerned. This is my own local community, and I can vouch for the fact that local people were just as concerned for the parents of the boys who had done this as they were for the parents of the girl who died.

There were very interesting dissonances of opinion among child researchers. Some emphasised the more or less accidental nature of such incidents and pointed out that children of five or six have little empathy and are unable to provide accounts of how others will respond in certain situations. When situations occur outside the context of relationships with which they are familiar, they cannot handle them and can quite easily get out of control. Other child researchers were inclined to see this as a sign of the declining mores in our society and the problems of parenting. In short, child researchers were no more able than anyone else to agree about the causes and were just as defeated by the horror of these events. Child psychiatry and the social services deal with the aftermath of such an incident.

When the young people concerned are over the age of 15, there is a double track response. There is still a heavy emphasis on investigation, on social work and on trying to find out the circumstances of the child. This is appropriate because our criminal law makes it incumbent on those dealing with a case to find out if there are any extenuating circumstances, and such considerations are particularly important for anyone under the age of 18. Many young offenders have extenuating circumstances: there is a link between unsatisfactory home situations and serious offences. The appropriate response is often viewed as being some form of treatment in an open care institution.

In Norway young people cannot serve a sentence together with adult offenders. It is impermissible for them to be placed in prison or in any kind of physical security until they reach the age of 16. There are between two and four cases a year in which, exceptionally, someone under 16 goes into a prison, and then it is viewed as a defeat for the system because there was no other alternative.

Advantages and Disadvantages

Norway has a very flexible and humane system that I admire very much. However, there are some possible disadvantages in a system that is so rigorously welfare oriented as Norway's. One of them is that children need to be protected from adults who insist on knowing the answers to their problems. It is not always an undiluted good to hand children over to the welfare and health systems to find out what is 'wrong with them'. A system that has no court provision for children below the age of 15 may to some extent fail to guarantee children's rights. Once the police have decided that the child has committed an offence, there is no way of disproving the police's view. There is none of the protection that some form of court hearing could give. In Norway no-one finds this very remarkable.

A system that sees treatment as an answer to children's seriously deviant behaviour to such an extent relies very heavily on social solidarity, the community's acceptance that treatment is appropriate and the community's restraint in not being vengeful. If you reflect that most people in Norway live in communities that are very small by the standards of most other European countries, the stigma attached to a serious offence committed in childhood will clearly last all your life. A small society does not ever forget. A system that relies on the social services to do the job must confront the fact that all services are far from perfect. They are staffed by people who make mistakes. In some ways a system that relies both on a judicial process and a welfare process has more safeguards because there are several parties involved.

On the other hand, the Norwegian system is blessedly free from the kind of ghoulish horrors that seem to have been attached to some cases in Great Britain in recent years. The spectacle of adults baying for blood when children have committed serious crimes is not an edifying one, and it is one that we have been spared.

The myth of the innocent child is a fundamental belief in our culture. When children prove not to be innocent, we adults get into very serious trouble. We either become vengeful or we attempt in some way to push the import of the events away from us. Professionals are just as prone to be phased, disturbed and upset by this as anyone else. Therefore it is very important to train professionals of all kinds—the police and the legal profession just as much as social workers and doctors—to try to cope with this. There are of course limits to how much training we can do to contribute to the better management of events that occur fairly rarely. Our notion of children's innocence prevents us from looking constructively at other aspects of the behaviour of children and young people—but it is very difficult to protest against culture. There may be an argument for a middle way between the extremes of the Norwegian system on the one hand and the British system on the other. There may be some advantages in defining criminal responsibility at, say, 13.

In Norway we have the same debate as is taking place in Britain and the same concern about violence among the young. In fact, violence among the young is not increasing very much, although it is increasing in the pages of the daily newspapers and on television. There is a lot of emphasis in the public debate in Norway on parents' responsibilities and much of this debate is fundamentally unrealistic. Children these days face a far more complex society than we did. So, rather than pose as an advocate of a Scandinavian welfare idyll, I would rather say to you: 'Learn from us, but do not learn too much.'

The Court System

We have a social court, not a family court, which considers alternative care for children who are found to be out of control and where parental care and control is inadequate, and which deals with issues of child protection. A child under 15 who committed a serious offence would be dealt with there. This social court has recently been changed in quite important respects. Nowadays it has a basically adversarial form. Lawyers attend for the various parties—i.e. for the state, for the parents of the child and for the child himself or herself—and a fairly strict procedure is followed. The party applying for alternative care is always the local authority.

For those over 15 years old we have a two tier court system with lower courts and higher courts. A serious offence would always go before a higher court, as would any case where the offender pleads not guilty. In the lower courts only the defendant, the judges and the advocates are present. The public are not allowed in and no report of the proceedings is made available. This means that the press cannot get hold of the contents of the hearing and, although they can report the sentence, courts almost invariably prohibit the publication of names.

In the higher courts the press have access and hearings are freely reportable, but the names of defendants are not. There is a system of appeal to a committee of the Supreme Court and appeals can be based either on the severity of sentences or on the application of the law. The Supreme Court never judges the issue of whether a verdict was correct or not.

Both the lower courts and the higher courts are composed of lay and professional judges. Occasionally the question of whether lay judgment is really appropriate arises. It is an endemic feature of the system that unpopular or curious verdicts cause anxious debate about this. All court proceedings are verbal and evidence has to be presented verbally. All evidence can be questioned by the defence. The judge has no inquisitorial function, unlike the position in some other European countries. The judge is a neutral person who has a professional background and who comes to the case for the first time when it is presented in court. Lay judges have the same role.

One very disturbing development in Norway, as in many other countries, is that the presentation of the prosecution and defence case through the media before the trial has become more and more widespread. This is a worrying trend and has given rise to serious concern. The peculiar unpleasantness of some cases that involve young people committing very serious crimes naturally leads the media to be especially interested.

Sentencing

Offenders under 18 very rarely go to prison. A judgment is made on a welfare basis about the appropriate regime for the young person and every effort is made to try to place them in such a setting in a residential home or residential institution, usually staffed by well qualified professionals.

Two-thirds of a sentence is served in the institution; but it is not unusual for young people to be released earlier than this to alternative forms of treatment or to pursue their education. The system is notably humane and there is no political interference with the length of sentences or the various decisions which can shorten the length of a sentence while it is being served. A prison committee is responsible for ensuring that such decisions are made: they are made in practice by professionals who know the child well, not by people who are higher in the bureaucracy.

All the concerns which relate to young people appearing in court are present in Norway. A court system is intimidating whether judges wear wigs or not. While the issue of children and young people as witnesses has been discussed fairly thoroughly in recent years because of child abuse cases, the very exposed position of the young person who is accused has been explored much less.

Children's development is a very erratic business. They may develop quickly for a time, then more slowly. At a given age, children have a wide spread of cognitive abilities, understanding of language, ability to maintain social situations and ability to cope with stress. The principle of individuation is very important. A family court situation like the one in Germany or a panel situation as in Scotland is fundamentally better suited to children's needs.

Research into telephone helplines for children, which have been seen as a very positive move towards empowering children, has shown that there are some grave problems associated with them. One of them is that children's understanding of the codes about communication often means that in telling you a secret, they expect you to do something about it. A child gives you trust by giving you a particular message. Children often tell secrets to others on the premise that they will help them, whether they are talking to a family friend or to a person employed by a court to find out the circumstances of a situation, and children may perceive implicit promises that are simply not there.

Children may experience forms of mild or even severe betrayal in the course of a process designed to find the truth. This in the end will be psychologically and spiritually an extra burden, and the experience may be wounding. These strictures probably apply to communication between children and fact-finders from a very early to a relatively late age. Although some form of criminal responsibility at ages lower than those that pertain in Norway may have benefits, it is certainly not beneficial in this respect. We are inclined to feel that when children become teenagers, their emotional and intellectual development is complete and they are able to sustain the burdens which these proceedings imply: there are indications that this is an over-optimistic view.

The main drawback of Norway's social court is that it is very formalised and procedural and there is almost no negotiation involved. I am very interested in the German family court system because it implies a rather broader framework for negotiation—that is to say, if a child has committed a serious offence, some form of negotiations with parents and others can be mediated through it, and that is certainly the import of the Scottish panel system.

In short, we have a welfare oriented system, in terms of punishment for young people over 15 and in total terms for those under 15. The procedural aspects of Norwegian practice raise the fundamental question of what children can sustain in respect of judicial procedure.

Dr. Graham Clifford is Senior Researcher at the Norwegian Centre for Child Research, University of Trondheim, Norway.

CHAPTER 17

The Dutch System

Judge Paul van Teeffelen

In the Netherlands a new Criminal Minors Code became effective on 1 September 1995. Two months later, on 1 November 1995, a new Civil Minors Code came into force. A feature of both laws is the reduction of the central position of juvenile court magistrates.

Arising from the need and demand to give youngsters protection, psychosocial help and justice, in the previous era the juvenile judge had become the focus for co-ordinating help and ensuring justice. The judge decides what is in 'the best interests of the child' in the specific case, whether civil or criminal. Thus he is both judge and co-ordinator of help and protection.

This model has been the subject of increasing criticism in the last two decades for the following three reasons. First, the welfare model is seen as being too paternalistic. Secondly, the youth's legal position in the criminal trial has not yet been specified in detail. The increasing independence, responsibility and emancipation of youngsters resulted in a greater emphasis on the youth's legal position. And third, increasing doubt and scepticism arose regarding the value and function of the welfare model in preventing youth crime. Solutions have to be found involving less care and more order.

In the new criminal law the juvenile judge is no longer the judge who takes charge of the case from the beginning till the end, being fully informed of the criminal case at each phase. The new law has less protective and pedagogic and more severe traits, although the minor receives more rights corresponding to the adult system. Beyond this, the new law contains an arrangement of alternative sanctions. Lesser offences do not go to a court hearing: only serious offenders will be punished there, and more severely. Until 1 September 1995 there was a maximum penalty of only six months. Now the maximum penalty for children between twelve and 16 years old is one year, and for 16 and 17 year old minors the maximum penalty has been raised to two years.

The result is that the gap between the criminal law for young people and adults has been reduced.

Different Ages

Children under the age of twelve are not considered criminally responsible. With the advent of the new criminal code, there was some discussion on this matter. According to the Minister of Justice the punishment of children up to the age of twelve is a task of the educators, especially their parents. There is no place for the public prosecutor. Besides, the Beijing Rules oblige countries to fix a minimum age for children's criminal responsibility: below that age they cannot be convicted of an offence, they have to be protected.

If the behaviour of those children is unacceptable for society, the Civil Minors Code is sufficient to intervene when their parents persistently fail to correct the behaviour of the child even with the voluntary help of social workers. In such a civil case the parents of the child are parties and they represent the minor before the juvenile court magistrates. It is possible that the child may have to be placed away from his family, in a youth treatment centre for instance.

The Criminal Minors Code applies to children between twelve and 18 years. The criminal law for adults can also be used for children of 16 and 17 years old. The criteria are: how serious is the case, what is the personality of the offender, and are there special circumstances in relation to the case putting the Criminal Adults Code into effect? Conversely, young adults between 18 and 21 years can be punished as minors if the case or the personality of the offender justifies this.

Even if the Criminal Adults Code applies to a child, the trial remains a juvenile trial. Only the sanctions are different, the sanctions for adult persons being used. A trial of a juvenile has its own character: the most important difference from an adult trial is the closed nature of the hearing. In principle formal hearings involving child defendants are closed to the public and the press.

The process is a criminal procedure; but the Crown prosecutor can stop the process before the formal hearing and can ask the juvenile judge to authorise supervision of the child on the grounds of danger to his or her physical or moral welfare. The crime can be a symptom of serious problems involving his carers in the family. The criminal process can be stopped and a civil process begun.

Agency Roles

The *police* can lock up the minor for six hours. After this time the *Crown prosecutor* can authorise his detention for three days and this term can be extended for another three days. The minor is held separate from adults. In the first three days of detention, the child will be visited by a *lawyer* and have free legal aid. The minor will be seen too by a social worker of the *youth protection council*. In most cases this social worker will contact the parents and the legal aid lawyer. The social worker will address a report to the Crown prosecutor, who can decide on the necessity of further detention of the child. The Crown prosecutor can stop the detention, and even the prosecution, when effective help for the young suspect has been organised.

Otherwise the Crown prosecutor authorises further detention. In that case the child will be brought before the *examining magistrate* (a juvenile court magistrate) within the first three days. This examining magistrate makes a decision about further detention for a term of ten days. Prior to his decision there is a hearing with the child and his parents.

The juvenile court magistrate can suspend detention immediately or after some days, and commit the minor to an *institution* to render help and support to him or her. During the pre-trial period the juvenile court magistrate can ask the youth protection council for a social inquiry report, especially about the youngster's personality, life history and other conditions of life.

In cases of violent crime there will always be an examination, requested by the Crown prosecutor: the examining magistrate will appoint one or more experts, for instance a *psychiatrist* or a *psychologist*. These experts can visit the youngster in custody. Sometimes the minor will be placed in a special *observation centre*.

After ten days, *three magistrates of the court* will consider the necessity of further detention. Most of these magistrates are not juvenile judges and are used to adult criminal cases. These magistrates can authorise detention for the next thirty days This term can be extended, for thirty days at a time. The youngster has a limited right of appeal to the *Court of Appeal* against these decisions. Within this period formal hearings have to start, to determine the facts of the case and to decide how to deal with the offender.

Initially the police have the power to decide on detention of the youngster, but soon afterwards one or more magistrates of the court are the competent authorities. On application by the public prosecutor, the examining magistrate and afterwards the three magistrates of the court are responsible for making decisions about the placement of the child pending a decision about whether to proceed to a formal hearing and pending the hearing's taking place. During the formal hearing, the same three judges are responsible for these matters.

In the new juvenile criminal law the Crown prosecutor is more independent, making the decision about whether to proceed to a formal hearing. Under the former law, the Crown prosecutor had to consult with the juvenile court magistrate and the youth protection council.

In the Netherlands we use the principle of opportuneness: this means that you can stop a prosecution if this is in the public interest. In making a decision many factors are taken into account. The decision is always dependent on the adequacy of evidence. The prosecutor will halt proceedings when there is a lack of evidence. Even if there is enough evidence, the prosecutor can decide to avoid a formal hearing. A reason for doing so can be the best interests of the child, especially when effective help for the youngster has been organised. Nevertheless the prosecutor may consider that the public is too shocked by the criminal act and decide on a formal hearing.

In the last decade much attention has been paid to the position of the victim. Sometimes the prosecutor will continue the prosecution for the sake of the victim, whereas some time ago there was more attention for the offender than for the victim. Nowadays the Crown prosecutor engages in conversation with victims of crimes and violence. Not only does this give him important information for the decision on what to do with the case, but it also demonstrates that he is willing to pay attention to the victims.

The Media

Generally the attitude of the media in reporting cases is an attitude of restraint, especially in relation to the identification of the child or other members of the offender's family. Of course in homicide cases the media pay more attention and, even when the press does not use names, in a little town everybody knows everything about the case.

Formal hearings are closed to the press. The president of the court can open the doors if in his judgement the public interest which justifies trying the case in open court is greater than the interest of the child and his parents in not being identified. However, the normal rule is a trial behind closed doors. There is usually less publicity than at the time of the offence, when the crime shocked the public.

Judge Paul van Teeffelen was a juvenile court magistrate at Breda from 1981 to 1993. He is now a member of the Court of Appeal at 's-Hertogenbosch.

CHAPTER 18

The Trial System in Holland

Judge Corinne Dettmeyer

In Holland defendants aged twelve or over are dealt with by a criminal trial, while offenders younger than twelve are brought before the family court. We have few children who kill, and I will therefore speak of serious crimes generally including armed robberies, knifings, rape and repeated burglaries of a serious nature.

When it is dealing with a serious crime, the court will consist of three professional judges, one of whom will be an experienced juvenile judge. They constitute a criminal juvenile court which is distinct from the adult court. When an adult and a juvenile commit a crime together in a way that means they have to be dealt with at the same time, the trial of both takes place in the adult court. However, that hardly every happens: usually they are split up and the adult goes before the ordinary criminal court and the young person before the juvenile criminal court. As in France, we have an instruction judge who gathers the evidence, hears witnesses in the presence of the defence lawyer and can have the child examined by psychiatrists, psychologists and social workers.

When the crime is a very grave one, the juvenile can be, and often is, held in pre-trial detention. In the Hague, which is one of the bigger courts, we have a court session every two or three weeks with something like seven or eight cases per session and 90 per cent of these will have been in pre-trial detention. If the crime is really serious, there is a lengthy previous criminal history and there is a suspicion that there is something wrong with the child mentally or psychologically, then not only do we ask psychiatrists to make a report but we also have the juvenile observed during his pre-trial detention. The maximum period of pre-trial detention is 104 days, which is spent in a youth detention centre where the doors are locked but there is a special regime involving work in groups, education, crafts, sport and psychiatric observation.

CHAPTER 19

The Treatment of Seriously Delinquent Young People in the Netherlands

Jelle Drost

A number of changes have occurred recently in the profile of juvenile delinquency in the Netherlands.

Surveys[1] suggest that young people start their criminal conduct at an earlier age and continue offending for longer periods. A small group of young people, the so called hard core, are committing increasingly serious offences. Young people are tending to become more violent. A growing proportion of the problem is caused by foreign young people,[2] particularly Moroccan young people. Crime among girls is increasing, but is only a fraction of the crime rate for boys.

While boys are committing serious crimes of violence more often (murder, manslaughter), the increase is mostly caused by types of crime (e.g. robbery with the threat of violence) in which physical violence is rarely actually used. Most of these young people end up in a juvenile offenders institution. At present there are 17 juvenile offenders institutions in the Netherlands. Together they can provide accommodation for more than 800 young people between the ages of 12 and 23. In the course of 1996 a number of new projects will be developed and existing ones will be expanded, so that the total capacity will reach about 1,350 places towards the end of 1996, distributed among 20 young offenders institutions, to which young people are sentenced by juvenile court magistrates. There are different sorts of institutions. The most important distinction between different types of juvenile offenders institutions is that between *detention centres* and *treatment centres*. The 17 detention centres and treatment centres can be broken down into eight state institutions and nine private sector institutions. The state institutions are the direct responsibility of the Ministry of Justice. The private sector institutions have their own boards of governors and are dependent on grants from the Ministry of Justice.

There is also a distinction between closed and open institutions. The detention centres are all closed. Closed means that the institution is secure. There are walls, fences, and sometimes even bars. Some of the treatment centres are also closed, but most of them are open. They do not have walls, fences or bars; access is reasonably free. The institutions differ from one another in their approach, but they all have the same basic goal: to prepare the youngsters as effectively as possible for their return to the community because a good new start is an important precondition for preventing reoffending.

In recent years much research has been done in the Netherlands into the characteristics of delinquent young people. In a research study of 383 youngsters admitted into judicial treatment centres, the following problem categories were distinguished:[3]

	Percentage	Average number of problems
Core group	35	15
Attachment problems	13	18
Runaways and drug users	12	19
Severe developmental disorders	11	20
'Hothead' group	6	20
Social and emotional problems	4	25
Multi-problem group	4	26

The core group is formed by juveniles with moderate problems in several areas, such as developmental disorders, attachment problems, social or emotional problems, delinquency, acting-out, drug use and running away. Yet their problems can only be judged as 'moderate' in comparison with their fellow inmates.

Each of the six other types of residents has its own focus on one or more specific problem areas. For example, the 'hothead' group shows the highest incidence of acting-out. Another group of residents, in which more girls than boys are found, mainly exhibits attachment problems. A third group, also composed mainly of girls, comprises runaways and drug users. Unlike the other types, these two groups contain the lesser offenders. A much more problematic group is formed by the juveniles with severe developmental disorders, some of them showing characteristics of psychosis as well. Comprising approximately 1 per cent of the population, these individuals have often committed many crimes. Juveniles with social and emotional problems form yet another small but problematic group. The last group can best be typified as a 'multi-problem group': these juveniles suffer from all the problems mentioned above.

An example: William

I will illustrate by means of a real example what may happen to a young person who ends up in a juvenile offenders institution. William is 16 years old. From his early years his mother was often away from home. During that time he did not know his father. According to his mother, the latter was a criminal. Mother has to earn a living by doing cleaning work. She regularly has a new partner. If, however, the partner reprimands William or beats him up, which occurs regularly, she shows him the door. Mother herself, however, is hardly able to give William her affection. She is often absent, is a regular pub crawler and leaves William alone while she is out drinking. In his fifth year the child protection agency intervenes when William, for the third time, is caught red handed stealing soft drinks in the neighbourhood shop. He is placed in a foster-family, which within six months has been driven over the edge by him and his mother. Mother wants to pay visits at irregular times and William appears to react badly to the affection of the foster-family. When the foster-family is in conflict with the mother, William becomes unmanageable.

He is again placed at home. During this period he regularly lives with his father whom he has looked for and has found. When there, he is often hit. Then things seem to improve for a couple of years. At the age of thirteen he is involved in a bag theft with a great deal of violence. Via a number of juvenile treatment institutions where he appears to be too violent, William is placed in an open juvenile offenders institution. Things go well there for a couple of months. With one residential child care worker in particular, there is a growing bond of friendship and William himself says that he has found a 'home' for the first time in his life. One evening, however, he and another pupil beat up the child care worker with a chair leg. He is sent to a detention centre for two weeks. After that, William is placed in a closed treatment centre.

A juvenile offenders institution has the task of executing punishment and of taking measures within a legal and political framework. The authority relationship laid down by the sentence characterises this task. It is not the intrinsic need of or request for help and care of the juvenile or his parent(s) that is most important, but giving satisfaction to the fulfilment of a judicial order. The juvenile offenders institutions are empowered to take over in part the role of the legal representatives of society. The institutions have the duty to realise this power.[4]

Underlying the placement of a young person in a juvenile offenders institution is judicial action. The juvenile court magistrate has intervened in parental authority by means of this action and has passed this authority in practice into the hands of the juvenile offenders institution. That has consequences for treatment. The treatment relationship is fundamentally different from a support relationship in a voluntary framework. The relationship is authority-based because of the judicial sentence and not based on the intrinsic need for help to the young person or parent(s); it is not based on motivation.[5]

The treatment, therefore, can be characterised as the fulfilment of a social and judicial task. A request for assistance is not the starting point, but the identification of shortcomings which need treatment. In this way a juvenile offenders institution is given responsibility for making decisions concerning the rearing of a young person and this includes competence to remedy deficient education.[6] Treatment should be qualified by these tasks.

Returning to William, when he is placed in a closed juvenile offenders institution as soon as possible after placement, a care plan[7] for the youngster is drawn up, based on a systemic view.[8] Development takes place within a situational context and there is a mutual interaction between the young person and his environment. The young person is often entangled in this context and should be helped to unravel this and to see things clearly. Of at least equal importance is the way this process makes the aims of treatment clearer to the care team. The more this context is mixed up in a youngster's perception, the more problematic the conduct.[9] Systems theory can be a valuable aid to mapping out this social context of the young person. In this way a good treatment plan can be drawn up. The care plan looks in outline as follows:

1. Personal image

1.1 The young person as an individual
1.1.1 Identity file
1.1.2 Family history
1.1.3 Development course
1.1.4 Physical aspects of conduct
1.1.5 Cognitive aspects of conduct
1.1.6 Emotional aspects of conduct
1.1.7 Social aspects of conduct
1.1.8 Didactic data, work experience, schedule for daily work

For William the following treatment goals are formulated:

Regulation of life rhythm
William has become accustomed to living at night and sleeping during
the daytime. By offering him a fixed life rhythm and day programme,
structure and safety are provided, by which a basis is laid for the
fulfilment of other necessities of life.[10]

Acceptance of social rules
William has lived in a sub-culture of his own for years[11] with private
rules and standards. He hardly knows the rules of society, as a result of
which he presents a danger for society. Not until he respects these rules
is the safety of society guaranteed and can he be admitted to an open
juvenile offenders institution.

Increase of social competency
Research has shown that there is a relationship between anti-social
behaviour, youth delinquency, conduct problems and behavioural
disturbances on the one hand and a lack of social skills, a deficit of
social competency, on the other.[12]

Other research[13] shows that youngsters in juvenile offenders institutions know only two ways of reacting to stress: beating up or running away. William has to learn that there are other ways to solve conflicts and problems.

Insight into the necessity of change in behaviour

Co-operation between the care worker and youngsters has a number of stages that must have been gone through in order to come to a working alliance:

- communication technique: the ability to send, receive and understand signals, verbal as well as non-verbal;
- the ability to bring about a relationship: there should be a mutual attainableness and the willingness to seek it;
- workability: this is mutual attainableness combined with the ability to bring about a relationship and the ability to use the treatment offered. That means realising that the treatment is useful and necessary.[14]

Offer of perspective

Research[15] shows that the perspective(s) of young people in such situations is gloomy. Their chances of getting a job are considerably lower than average, while the chance of running into problems (running away, using drugs, drifting), or creating problems themselves (vandalism, theft and other crimes), is comparatively much greater. The offer of education directed towards a place in the labour market presents an important perspective in the life of young people in juvenile offenders institutions.[16]

William's stay in a secure treatment institution, however, is not a goal in itself. The security is used only to make him accessible to treatment and to take away the obstacles which have led to his placement into a closed setting. The security ought to be for the shortest possible time. In this connection the 'phased' treatment in Dutch youth care has an important place. The transition from closed to open treatment often turns out to be too large a step. It is difficult for William to handle the comparatively greater freedom in the open setting, so that the results achieved in the closed institution are at risk of being reduced to naught.

As an intermediate stage there is the possibility of a private establishment. This is not characterised in the first instance by means of security by buildings (though the building ought to have the capability of being locked) but by means of very intensive care of William by the child care worker. William cannot move freely outside and is obliged to keep to strict rules and agreements. From this starting point they work bit by bit towards more freedom and more responsibility, after which a transfer to an establishment with a more open character may take place. This phased approach, the treatment aims which will be pursued, the timetable and the testing procedures will be referred to in the care plan.

At the end of his treatment William can make use of a reintegration project, for instance in the shape of supported lodgings whereby he lives in a room on the site of the institution or in a neighbouring town and receives a decreasing amount of care from an appointed assistant. When the placement agency as well as the appointed worker think that William has become sufficiently independent, the placement can be ended. Then William will be dependent on less intensive forms of support.

In Dutch youth care a great deal of attention is given to the planning of a system of verifiable quality. Therefore a number of research studies are being carried out into the effects of treatment in juvenile offenders institutions. Results will be available in 1996.

Feelings of insecurity in Dutch society are increasing. Therefore there is an increasing demand for closed institutions and the number of available places will increase because new institutions are under construction and existing ones are being enlarged.

The treatment of young people, however, ought to be the central point in this process. Security may be no more than a temporary means to project society against the behaviour of the youngster or the youngster against society or himself. However, the creation of a working alliance[17] should be emphasised, by which means meaningful treatment of the young person can be realised in his social context. Security as a beginning of treatment is acceptable, but only if it is for as short a time as possible.

Jelle Drost is a staff member of the Orthopedagogical Centre De Marke, a private juvenile offenders institution for boys and girls aged twelve to 23 in the east of the Netherlands

ENDNOTES

1. Nijboer J., Trends, theorieen en beleid Ontwikkellingen in Jeugdcriminaliteit, *Tijdschrift voor criminologie*, 37, 108-123 (1995).
2. Coming from Surinam, a former Dutch colony, and from the Mediterranean area.
3. Boendermaker L., *Jongeren in justitele behandelinrichtingen*, Ministerie van Justitie: W.O.D.C., 1995.

4. Raamwerk voor Justitiele Jeugdinrichtingen, 1994.
5. Jonker A., (Ortho)pedagogische thuishulp in de jeugdhulpverlening en jeugdbescherming, 9-16, in J.E. Rink, R.C. Vos (eds.), *Justitiele en niet-justitiele orthopedagogische thuishulp in Noord-Nederland*, Leuven-Apeldoorn, Garant, 1992.
6. Rink J.E., *Pedagogical mismanagement and orthopedagogy*, Leuven-Apeldoorn, Garant, 1995.
7. Drost J., *Planmatig behandelen in een Jutitiele Jeugdinrichting*, interne nota De Marke, 1995.
8. Drost J., Systeemtheorie als leidrand voor gezins en residentiele behandeling, *Nederlands tijdschrift voor opvoeding, vorming en onderwijs*, 11, 45-56, 1995.
9. Drost J., Ervaringsleren in de orthopedagogische situatie, in P.v.d. Doef ed., *Interdisciplinariteit in de jeugdhulpverlening en adolescentenzorg*, 96-107, Amersfoort/Leuven: Acco, 1992.
10. Maslow A.H., *Psychologie van het menselijk zijn*, Rotterdam: Lemniscaat, 1994.
11. Janssen J., *Jeugdcultur*, Utrecht: De Tijdstroom, 1994.
12. Bartels A.A.J., *Orthopsychiatrische Kliniek voor jongeren en jongvolwassen* (programma-opzet, uitgangspunten en basisprincipes), Amsterdam/Duivendrecht: Paedologisch Instituut, 1992.
13. Vos R.C., *De houding van jongeren in detentie t.o.v. sociale grenzen*, Groningen: Kinderstudies (Ph.D. thesis), 1991.
14. Drost J., *Onderzoek naar het in kaart brengen van aandachtspunten die van belang zijn om de weder zijdse bereikbaarheid (working alliance) tussen jougeren* (in preparation).
15. Schuyt C.J.M., *Kwetsbare jongeren en hun toekomst*, Amsterdam: Ministerie van Volksgezondheid, Welzijn en Sport, 1995.
16. Damen E. and Jol C., Generatie Nix opgevoed door de realiteit, *Index, Feiten en cijfers over onze samenleving*, 2, 30-31, 1995.

CHAPTER 20

The French Trial System

Yves Lernout

In describing the workings of the French penal system as applied to minors who commit the most serious offences, the risks of confusion and misunderstandings are numerous. For example, the very word *crime*, in French, qualifies the gravity of the offence committed. Only the most serious offences are classified as *crimes*. These incur the heaviest sentences following a specific procedure called 'criminal procedure'. Murder, rape and armed theft are considered *crimes,* whereas ordinary theft and deliberate violence without aggravating circumstances are considered misdemeanours (*délits*).

It is therefore the classification of the offence as a crime or misdemeanour which will determine the type of procedure followed. In the first case, the procedure will lead to the High Court (*Cour d'Assises)* which judges *crimes* (if the accused is over sixteen). The youth court *(tribunal pour enfants)* is restricted, where *crimes* are concerned to dealing with young people under sixteen years old. A specially composed High Court is set up for those accused young people aged 16-18, called a Youth High Court *(Cour d'assises des mineurs).*

In the case of misdemeanours, there is a criminal procedure pertaining specifically to minor offences. The case will go to the court of summary jurisdiction, *tribunal correctionel,* for over-eighteens or to the youth court for under-eighteens. Thus it is necessary to take account both of the young offender's age and of the designation given to his offence in order to determine the appropriate procedure to be followed.

In France, as in many other countries, penal law with regard to minors has emerged as a derogation from adult penal law. At first it was seen as a way of applying the law less harshly to young offenders than to their elders. In time a specialised executive jurisdiction emerged to go with the already specific minors' law. Children gradually acquired their 'own' law and their 'own' judge. However, the graver the offence committed by a minor, the less it becomes acceptable to judge him on the basis of his age. And so it is that criminal procedures as applied to such minors depart somewhat from the principles and the usual rules of procedure governing them. In short, when a minor commits murder or rape, the procedure will more closely resemble that applied to adults, while still drawing on the basic principles regulating minors' penal law.

162

Another difficulty in understanding the French system arises from the obligation, where crime is concerned, for the *juge d'instruction* (examining judge) to intervene. He does this after the police action and before trial. This is viewed by some as an original and interesting institution, by others as a sort of legal monstrosity. This judge has the duty of investigating the case in order to get as near as possible to the truth of the matter. Neither policeman nor prosecutor, he works from the public prosecutor's indictment and has various police services, experts etc to work with him, in order to make a thorough study of the evidence. He is the one who will officially inform the young person of what he is charged with. A criminal investigation may last several months, even years, before the crime comes to trial. This 'odd-ball' judge does not judge (in the strict sense of the word), but his action may determine what follows, that is to say the actual judgement pronounced later by other judges (in the youth court if the young criminals are under 16, in a youth high court if they are between 16 and 18).

The Main Principles: Specificity and Specialisation

The specificity of minors' law is based essentially on the priority given to reformative measures. This principle was already set down in Clause 2 of the February 2, 1945 Ordonnance concerning juvenile delinquency, a fundamental and, for some analysts, a founding text for minors' law:

> The youth court and the youth high court will pronounce, for a given case, measures of safety, care, supervision and reform which seem appropriate.

> They can however, when the circumstances and the offender's character justify it, pronounce a penal sentence on minors over thirteen years old.

In short, the judge must give reformative measures priority and it is only when the circumstances, coupled with the offender's character, make it necessary that he will be able to pronounce a penal sentence. We sum this up by the formula 'reform rather than prison' or again 'reform is the rule, prison the exception', or even more precisely the *ultima ratio*. This is a generally accepted principle throughout Europe. In France youth judges and other professionals in this field, eg psychologists, consider reform to be incompatible with any type of institutional confinement. Despite on-going debate on this subject, there no longer exist places labelled 'reformatory' or 'rehabilitative' whose doors and windows are locked and barred. It is the dominant opinion in

French professional spheres that it is the authority and persuasion of the *éducateurs* (social workers) combined with the relevance of the reform programme which must restrain young people rather than locks and bars.

The majority of French welfare officers believe the function of custody to be incompatible with the function of reform. Furthermore, most jurists consider that a spade should be called a spade, and so a place you cannot get out of is . . . a prison.

It would be true to say the French experience of 'reformatory prisons' followed by 'detention centres' has shown that such places soon become dumping-grounds where the most difficult young people end up spending lengths of time in no way connected to the initial intention of reform. Knowing the young offender well is crucial for compliance with the notion of reform as a priority. This is why, even before the debate over 'detention centres' became so acute, the 1945 Act had already made it impossible to judge a child offender without first thoroughly investigating his character and background. He cannot therefore be taken to court by an emergency procedure. The 'emergency appearance' procedure is reserved for adults. Indeed, the implicit reasoning of the authors of the 1945 Act is that, when a minor breaks the law, he reveals a situation needing special attention in order to provide him with help, to prevent recurrence and to protect society. To these ends, an inquiry into his character is undertaken in order to get to know him as well as possible. Meeting these ends also justifies handing his case file over to a judge before the actual trial. This judge may take decisions on reformatory measures on a provisional and invariably reviewable basis.

During this preparatory phase of the trial, while drawing on his general knowledge of juvenile delinquents as well as his understanding of the problems encountered during childhood and adolescence, the judge must also get to know the arrested child better so as to ensure that appropriate measures are ordained.

Taken together, all these considerations explain the specialisation of minors' jurisdiction. The key man here is the *juge des enfants* (children's judge). This judge needs to be a specialist in order to understand young people and also to know about related available rehabilitative measures and establishments, appropriate techniques, experts' reports, psychological and psychiatric treatment.

The children's judge, while remaining a judge (he is a professional, recruited in the same way as other judges), becomes a childhood specialist. He will supervise legal and judicial aspects of the rehabilitative measures undertaken in compliance with his orders. He will also continue to broaden his knowledge of childhood by following procedures concerning the protection of endangered children (cases where the health, security and morality of a child are threatened) which are called *procédure d'assistance éducative* (child welfare procedure).

Jean Chazal, who was the main instigator of modern minors' law, used to say of this judge: 'He is in close contact with life'. Understanding the young person was seen by the legislature to be important enough to justify appointing the same judge (the children's judge) both to the preliminary enquiry and to the trial. Therefore young people who have committed offences other than *crimes* will be judged at their trial by the same children's judge who has already led the initial inquiry *(l'instruction)*. He will pass judgement either alone in chambers, or in a youth court in which he presides.

This continuity, though it is an exception to the usual rules, provides for a better understanding of the young person, even if it shocks some jurists who see it as contrary to the rule of impartiality. However, in a case involving a Dutch children's judge *(Nortier v Holland, 24 August 1993)*—who likewise holds a double function, that of examiner and judge—the European Court of Human Rights deemed this suspicion of bias on the part of the judge to be unjustified. This continuity does not apply in criminal matters, as explained below.

Exceptions to the principles governing youth penal law during the preliminary stages of the young offender's trial
In criminal procedure, unusual rules start to be applied from the moment the young suspect is arrested. First, the *garde à vue*, a period of police custody before being charged, is allowed in the case of a criminal act even if the child is under thirteen (from ten to 13 he may be detained for ten hours, renewable once, after being brought before the Public Prosecutor).

At the end of the police custody period, if the Public Prosecutor decides to indict the young person for a *crime*, he will have no choice but to open a preliminary investigation *(instruction)* which can only come before an examining judge *(juge d'instruction)* and not a children's judge.

Here the continuity mentioned earlier will not occur. Indeed, the job of the *juge d'instruction* is to get to the truth of the matter before the trial, to make his case by collecting as many relevant facts as possible in order to bring to light not only the true facts of the crime but also the true character of the young person. Unlike the children's judge, the *juge d'instruction* will not be present at the actual trial. If he were, it would cause the judgment to be nullified.

Here we have a different reasoning from that which takes into account the young person's best interests through a better understanding of him. Even though the enquiry may take months, or even a whole year, during which time the *juge d'instruction* will often meet the young person and question him not only about what he has done but also about who he is, the resulting knowledge will be transmitted through a case file and not by the judge in person. Here we see a more traditional role than the one which has emerged for him in the youth jurisdiction.

Moreover, whereas the procedure involving the children's judge stands out as being somewhat informal, giving the young person a chance to express himself and to relate to the judge, a criminal inquiry (*instruction*) will follow far more strict and formal rules.

This *juge d'instruction* will be a 'specialist in juvenile matters' (*juge d'instruction des mineurs*) but, with the exception of a few major law courts, the youth *juge d'instruction* will not necessarily be a childhood specialist and, if he happens to be one, it will more likely be due to his personal career than to an obligation imposed by the law.

After the period of *garde à vue* (police custody), and if the Public Prosecutor has decided to prosecute the young offender for a *crime*, the enquiry starts off with the *mise en examen*: the *juge d'instruction* must inform the young person of the accusation made against him. The presence of a lawyer becomes obligatory at this stage (whereas during the period of police custody the lawyer may meet the young person but cannot be present during police questioning).

Immediately following the *mise en examen*, the *juge d'instruction* will proceed to a preliminary interrogation if the young person agrees to it, still in the presence of his lawyer. At the end of this interrogation, the judge must ask himself the terribly difficult question: what am I to do with this young person? Let us take a case of rape or murder. The young person may have admitted guilt, or perhaps the evidence against him is very strong (material proof, witnesses, etc). The law prescribes reformatory measures as a first choice, but there is also risk of intimidation of witnesses or victims to be taken into account, *trouble de l'ordre public* (disturbance of the peace), and risk of further crimes.

Before taking his first decision, the *juge d'instruction* is under an obligation to get a written opinion from the *Service Educatif Auprès du Tribunal*. This service belongs to the Ministry of Justice, that is the state. The youth welfare officers attached to this service will meet the judge in his office and propose a reform programme based on their hastily acquired knowledge of the young person, his background and family, plus perhaps further information gathered from other social reform services which have already had dealings with him. But this is a very difficult endeavour. It often seems unthinkable to suggest his returning

166

home that same evening to his parents, considering the gravity of the offence or even the family context. Moreover, rare and few are the establishments willing to take particularly difficult young people. Nor are they equipped for this, since the French reformatory establishments do not take minors even when they have committed serious crimes. If the young person *mis en examen* is sent to an establishment other than a prison, no-one can guarantee he will stay there. His remaining there will not be due to any closed doors or prison guards. Once again, encouragement and persuasion combined with a tenacious will to reform are the sole tools to be used to achieve success.

The prescribed purpose of a reform establishment is to be as different as possible from a prison, and to attain this by avoiding any form of confinement. Paradoxically, this explains why, for the most serious crimes, prison is often considered as a solution. Only recently have specialised youth prisons come to exist throughout France. Regrettably, however, these youth prisons resemble other prisons— with a few differences. In short, there is often an impossible choice between an old-fashioned prison system and an uninspired reform system. One must also understand the reticence encountered not only about the use of prison, but also about the use of a reformatory institution which may, in order to reform him, detain a young person for an inevitably indefinite period, since it depends on his personal development. This debate is on the same lines as the one now going on in France about methods based on behaviourist theories.

The *juge d'instruction* also receives the prosecutor's requisitions. If the judge is considering imprisonment, then there will immediately be a debate in his office on the question of temporary imprisonment on remand.

The judge will come to a decision after hearing the prosecutor, the young person's lawyer and the young person himself. What I am describing is neither a trial nor a formal hearing. It takes place in the judge's office. Nobody, except the child's lawyer, wears the black robe symbolic of judges and prosecutors. The hearings are not made public at this stage (this also applies to adults). Both investigation and enquiry are confidential.

The initial decision of the *juge d'instruction* concerning temporary custody can be modified at any time. The young person's lawyer will be sure to ask for his release. New submissions may be made during the course of the enquiry based on, for instance, expert psychological or psychiatric appraisal. Also youth welfare officers may suggest placing the young person elsewhere, after visiting him in prison and discussing this with him. There may be a wide range of suitable places to choose from other than establishments run by the Ministry of Justice. He could

In both the youth court and the current Youth High Court, the proceedings are conducted with great solemnity. In the High Court, formalism is taken to the extreme (in order, above all, to avoid a *pourvoi en cassation,* an appeal to the Supreme Court). The proceedings are very lengthy. They start with the reading of the bill of indictment by the clerk of the court. The facts of the case, its investigation and the whole inquiry are gone over in great detail by the President. He enjoys wide powers in conducting the proceedings and questioning witnesses and experts. The Public Prosecutor (what might be termed the *accusation*), as well as the barristers representing the young person and the victim or victims, similarly all play their part. Any minor accused of crime must compulsorily be represented by a barrister. If he does not himself choose one, then the *Batonnier de l'Ordre des Avocats* (that is the elected representative of the barristers to the court) will appoint one for him.

The only people admitted to proceedings before the Youth Court and the Youth High Court are: witnesses, close relatives, the tutor or legal representatives of the young person, the barristers, representatives of reform services or institutions, youth welfare officers and educators. Reporting the proceedings through the press is forbidden and punishable, just as is any form of publication (written or televised) of the identity or personal details of the young person.

Up to now this rule protecting criminal minors' anonymity has been fairly well respected, but the first breaches of the principle are beginning to appear. Easy identification of the young person is made possible by on the spot reporting, immediately following his arrest, outside his school or with close neighbours. Some journalists, under the pretext of a 'better understanding of what has happened', will not hesitate to interview close relatives of minors charged with criminal acts. The pressure of public opinion and the fierce competition between television networks tend to encourage this kind of transgression, just as does the near total lack of sanctions.

During the hearings before the court, any expert may be called, whether or not he has participated in the preliminary phase. So too can those people who have taken change of the minor up to the trial. Their opinions matter. Experts, in particular psychologists and psychiatrists, can be questioned not only regarding pathological factors and the personality of the minor, but also on the relevance of various proposed types of reformatory or therapeutic action. They may go beyond a diagnosis and put forward a prognosis.

On those occasions where the young person is already attending a reform or care establishment before the trial, it is particularly helpful to hear from the people who are in regular contact with him, the care or welfare officers. They can describe his behaviour patterns, his progress, attempts at rehabilitation, programmes, set-backs, and perhaps his first successes. The family may also be heard, to derive further information. Each of these may be heard at the request of the prosecutor or the defence counsel, and also of the President of the Court.

One important difference between the youth court and the High Court is the totally oral nature of the procedure before the High Court. This is so even to the extent that, when the jury retires to deliberate together with the three professional judges, all written records remain elsewhere with the clerk of the court.

Reasons do not have to be given for the findings of the High Court. This is the reign of deep seated conviction, *l'intime conviction!* The findings of the youth court, on the other hand, do have to be justified and must be particularly well founded if a custodial sentence is involved.

When the jury returns, it pronounces at the same time the verdict and the sentence or reform measures. If the minor is found guilty the jury must answer the question 'should the accused receive a penal sentence?' If the answer to this is yes, a second question follows: 'should the accused be denied the benefit of the reduction of sentence covered by the 2.2.45 Act?', that is one half of the sentence incurred for adults.

Therefore, by answering 'yes' to these two questions, a High Court may end up by completely ignoring the special youth law in the specific case before it. I underline the fact that three professional judges, including the President, take part in the vote. So through the expedient of the answer to these two questions, a minor in France may theoretically be condemned to life imprisonment.

Sentencing

Throughout the entire criminal trial, one of the key questions is that of the future of the young person: what will become of him? 'In France, the most frequent alternative choice is whether or not to order imprisonment. A reform establishment will not deprive the young person of his liberty, due to the open character of French establishments. He may also be placed in a foster-family. He would then be under the supervision of a service or an association which manages the placement and ensures the follow-up of both the minor and the foster-family. Usually this type of placement involves some form of therapy work with the minor.

The option called *liberté surveillée* puts the youngster back into his own family under legal supervision, follow-up and educational assistance. The welfare officer in charge must ensure the proper social and personal rehabilitation of the child during this period of supervision. His task is a long term one; it involves establishing progressively a climate of trust between the youth and his welfare officer. Another option is the 'double-purpose' sentence, which is a combination of (suspended) imprisonment and social-educational supervision. This has the advantage of a stated custodial sentence (partly or wholly suspended) combined with reform under supervision. The conditions attached to the suspended sentence may include education or vocational training, medical treatment and compensation of victims. This implies that, should the minor fail to comply, he must suffer the punishment which has been suspended, either by going to or returning to custody for that part of the sentence which has been suspended. This type of sentence, initially introduced for adults, eases the impossible choice which would often have to be made between custody and reform measures. By choosing a suspended sentence with supervision, we are in effect choosing punishment but without really abandoning the idea of supervised reform. It is, in a way, stretching the traditional principle of youth law, but it also often avoids making a custodial sentence the only option.

The term of custody fixed by the court may be reduced to a certain extent by means of good conduct allowances or through a conditional discharge. This is not a right reserved to minors. However, conditional discharges are seldom granted and, in the case of *crimes*, the trend is further decreasing. The children's judge will be consulted, but the decision will be taken at a higher level in the Ministry of Justice.

A different type of decision-making applies where placements in reform centres are concerned. At a later hearing, the youth court may go back on decisions it has taken previously. Similarly, the children's judge responsible for the follow-up of the decision may, if the decision provides for it, change the conditions of the educational placement. This possibility of revising the educational options to the youth's benefit is essential because what is right and fair at a given time may cease to be so. This is why it is very useful for the children's judges to sit in the High Court, to prevent its making decisions which will determine too rigidly the youth's future for years to come. For an educational measure to be both effective and long-lasting, it must be flexible enough to allow modification, keeping pace with the youth's own personal development. What is essential is that the court sets out the overall objective of the measure and its framework.

Victims and their families may either be present or represented at the trial. They may form what is called the *partie civile* and may intervene, plead, claim damages and interest payments. There is even a commission for the compensation of victims in case the author of the crime is insolvent. Despite all this, victims of crime often feel forgotten, ignored and seem to resent that the perpetrator of the crime gets more attention than the victim himself. During the recent trial of a 14 year old adolescent accused of murdering a classmate, the lawyer for the victim's family said: 'Everybody is asking about what provisions have been made to accommodate Leila but we seem to have forgotten that the only accommodation for Sabrina (the young girl who died) is a coffin in a cemetery.'

I consider that one of the important elements in any system of justice is to confront the young perpetrators with the pain of their victims. The justice system can carry out its mediation obligations only if the law takes the suffering into account. The problem, particularly where minors are concerned, is that suffering is felt on both sides and it is often intolerable for one side to have to see that of the other.

Trials of young criminals are attracting media interest to an extent which is both understandable and dangerous. Certain crimes—for example those occurring in suburbs already caught up in problems connected to violence and mob confrontations with the police—are becoming social issues. Beyond the individual himself, it is the whole of society—or, even more perniciously, one or another social group—which is on trial, all the more so since many of the young people involved differ from the majority in their culture, religion or colour. This is a dangerous situation, since the whole characteristic of justice is to individualise. Human beings are put on trial, not cases. Exemplary trials are even less appropriate where minors are concerned. Each individual has a past, composed of his own personal and collective experience, which, if taken into account, may contribute to a better understanding of him. He also has a future, and this future cannot be seen as being just that bit of his lifetime, necessarily limited to the length of his sentence, during which he is banned from society.

Public opinion is versatile. One day it weeps for the victims and cries vengeance, sometimes more than the victims themselves want. The next, it decries prison as a 'school of crime'. Nothing could be more dangerous than trying minors under the spotlight of the mass media and following rules dictated by them. Justice is something quite different—and it is essential that tomorrow's citizens should be taught this.

Yves Lernout is the Premier Juge d'Instruction, Tribunal de Grande Instance, Avignon, France

CHAPTER 21

Juvenile Justice in Slovakia

Judge Annamaria Brunovska

Last year in Slovakia we had just one case in which a young person killed another young person, and this case was connected with issues of nationalism. There were 13,000 criminal offences last year, but more than 11,500 of these were minor offences: we do not have many cases where children commit serious violent crimes.

The law in Slovakia derives from Roman law. It is very similar to that of Austria and Germany and our legal procedures concerning children are similar. The basis of the present law dates back to 1962, since when there have been many changes and a major recodification after the revolution in 1992. At that time Czechoslovakia was still in existence, as a result of which the law is the same for Czechs as it is for Slovaks.

Children have the same legal rights as adults in our system, but there are also special regulations which affect children in both criminal and civil court proceedings. The age of criminal responsibility is 15, and children younger than this who commit offences are dealt with in a civil court. In such cases children cannot be imprisoned, but can only be placed in special child care establishments which provide education and therapy. Only children aged 15 to 18—we still call them 'children' as well as 'juveniles'—are criminally responsible. During the police investigation of the crime, children have more rights than adults. Throughout the process the child is always in the presence of a person from the social welfare office, which is always informed in relation to both criminal and civil proceedings and is party to the proceedings up to the trial.

In a criminal trial the child has the same rights as other parties, namely to appeal, to give evidence, to call witnesses and to receive written decisions. The child is entitled to have an advocate, paid for by the state if he cannot afford to pay for representation. From the outset the advocate must be informed, as must the parents or the person responsible for the child, and they participate in the proceedings throughout the process. The child cannot be held in prison during the pre-trial proceedings unless there is no alternative to prevent a dangerous situation or in a serious case.

proceedings code provides that the other agencies should always co-operate with the social welfare service in order to find out about the juvenile's background, moral welfare, family problems and education. Since the revolution we have also had other non-governmental organizations which may work with the state to provide help to the child. This information about the child's background is very important for decisions at every stage, including decisions about sentence, because except in serious cases the child must not be sentenced if the court can show that there are organizations which can work to ensure that he will not offend again.

If a child aged under 15 commits a crime, it is always dealt with in civil proceedings by the guardianship court. In these cases the court can proceed without an application (whereas normally in civil proceedings the court must receive a suit). The judge or judges can prohibit the press from reporting the case. In some cases the child is excluded from the courtroom where there is evidence that may be deleterious to the welfare of the child.

This issue is not discussed a great deal in our country. Most juvenile crime is minor and Slovakia has so many other problems that it does not receive much attention. Also, professionals consider that the system for dealing with young offenders works well. These cases are usually dealt with by professionals with a great deal of experience in this field, especially in the criminal process. They are mainly judges and social welfare workers of long standing, and some judges have received special training in how to interview and deal with children.

In 1990 Czechoslovakia ratified the European Convention on Human Rights, which we also incorporated into the constitution of Slovakia in 1992. This did not necessitate any change in our criminal or family law because both were compatible with the European Convention.

Annamaria Brunovska is a district court judge in Bratislava, Slovakia, and a representative of the Association of Slovak Judges

CHAPTER 22

Child Criminality in Latvia

Uldis Kinis

Latvia was founded on 18 November 1918. From 1918 to 1940, Latvia was a country with a highly developed court and legislative system. All this was lost after 1940, when Latvia was occupied by the USSR. During the next 50 years we could not develop our court and legislative system, because during this period, as part of the USSR legislative and court system, we had no independence.

On 21 August 1991 our Parliament proclaimed our independence from the USSR and, since that time, we have started to reorganise our legislative and court system. One inheritance from the USSR is a lack of understanding of free market relations. The results have been harsh—many big factories closed, many people lost their jobs and became unemployed, the gap between rich and poor became very great. In the countryside all collective farms were liquidated. As a result the majority of people who live in the countryside lost their jobs and remain without any money. The rate of alcohol abuse has increased. In Latvia we also have a difficult problem with children who are mentally ill and children in special schools.

All these problems are reasons why child criminality is high in Latvia.

Statistics

2.6 million people live in Latvia. Each year the seriousness of child offending increases. In the first nine months of 1994 there were 28,264 offences in Latvia, of which 1,483 (4.97 per cent) were committed by children. In the equivalent nine month period in 1994, there were 30,176 offences of which 1,033 offences (3.42 per cent) were committed by children.

Serious offences registered in the first nine months of 1995 were 14,081 of which 970 (6.88 per cent) were committed by juveniles. In 1994 the figures were 17,148 and 711 (4.15 per cent) respectively. The figures for murders and causing serious bodily injuries were:

	1995	1994	1993
Murders	9	13	6
Serious bodily	17	15	14

At present 3,014 children aged from seven to 18 are supervised from the police office: this means that these children are suspected or guilty of offences. We have found that 81.8 per cent of juveniles were neither working nor studying at schools at the time they committed offences.

Latvian Criminal Legislation

Article 10 of the Latvian Criminal Code stipulates that criminal responsibility starts for children when they are 14 years old for serious offences (for instance, murder, rape, robbery, serious bodily injuries, larceny, hooliganism). For other offences criminal responsibility for juveniles starts from the age of 16.

Criminal Procedure

There are three levels of court system in Latvia:

(i) the lowest court—the district court—has jurisdiction for ordinary crimes, including crimes committed by juveniles
(ii) the regional court has jurisdiction for all serious crimes including murders. It is the appeal court for district courts' decisions
(iii) the Supreme Court is an appeal court for regional courts' decisions.

There are no special courts for juveniles in Latvia: it is the duty of ordinary courts to deal with them.

Penitentiary

There is one type of penitentiary for juveniles in Latvia, with separate provision for girls and boys. The penitentiary does not separate juveniles who have committed serious crimes from others. This is a serious problem, but provision depends on the state budget, which is poor. There is no form of establishment for children who are guilty of criminal actions, but have not reached the age of 14.

Uldis Kinis is Chief Judge of Kuldiga District Court, Latvia

CHAPTER 23

The Canadian Legislative Response to Children Who Kill

Mary-Anne Kirvan

No other offence will put youth justice systems to the test more than the offence of murder. Neither, perhaps, will any other offence tempt governments more to make exceptions or deviate from principles generally applicable to youths who engage in criminal conduct.

At this juncture in the evolution of youth justice, many countries seem to be striving for youth justice systems whose practices as well as their written laws hold out the best promise of meeting two very distinct goals. After I have outlined Canada's legislative history with respect to adolescents who kill, I believe you will arrive at least at a tentative conclusion of why Canada's course has been as strained as it has. I would submit that the pressure communicated by many Canadians to their elected Members of Parliament to reform the law applicable to youth crime in Canada, the Young Offenders Act, is based in part on the failure to acknowledge two very distinct goals when we respond to criminal behaviour by youths. One involves holding them accountable for their wrongdoing through a process that is fair and equitable. The second goal we expect the justice system to play a role in is contributing to safe, secure communities. It would seem that many of the tensions around the Young Offenders Act have arisen, in part, because of the tendency to believe that altering the seriousness of our response to crime, particularly crimes like murder, will contribute to this second goal of safe, secure communities. Some know it, but many do not, that ratcheting up the penalties will not increase the degree of safety or reduce the amount of serious crime, murder included.

Capturing the Canadian experience is a daunting task because our statutory laws have not stood still for long at all. Of course, this means that the jurisprudence has not developed to the extent that one would like, in order to provide guidance and to permit evaluation. It also means that the infrastructures required to support our youth justice system, including other child serving systems, have not developed sufficiently in most of the country, and without this the law does not have the optimum chance of being seen to work in the eyes of the professionals in the system, and also in the eyes of the public.[1]

Highlights of the Young Offenders Act

The Young Offenders Act is the law that applies to all young people in Canada who have been charged with any criminal offence between the ages of 12 and 17 years inclusive at the time of the alleged offence. This law was passed unanimously by Parliament in 1982 and brought into force on 2 April 1984. It was the culmination of over two decades of intensive study and consultation, and was heralded as a major social reform initiative. It replaced the 1908 Juvenile Delinquents Act, a law which was characterised by a distinctive child welfare oriented philosophy, a strong treatment orientation, indeterminate sentences to be served until rehabilitation had been achieved, informality of procedure and very considerable discretion. It had a minimum age of seven years but there was a presumption of incapacity for children between the ages of seven and 13 years inclusive, which could be rebutted.[2] At the upper end of the age scale, the majority of provinces included youth only up to the age of 16 in their youth system.

Canada's Young Offenders Act constitutes a clear departure from its predecessor. Unmistakably criminal law and not child-welfare legislation, the Act recognises the objectives of protection of the public and accountability for one's criminal acts. It is, however, different from the criminal law applicable to adults in several critical respects. First, while it recognises that young persons must be held accountable for criminal acts, they need not always be held accountable in the same manner or to the same extent as adults. The principle of limited accountability is most clearly reflected in the time limitations imposed on the use of custody. For most offences, the sentence cannot be longer than two years. For offences where punishment for an adult would be life imprisonment, the maximum disposition under the Young Offenders Act is three years in custody, with murder being the only exception as of 1992, unless the youth's case is transferred to the adult court. Second, the Act extends rights and safeguards to youth that go beyond those enjoyed by adults, including the right to least possible interference with their freedom.[3] Most important, the Act recognises that youths, by virtue of their adolescence, have special needs and circumstances that must be considered when any decision is made pursuant to the Young Offenders Act. The Declaration of Principle requires that the limited maturity and dependency of youth be taken into account, and that decisions made about youth reflect their 'special needs'.[4] While the Declaration contains a number of elements or principles which may initially appear to be contradictory, it is suggested that as a whole it provides a framework within which, at times, competing elements must be balanced and applied to a particular fact situation.

The Declaration has been amended with effect from 1 December 1995, and the goal of promoting responses which are effective is at the heart of two key changes. One change will recognise that crime prevention is essential to the longer-term protection of society. Therefore, the underlying causes of youth crime must be studied and multidisciplinary approaches to identifying and responding to young persons at risk of criminal behaviour must be developed. Secondly, the changes recognise the mutually supportable goals of protection of the public and rehabilitation by clearly stating that the protection of society, a primary objective of the criminal law, is best served by rehabilitation, whenever possible, of young offenders. Further, the new principle specifically speaks about rehabilitation being achieved by addressing those needs of a youth that are linked to the youth's offending behaviour, thereby enshrining the goal of effectiveness. These principles, found in section 3 of the Young Offenders Act, are to guide the interpretation and implementation of the Act. [5]

For an Act so young, it has been amended three times—in 1986, 1992 and 1995—and the last two of these amending Bills have addressed the issue of youths who are charged with murder. In fact, the 1992 Bill dealt virtually exclusively with the test for transferring a youth from the youth justice system to the adult justice system and with sentences for youths convicted of murder in both the youth and the adult justice systems. Bill C-37, 'An Act to Amend the Young Offenders Act and the Criminal Code', which was given Royal Assent on 22 June 1995 and came into force on 1 December 1995, also focuses largely on serious offenders, and in particular addresses the consequences for murder.

Statistical Snapshot of Youth Violence

No doubt you must be wondering what environment prompted such a flurry of legislative action. Let me speak first then to the incidence of murder by adolescents and some highlights as to the nature of youth murders in Canada.

To create an overall context, in 1994:

- Of all Criminal Code offences reported by police in Canada, 11 per cent were violent offences (*Uniform Crime Reporting Survey, 1994*, Canadian Centre for Justice Statistics).
- Of charges for violent offences, homicide (including first degree, second degree, manslaughter and infanticide) accounted for 0.2

180

per cent (total of 596 homicides). The majority of violent offences were minor assaults (*Uniform Crime Reporting Survey, 1994*, CCJS).

- Canada's homicide rate (2.0 per 100,000 persons) was one-quarter that of the United States (9.0 per 100,000 persons), but is generally slightly higher than most European countries (eg 1.4 per 100,000 in England and Wales) (*Homicide in Canada*, CCJS Juristat, 1995).

In addition, youth statistics demonstrate that:

- While youths aged 12-17 represent approximately 8 per cent of the Canadian population, they accounted for only 5 per cent of those charged with Criminal Code offences in 1994, and for 14 per cent of those charged with violent offences. (*Uniform Crime Reporting Survey, 1994* CCJS).[6]
- Of all crimes committed by youths, less than two out of 10 are violent offences, and minor assaults (ie pushing etc) account for about one-half of these 'violent offences' (*Uniform Crime Reporting Survey, 1994*, CCJS).
- Over a thirty year period, 1961 to 1990, there were 794 murders committed by youths in Canada—most involving 16 and 17 year olds, only 18 per cent involved children under 15 years of age (Silverman, R. and Kennedy, L, 1993, *Deadly Deeds: Murder in Canada*, p. 164).
- During the last ten years, youths accounted for an average of 8 per cent of homicide suspects (*Homicide in Canada*, CCJS Juristat, 1995).
- Of the 30 homicide cases heard in youth courts in 1993/94, 13 resulted in guilty decisions, six were transferred to adult court, seven were withdrawn, three were stayed and one was found not guilty (Department of Justice, *Youth and Justice*, 1995).

The following provides some characteristics of youths charged with homicide:

- Although Aboriginal persons account for about 3 per cent of the population of Canada, approximately one-third of youth charged with homicides are Aboriginal (Meloff, W. and Silverman, R.A., 'Canadian Kids Who Kill', *Canadian Journal of Criminology*, January 1992, pp 15-34).
- Similar to adults, about nine out of ten homicides committed by youths involved male accused (*Uniform Crime Reporting Survey, 1994*, CCJS).

- Similar to adults, the largest proportion of youth homicides involved firearms (35 per cent), followed by stabbings (30 per cent) and beatings (22 per cent) (Meloff Silverman, 1992).
- Of homicides committed by youth, almost one-half of the victims are family members and approximately one-third are friends/acquaintances (Silverman and Kennedy, 1993, p.165).
- Personal motives (ie arguments or revenge) appear to be the most frequently reported reason for youth homicides (*Teenage Victims of Violent Crime*, CCJS Juristat, 1992).
- Many homicides committed by youths appear to be motivated by other criminal offences. For youth younger than 15 years of age, 14 per cent of the homicides were motivated by theft/robbery and 3 per cent were sexually-related. For youths aged 15-17, 22 per cent were motivated by theft/robbery and 7 per cent were sexually-related (Silverman and Kennedy, 1993, p. 165).

Environment as Portrayed by the Media

I have just attempted to create a snapshot for you of Canadian reality in terms of adolescent violence. Let me briefly paint the picture portrayed to the public via the media. My intent is to provide you with glimpses of the patterns of media coverage over this past decade. A case which attracted nationwide attention fairly early in the life of the new Young Offenders Act was one involving the release of a young man who had murdered his father, mother and sister, after he had served the then maximum sentence of three years. One indelible memory was the headline of a tabloid paper which asked 'Are these killer eyes looking at you?' This case generated issues not only of the adequacy of three years for three murders but also of the legitimacy of the prohibition on publication.[7]

Throughout this period, coverage has generally speaking been focused virtually exclusively on sensational cases and a great deal of the material is inadequate and often erroneous. The most common mistake is a description of the maximum sentence available for youths convicted of murder. Up until the changes in 1992, it was presented as three years and now as five years, with no mention of a process which would result in the youth being possibly incarcerated for life. Further, the mandatory sentence of life imprisonment which is imposed on youths who are transferred and convicted of murder is normally depicted in terms of when the youth is eligible for parole. The misperception of leniency is made much clearer with an example comparing the fates of a 15-year-old and a mature 40-year-old who are both convicted of murder in adult court and who hypothetically have the same life expectancy of 75 years.

When informed that the 15- year-old may serve 25 more years than the 40 year old, the message seems to strike a chord.

Current Law Relating to Youth Who Murder

Let me now outline those provisions in the Young Offenders Act which are most relevant to youths charged with murder and which have not been subjected to change. You will see that the basic approach to youths involved with murder has remained the same—that is, Canada has a hybrid approach, and there are three components which need to be looked at in combination to understand it. These are the sentence for murder in youth court, the procedure for transferring a young person's case to adult court, and the sentence and parole eligibility provisions where a youth is transferred and convicted of murder in adult court:

- Youths charged with murder may be dealt with in the youth court, and must be if they were under the age of 14 years at the time of the offence.
- The sentence in the youth court, which has jumped from three to five to ten years, is subject to annual reviews by a youth court, and more if grounds exist, and the youth may be released earlier.[8]
- An application, typically initiated by the Crown prosecutor, may be brought before a youth court judge to have a youth charged with murder transferred to the adult court. This process is also available for other offences. For a youth to be eligible for transfer to adult court, the youth must have been 14 years of age a the time of the alleged commission of the offence.
- The transfer application is decided using an individualised approach. The court considers a list of factors[9] and the rules of evidence are relaxed, although the courts are certainly called upon to consider the extent to which opinion and hearsay evidence are admissible in hearings of transfer applications. The focus of inquiry is not on the guilt or innocence of the youth.
- Should a youth be transferred for murder, he or she is subject to the same sentence as an adult would be but there are differences, as of the 1992 changes, in terms of the youth being able to apply for early release. Two distinct tools to gather this information are provided: a pre-disposition report and a more specialised medical/psychological/psychiatric report.[10]
- Hearings are open to the public unless the court orders the exclusion of some or all members of the public. There is, however, a ban on the publication of any information serving to identify the young person.[11]

183

There is no jurisdiction under Canadian criminal law to deal with children under the age of twelve years who have been accused of murder. This policy continues to be highly controversial and you can be assured that England's 1993 experience with the slaying of a toddler by two 10-year-old boys fuelled the debate. At the present time, children involved with murder would be subject to the child protection and health laws of the province or territory. More information on this issue is provided in the endnotes, including reference to a recent and very thorough examination of the matter[12] and some data on the incidence of violence by this age group.[13]

Sentence for Murder in the Youth Court

The 1992 changes increased the sentence for a young person convicted of murder in youth court from three to five years for murder, whether first or second degree.[14] From 1984 to 1992, the maximum sentence available in the youth court was three years. A rather unique hybrid form of sentence was introduced to achieve two goals: restrict the use of custody to a maximum of three years, but provide for additional supervision, support and control by the addition of a maximum of two more years to be served in the community. This decision seemed closely to reflect the thinking presented in a consultation document prepared by the Government of Canada in 1989 which set out the concerns of clinicians with lengthy custodial terms for adolescents, including custodial terms of over three years. In short, it was generally thought that a three year period was sufficient, given well structured and individualised programming. It was, however, recognised that for those cases where virtually all three years were spent in custody, some form of supervision following the three years of institutional life would be required.[15]

In short, the sentence for murder was increased by 66 per cent when the 1992 changes came into effect.

Transfer

The 1992 Bill also altered the test to be applied by the specialised youth court when considering whether or not to transfer a youth's case to the jurisdiction of the adult court. The test which had been in effect from 1984 to 1992 authorised the court to transfer a case if it 'is of the opinion that, in the interest of society and having regard to the needs of the young person' the youth should be dealt with in the ordinary court. The objectives of amending the transfer test were to provide greater clarity and equality in the interpretation of the law. [16]

The Honourable Kim Campbell, Minister of Justice at the time of the enactment of Bill C-12, explained the changes to the test as follows:

> The test for transfer is a two-step test. Where the judge determines that both needs can be met in the youth system, the discretion to transfer is gone. It is only where both needs cannot be met that the decision to transfer becomes one available to the judge . . . it is a clearer test and it is one that says there will be no transfer if both goals of rehabilitation and public safety can be met within the youth system. [17]

Sentence Where a Youth is Convicted of Murder in Adult Court

Until these 1992 changes, the sentence for a youth who had been transferred and convicted of murder was the same as it was for adults, including the periods which had to be served before being eligible to apply for parole. The Criminal Code imposes mandatory life imprisonment with no eligibility to apply for parole for 25 years in the case of first degree murder, and a period of 10 to 25 years to be determined by the sentencing court, in the case of second degree murder. [18]

The 1992 changes brought about significant change, not in the life imprisonment sentence, but to the periods to time that a youth convicted of murder would have to serve before applying for parole—these were very markedly reduced. For both first and second degree murder, the adult court judge, with or without a jury, would determine the number of years the youth would have to serve between the period of five and ten years.

Placement of Youth Convicted of Murder

For youths accused of murder in the youth court, the Act requires that they be detained and incarcerated separate and apart from adults. [19] An exception is made at the pre-trial stage where a court is satisfied that a given youth '. . . cannot, having regard to his or her own safety, or the safety of others, be detained in a place of detention for young persons; or no place of detention is available within a reasonable distance'. [20] The Act, however, does provide for the transfer of a youth from a youth facility run by the provinces at any time after the youth has reached the age of 18 years. [21]

185

It is of interest to note that the Bill, as first introduced, failed to address the issue of placement but in response to very considerable pressure, strongly aided by the recent ratification of the United Nations Convention on the Rights of the Child, there were amendments made to bring Canada's law closer to conformity with Article 37. The 1992 changes create a presumption in favour of a youth under the age of 18 years being detained in the youth system but this presumption is rebuttable. [22]

In terms of youths who have already reached the age of 18 years before their case is ordered to be transferred, there is a legislative presumption[23] that they will be detained prior to trial in adult facilities but application may be made to the court to have such an accused reside in youth facilities on the same grounds of best interests of the young person and safety of others.

For youths who are convicted of murder in an adult court, the 1992 changes were welcomed as they required the decision about placement to be made in open court, not administratively as had been the case, and the court would have the benefit of comparing programmes from the youth, provincial adult (for sentences of two years less a day) and federal penitentiary systems and making the best choice having taken specified factors into account.[24]

I have outlined the key changes to the law applicable to youths charged with murder and would now like briefly to comment on their cumulative effect. The changes reveal the complexities inherent in policy making where there are two distinct approaches in competition. The legislative process which culminated in the 1992 changes revealed the competing concerns and these remain today. Clearly, the original impetus for amendments to the law came from those who sought 'firmer' responses to youths engaged in violent crime.[25] Others, however, sought change of a more profound nature that would focus on addressing underlying causes.[26]

A summary of the most notable reasons for change is provided in the document but three main reasons were the belief that a three year sentence was insufficient and contributing to a loss of public confidence in our justice system, that the choices between three years in the youth system and life in the adult were too disparate, and that the test for transfer was not sufficiently clear.[27]

At the end of the day, I think it fair to say that the 1992 amendments were generally received with mixed views[28] and scepticism as to how the changes would be interpreted by the courts. Hindsight has dictated that these changes were not to be viewed as adequate for long in the face of enormous political and public pressure for change. The changes in short reflected an effort to meet very diverse, often polarised needs, in a principled way that remained faithful to an individualised approach, and to the joint objectives of protection of the public and rehabilitation. The United Nations Convention on the Rights of the Child had just been ratified and its influence positively felt in some amendments to the Bill, most notably the inclusion of rehabilitation in the test for transfer and a much more open process to arrive at the placement issues related to youths who are transferred to the adult court.

Application of the 1992 Law

Let me now give you a few examples of how the 1992 laws have been interpreted. The first case arose in Quebec, a province which stands out for its strong philosophical and programming commitment to young offenders. A 14-year-old was charged with the first degree murder of his brother and parents. The youth court ordered the youth transferred and the Court of Appeal upheld the order. The evidence before the court revealed a seriously disturbed youth who would be a danger to society without a minimum of five years of in-care psychiatric treatment. At the transfer hearing, the psychiatrist reported that the youth was of above average intelligence and had no problems in terms of abstract thought, comprehension or logical reasoning. However, he had a very immature and very disturbed personality and showed no interest in or compassion for others. The most alarming and striking feature noted was his inability to appreciate the impact of his actions on others or to empathise with his victims. The risk of reoffending in a similar manner was considered not to be very high. However, it was the psychiatrist's opinion that the youth would require specialised help to change his attitudes and ways of reacting to others. The psychiatrist concluded that a period of between five and seven years in a secure institution was required for the purposes of rehabilitation.[29]

The second case follows the same approach of interpreting the transfer test to focus on the two factors of rehabilitation and protection of the public in terms of the youth's potential future dangerousness. In the Ontario decision of *R. v C.B*,[30] Robins J.A. of the Ontario Court of Appeal wrote:

> The transfer order test set out in s16(1.1) limits the "interest of society" concern to two identified objectives—the protection of the public and the rehabilitation of the young person. Other factors which may also pertain to the "interest of society", such as general deterrence, the gravity of the offence and the circumstances surrounding its commission, and the need to maintain and promote public confidence in the administration of justice, on

the court's interpretation of s16(1.1), cannot in themselves provide the basis for transferring a young offender to adult court.

In a recent analysis of the case law subsequent to the 1992 amendments,[31] the interpretation just outlined above appears to be followed generally in the Courts of Appeals of three of Canada's ten provinces, these being Ontario, Nova Scotia and Quebec. By contrast, however, a broader interpretation has also been given to the test by numerous judges who have interpreted it in a broader manner on the basis that the test does not expressly state what is to occur if protection and rehabilitation cannot both be reconciled, and further that the language is such that other factors such as general deterrence and public denunciation of violent behaviour may rightfully be considered.[32]

Let us briefly look at how the change in law is reflected in practice:

- In 1993/94, 63 youths were transferred to the adult court. Only six of these were for murder/manslaughter.[33]
- Youth admissions to adult federal custody have declined dramatically since the implementation of the Young Offenders Act (see *Tables 1* and 2 below). For instance, prior to implementation of the Act, on average 80 youths were admitted each year, whereas in 1991-92 there were only seven, in 1992-93 only one, in 1993-94 only eight, and in 1994-95, 21.

Table 1: Major Admitting Offences for Youth Admissions to the Federal Adult Correctional System (1978-1983)

	Homicides and attempts	Other violent offences	Robbery	Break and enter	Other property offences	Other offences	Total offences
Ages 15-17							
Pre-YOA period (1978/83)	16	55	146	143	25	55	440
Transition period (1983/88)	10	43	72	63	7	18	213
Post-YOA period (1988/93)	3	3	6	4	0	1	20
Total	29	104	224	210	32	74	673
Ages 18-19							
Pre-YOA period (1978/83)	64	240	821	668	153	259	2205
Transition period (1983/88)	71	231	538	632	108	209	1789
Post-YOA period (1988/93)	61	202	339	306	42	141	1091
Total	196	673	1698	1606	303	609	5085

Table 2: Major Admitting Offences for Youth Admissions to the Federal Adult
Correctional System (1993-1995)

	Homicides and attempts	Other violent offences	Robbery	Break and enter	Other property offences	Other offences	Total offences
Ages 15-17							
1993/94	1	0	5	1	0	1	8
1994/95	5	4	8	2	1	1	21
Total	6	4	13	3	1	2	29
Ages 18-19							
1993/94	29	104	121	119	59	35	467
1994/95	26	94	107	106	51	47	431
Total	55	198	228	225	110	82	980

Law Relating to Youths Who Murder as of 1 December 1995

In spite of what seemed in 1992 to be significant change, every political party leading up to the federal election in the fall of 1993, one and a half years after the amendments were brought into effect, campaigned vigorously with respect to law and order issues, and in particularly the Young Offenders Act.

Thus, on 2 June 1994, the newly elected government introduced Bill C-37, An Act to Amend the Young Offenders Act and the Criminal Code, Chapter 19 of the Statutes of Canada, 1995 and it came into force on 1 December 1995. In the context of murder, several substantive changes were made.

Sentence for Murder in Youth System

Where a youth is convicted of murder in the youth system, the maximum sentence for first-degree murder has been raised from five to ten years, with a maximum of six years to be served in custody and the remainder in the community under intense supervision. For second-degree murder, the maximum is seven years, with a maximum of four years in custody. In both of these cases, the youth may serve the full period of ten to seven years if there are risks of serious personal injury to others. The laws were also changed to allow for the indefinite detention of youths with records of the most serious crimes such as murder.

In short, the Government now believes that the existing sentences were totally inadequate to reflect society's values on the sanctity of life.

Transfer and Sentences for Youth Convicted of Murder in Adult Court

The changes to the Young Offenders Act which come into effect on 1 December 1995 are significant in respect of transfer and the consequences of a conviction for murder in the adult court. Important other changes to the Young Offenders Act also came into effect.[34]

Sixteen and 17-year-old youths charged with offences of serious personal injury (murder, attempted murder, manslaughter, and aggravated sexual assault) will be tried in adult court unless the youth can show that the youth justice system is appropriate to meet the objectives of both protection of the public and rehabilitation.

This is a marked departure from treating all youths eligible to be transferred to the adult court equally. Rather than the onus being on the Crown, the onus will now shift to the accused youth. This means these youth will be dealt with as adults unless they convince the court that the objectives of protection of the public and rehabilitation can be achieved by the time periods available in the youth system. The Honourable Allan Rock, Minister of Justice and Attorney General of Canada, in response to considerable concerns in the Senate, justified the position on several fronts:

> This Act provides Parliament with the opportunity to say, as a matter of policy, that the issue (transfer) should be considered in every such case . . . It will not leave it to the Crown attorney . . . given the seriousness of the crime, the allegation, and the age of the alleged offender, it (transfer) should be considered in every case. Parliament is saying that the matter should go to adult court unless the court decides he should be tried in youth court.

We are attempting to reflect the strongly held view on the part of many Canadians that a different approach should be taken, but leaving the decision in the youth court, to ensure that the matter is considered. If I am 16 and charged with murder, I will go to adult court unless I bring forward an application. The youth court will then take those matters into consideration, but no longer at the option of the Crown attorney, rather by operation of statute.

The approach of the purist might be to say that the Act (the Young Offenders Act) will apply to people who are 16 and 17 years of age. That would make it straightforward, cut and dried. We have not done that. We have taken a little from the realm of both (ie youth and adult) to produce a hybrid result.

We should pay regard to the opinion of many Canadians . . . They see violent crime by 16 and 17 year olds and they want to see a response in the system that is consistent with accountability.

- This change in the transfer provision would mean that, in the most serious cases, legitimate societal demand for accountability would be reflected in a new approach to the question of transfer for that very limited number of people. It does not say that they will be transferred. It does not say it is a foregone conclusion. It will be determined by a youth court judge with all her insight into the statute and resources available. [35]

For young persons who are transferred to the adult court and convicted of murder, the sentence remains a mandatory one of life imprisonment. The provisions permitting transferred youths to apply for parole earlier than adults convicted of murder remain, but an important distinction has been made between young offenders under 16 years of age and those 16 years of age or more.

For the younger youth who are convicted of murder in adult court, they are eligible to apply for release after serving from five to seven years, depending on what period the sentencing court will order. The applicable Criminal Code is silent as to the criteria to be applied, thereby giving the judges virtually unfettered discretion. With respect to 16 and 17-year-olds the distinction between first and second degree murder, which was removed in 1992, is restored with the result that youth convicted of murder will have to serve a mandatory ten year period before applying for parole. Where a youth is convicted of second degree murder, the youth must serve seven years before applying. [36]

Conclusion

Let us stand back and attempt to comprehend this rapid evolution of youth justice in Canada, particularly with respect to murder.

As with other very controversial issues, it is to be expected that there will be a range of views as to how a society should best respond where adolescents breach the most fundamental societal value—the right to life. At the outset of this paper, it was suggested that the pressure for reform has come about, in part, because of a failure adequately to distinguish between two very different goals—these being holding youths accountable and contributing to safe, secure communities.

Clearly, there are a number of lessons learned. It seems as though we modernised parts of our system to reflect values of openness, accountability and access, and this was reflected in the changes to the law which provided for youth court proceedings being open to the public and to the media. But we, collectively, have done a very poor job of informing the Canadian public about our youth justice system, its goals, its limits, the roles and responsibilities of other systems and institutions to protect society, including the vital necessity of early identification of problem behaviour and appropriate response. This point was brought home to the Government by witness after witness who testified before the House of Commons and Senate Committees holding hearings on Bill C-37.

A second lesson is that we must decide as a society whether we wish to treat adolescents distinctly because of their developmental stage or treat them as adults, particularly in the extreme case of murder. We have made the decision in many of our laws that these youth should not have the same freedom of decision-making as adults until they reach the age of majority —our laws with respect to the purchase of cigarettes, alcohol, firearms, voting, and those governing adult sexual relations with adolescents all provide examples. There is a danger in sending out mixed messages to adolescents and we have work to do here. The philosophy of a distinct youth justice regime must be reconciled with the two goals of holding youth accountable and achieving safer, more secure communities.

Our challenge, at this juncture, is to look at our response to youths who murder within this broader context.

Mary-Anne Kirvan, is Senior Counsel at the Canadian Department of Justice, Ottawa. The views expressed in this paper are those of the author alone and may not necessarily reflect the views of the Department of Justice (Canada)

ENDNOTES

1. To appreciate the challenges of implementing this law, one must understand Canada's federal structure. While the federal government is responsible for enacting the criminal law, the ten provincial and two territorial governments are responsible for its administration. Thus, decisions with respect to programmes, allocation of resources and integration of youth justice with other child/youth serving institutions are determined by the provinces and territories.

2. This presumption could be rebutted if there was evidence to establish that the child had sufficient intelligence and experience to 'know the nature and consequences of the conduct and to appreciate that it was wrong': Criminal Code, section 13 which was repealed by the Young Offenders Act, section 72.

3. The Act legislates these safeguards and they include limits on dispositions (s20), involvement of parents (ss9, 10, 20), bans on publication of identity (s38) and restrictions on use of records (ss40-6).

4. Canada's juvenile justice system is premised on a fundamental assumption that young persons have special needs by virtue of their adolescence. These needs will vary, depending on a youth's level of biological, psychological, and social development. The term 'special needs', therefore, encompasses the needs of youth to form positive peer relationships, to develop appropriate self-esteem, and to establish an independent identity; it also extends to their health, educational, and spiritual needs. Over and above the needs of and developmental challenges facing all adolescents, the Act recognises the importance of identifying the additional needs of youth who may be suffering from such problems as a 'physical or mental illness or disorder, a psychological disorder, an emotional disturbance, a learning disability or mental retardation' [s13(1)(e)]. For further analysis of the Young Offenders Act from the perspective of special needs, see: Kirvan, MA, *Canada's Young Offenders Act, The challenge of responding to one of its central principles that youth have special needs*, in Junger-Tas, J. Boendermaker, L. van der Laan, P. *The Future of the Juvenile Justice System*, p. 223, Acco, 1991.

5. Declaration of Principles, section 3 of the Young Offenders Act:

'3.(1) It is hereby recognised and declared that -

(a) crime prevention is essential to the long-term protection of society and requires addressing the underlying causes of crime by young persons and developing multi-disciplinary approaches to identifying and effectively responding to children and young persons at risk of committing offending behaviour in the future;

(a.1) While young persons should not in all instances be held accountable in the same manner or suffer the same consequences for their behaviour as adults, young persons who commit offences should nonetheless bear responsibility for their contraventions;

(b) society must, although it has the responsibility to take reasonable measures to prevent criminal conduct by young persons, be afforded the necessary protection from illegal behaviour;

(c) young persons who commit offences require supervision, discipline and control, but because of their state of dependency and level of development and maturity, they also have special needs and require guidance and assistance;

(c.1) **the protection of society, which is a primary objective of the criminal law applicable to youth, is best served by rehabilitation, wherever possible, of young persons who commit offences, and rehabilitation is best achieved by addressing the needs and circumstances of a young person that are relevant to the young person's offending behaviour;**

(d) where it is not inconsistent with the protection of society, taking no measures or taking measures other than judicial proceedings under this Act should be considered for dealing with young persons who have committed offences;

(e) young persons have rights and freedoms in their own right, including those stated in the Canadian Charter of Rights and Freedoms or in the Canadian Bill of Rights, and in particular a right to be heard in the course of, and to participate in, the processes that lead to decisions that affect them, and young persons should have special guarantees of their rights and freedoms;

(f) in the application of this Act, the rights and freedoms of young persons include a right to the least possible interference with freedom that is consistent with the protection of society, having regard to the needs of young persons and the interests of their families;

(g) young persons have the right, in every instance where they have rights or freedoms that may be affected by this Act, to be informed as to what those rights and freedoms are; and

(h) parents have responsibility for the care and supervision of their children, and, for that reason, young persons should be removed from parental supervision either partly or entirely only when measures that provide for continuing parental supervision are inappropriate.'

Passages in bold print have effect from December 1, 1995.

6. Young adults aged 18-24 years account for about 10 per cent of the population, but are involved in about 22 per cent of the violent incidents reported to police. Persons aged 25-34 account for a further 17 per cent of the population, but account for 33 per cent of the persons accused in violent incidents.

7. This case appeared to be a major impetus and was relied upon by the Attorney General of the day in one province to urge tougher measures. What was largely left unsaid to the public was that the options available in law to ensure longer removal from the public if necessary had never been resorted to because of a mistaken sense of conviction on the part of

194

both the defence counsel and the Crown that the youth would be found not guilty by reason of mental disorder and subjected to indefinite confinement.

8. Section 28 of the Act states:

'28. (1) Where a young person is committed to custody pursuant to a disposition made in respect of an offence for a period exceeding one year, the provincial director of the province in which the young person is held in custody shall cause the young person to be brought before the youth court forthwith at the end of one year from the date of the most recent disposition made in respect of the offence, and the youth court shall review the disposition.

(2) Where a young person is committed to custody pursuant to dispositions made in respect of more than one offence for a total period exceeding one year, the provincial director of the province in which the young person is held in custody shall cause the young person to be brought before the youth court forthwith at the end of one year from the date of the earliest disposition made, and the youth court shall review the dispositions.

(3) Where a young person is committed to custody pursuant to a disposition made under subsection 20(1) in respect of an offence, the provincial director may, on the provincial director's own initiative, and shall, on the request of the young person, the young person's parent or the Attorney General or an agent of the Attorney General, on any of the grounds set out in subsection (4), cause the young person to be brought before a youth court

(a) where the committal to custody is for a period not exceeding one year, once at any time after the expiration of the greater of

(i) thirty days after the date of the disposition made under section 20(1) in respect of the offence, and

(ii) one third of the period of the disposition made under subsection 20(1) in respect of the offence, and

(b) where the committal to custody is for a period exceeding one year, at any time after six months after the date of the most recent disposition made in respect of the offence,

or, with leave of a youth court judge, at any other time, and where a youth court is satisfied that there are grounds for the review under subsection (4), the court shall review the disposition.

(4) A disposition made in respect of a young person may be reviewed under subsection (3)

(a) on the ground that the young person has made sufficient progress to justify a change in disposition;

(b) on the ground that the circumstances that led to the committal to custody have changed materially;

(c) on the ground that new services or programs are available that were not available at the time of the disposition;

(c.1) on the ground that the opportunities for rehabilitation are now greater in the community; or

(d) on such other grounds as the youth court considers appropriate.'

Passages in bold have effect from December 1, 1995,

9. Section 16(2) of the Act states:

'In making the determination referred to in subsection (1) or (1.03) in respect of a young person, a youth court shall take into account
(a) the seriousness of the alleged offence and the circumstances in which it was allegedly committed;
(b) the age, maturity, character and background of the young person and any record or summary of previous findings of delinquency under the Juvenile Delinquents Act, chapter J-3 of the Revised Statutes of Canada, 1970, or previous findings of guilt under the Act or any other Act of Parliament or any regulation made thereunder;
(c) the adequacy of this Act, and the adequacy of the Criminal Code or any other Act of Parliament that would apply in respect of the young person if an order were made under this section to meet the circumstances of the case;
(d) the availability of treatment or correctional resources;
(e) any representations made to the court by or on behalf of the young person or by the Attorney General or his agent; and
(f) any other factors that the court considers relevant.'

Passage in bold came into force December 1, 1995.

10. The pre-disposition report must be ordered where transfer is being considered. The Act requires that certain information be included in such a report including the results of an interview with the youth, and parents, if possible; the results of an interview with the victim where applicable and reasonably possible; the age, maturity, character, behaviour and attitude of the young person and willingness to make amends; any plans advanced by the youth to change his conduct, participate in activities, improve himself; the history of previous encounters with the law and the response of the youth to the prior interventions ordered by the court; the availability of community services and the receptiveness of the youth to participate; the relationship between the youth and his parents and the degree of control and influence of the parents over the youth; and the school/employment record (section 14(2) of the Young Offenders Act).

The second tool available to the youth court to ascertain the special needs, if any, of a youth is the specialised medical, psychiatric, or psychological assessments prepared by qualified professionals in the respective disciplines. The circumstances of a given case may in fact necessitate the involvement of a multi-disciplinary team. These reports are available in a number of specified circumstances, including consideration of a transfer hearing. Of significance is that the court can order an assessment without any consent where the court has reasonable rounds to believe that the young person may be suffering from a physical or mental illness or disorder, a psychological disorder, an emotional disturbance, a learning disability or mental retardation, and the court believes a medical, psychological or psychiatric report might be helpful in making a decision about sentence or about the transfer of a youth's case to adult court. The specialised nature of these reports allows for the needs of a youth pertinent to his/her offending behaviour to be identified, a necessary prerequisite to the selection of the most appropriate intervention to promote rehabilitation and secure protection of the public.

11. **Section 38 of the Young Offenders Act.** Changes to the Young Offenders Act which take effect on December 1, 1995 do permit an application to be made to the youth court to disclose the identity of a young offender where the court is satisfied that such disclosure is necessary in the interests of safety:

'38. **(1.5) The youth court may, on the application of the provincial director, the Attorney General or an agent of the Attorney General or a peace officer, make an order permitting the applicant to disclose to such person or persons as are specified by the court such information about a young person as is specified if the court is satisfied that the disclosure is necessary, having regard to the following:**

(a) the young person has been found guilty of an offence involving serious personal injury;

(b) the young person poses a risk of serious harm to persons; and

(c) the disclosure of the information is relevant to the avoidance of that risk.'

12. Children under 12 years who have committed acts that would, but for their age, bring them within the jurisdiction of the criminal law, would be subject to the health and/or child protection laws of the province. These laws vary, and recommendations have been made for them to be made uniform, that provincial capacity to act where a child is clearly a risk to the safety of others be made very clear, and that concerted steps be made to educate the public and professionals of such measures in order that their confidence be earned in terms of state preparedness. An alternative option which has been advanced, almost since the coming into force of the Young Offenders Act in 1984, is that of lowering the minimum age, and 10 years appears to be most often suggested. Bala, Nicholas, *Responding to Criminal Behaviour of Children Under 12: An Analysis of Canadian Law and Practice*, 1994, prepared for the Department of Justice (Canada), thoroughly examines the issue of present capacities of provinces and territories to respond appropriately where children under 12 years of age are engaging in serious and/or violent behaviour.

13. Some police departments report offences committed by children under 12 years of age. Among a sample from 27 cities, of those children under 12 who were alleged to have committed an offence, 7 per cent were for violent offences, mostly minor assault. There have been no reported incidents of homicide among this age group (Clark, B.M. and O'Reilly-Fleming, T., 1994, *Out of the Carceral Straitjacket: Under 12s and the Law*. Canadian Journal of Criminology, 36(3), 305-328).

14. The statutory definitions of first and second degree murder are as follows:

'231. **(1) Murder is first degree murder or second degree murder.**

(2) Murder is first degree murder when it is planned and deliberate.

(3) Without limiting the generality of subsection (2), murder is planned and deliberate when it is committed pursuant to an arrangement, under which money or anything of value passes or is intended to pass from one person to another, or is promised by one person to another, as consideration for that other's causing or assisting in causing the death of anyone or counselling another person to do any act causing or assisting in causing that death.

(4) Irrespective of whether a murder is planned and deliberate on the part of any person, murder is first degree murder when the victim is

(a) a police officer, police constable, constable, sheriff, deputy sheriff, sheriff's officer or other person employed for the preservation and maintenance of the public peace, acting in the course of his duties;

(b) a warden, deputy warden, instructor, keeper, jailer, guard or other officer or a permanent employee of a prison, acting in the course of his duties; or

(c) a person working in a prison with the permission of the prison authorities and acting in the course of his work therein.

(5) Irrespective of whether a murder is planned and deliberate on the part of any person, murder is first degree murder in respect of a person when the death is caused by that person while committing or attempting to commit an offence under one of the following sections:

(a) section 76 (hijacking an aircraft);

(b) section 271 (se<ual assault);

(c) section 272 (sexual assault with a weapon, threats to a third party or causing bodily harm);

(d) section 273 (aggravated sexual assault);

(e) section 279 (kidnapping and forcible confinement); or

(f) section 279.1 (hostage taking).

(6) [Repealed. R.S.C. 1985, c27 (1st Supp.), s35]

(7) All murder that is not first degree murder is second degree murder. R.S., c. C-34, s214; R.S. c.C-35, s4; 1973-74, c.38, s2; 1974-75-76, c.105, s4; 1980-81-82-83, c.125, s16; R.S.C. 1985, c.27 (1st Supp.) ss7(2)(b), 35, 40(2).'

15. Notwithstanding the conviction of clinical and correctional professionals that the youth justice system is the most appropriate for the vast majority of youth, the insufficiency of research into the effectiveness of interventions was readily acknowledged. The recognised limitations of institutional life were stated to include the following:

- institutionalisation can promote immaturity because it prevents development;
- due to separation from family and community, institutionalised adolescents develop their own subculture which is different from the normal adolescent community. This difference poses another hurdle which impedes successful reintegration and which must be overcome;
- an institutionalised youth may often suffer a major educational lag notwithstanding the efforts to ensure educational programming. This

is so because the youth's frame of reference is the institutional classroom and, accordingly, some youth settle for a lower standard for themselves and the institution sets a lower standard; and
- youths are prevented by virtue of their incarceration from socialising in the manner of normal adolescents, including the development of appropriate relationships. (*The Young Offenders Act: Proposals for Amendments*, Consultation Document, Department of Justice (Canada), page 18).

16. The text in effect as of May 1992 is as follows:
'... the court shall consider the interest of society, which includes the objectives of affording protection to the public and rehabilitation of the young person, and determine whether those objectives can be reconciled by the youth remaining under the jurisdiction of the youth court, and if the court is of the opinion that those objectives cannot be so reconciled, protection of the public shall be paramount and the court shall order that the young person be proceeded against in ordinary court in accordance with the law ordinarily applicable to an adult charged with the offence. [Section 16(1.1) of the Young Offenders Act]. This change must be viewed in the context of changes made to the sentence for murder in youth court as it was restructured to provide both greater opportunity for rehabilitation if required, and greater protection through a prolonged period of supervision upon reintegration into the community. If the court determines that it can meet these two objectives, that is the end of the matter and the youth remains in youth court.'

17. Senate Committee on Constitutional Affairs, April 7, 1992, Issue 12, page 34.

18. Supra, note 15.

19. Sections 7(2) and 24.2(4) of the Act state:
'7(2) A young person referred to in subsection (1) shall be held separate and apart from any adult who is detained or held in custody unless a youth court judge or a justice is satisfied that
(a) the young person cannot, having regard to his own safety or the safety of others, be detained in a place of detention for young persons; or
(b) no place of detention for young persons is available within a reasonable distance.'
'24.2(4) Subject to this section and section 24.5, a young person who is committed to custody shall be held separate and apart from any adult who is detained or held in custody.'

20. Subsection 7(2) of the Young Offenders Act (see footnote 19).

21. The intent of this provision is that youth 18 years of age or more be appropriately placed for the sake of youth residents and of the older 'young offender' whose needs may be better met by the provincial adult correctional system. In Canada, provinces are responsible for the administration of places of custody for youth, and for adults who have received sentences of two years less a day. The federal government is

responsible under the constitution for care and supervision of adult persons convicted to custody for terms in excess of two years.

22. Section 16.1(1) sets out the test that must be satisfied for a youth who has been transferred and is under the age of 18 years to be detained in an adult place:

'16.1(1) Notwithstanding anything in this or any other Act of Parliament, where a young person who is under the age of eighteen is to be proceeded against in ordinary court by reason of

(a) subsection 16(1.01), where no application is made under that subsection,

(b) an order under subparagraph 16(1.1)(b)(i), or

(c) the refusal under subparagraph 16(1.1)(b)(ii) to make an order, and the young person is to be in custody pending the proceedings in that court, the young person shall be held separate and apart from any adult who is detained or held in custody unless the youth court judge is satisfied, on application, that the young person, having regard to the best interests of the young person and the safety of others, cannot be detained in a place of detention for young persons.'

Came into force December 1, 1995.

23. The statutory presumption reads as follows:

'16.1(2) Notwithstanding anything in this or any other Act of Parliament, where a young person who is over the age of eighteen is to be proceeded against in ordinary court by reason of

(a) subsection 16(1.01), where no application is made under that subsection,

(b) an order under subparagraph 16(1.1)(b)(i), or

(c) the refusal under subparagraph 16(1)(b)(ii) to make an order,

and the young person is to be in custody pending the proceedings in that court, the young person shall be held in a place of detention for adults unless the youth court is satisfied, on application, that the young person, having regard to the best interests of the young person and the safety of others, should be detained in a place of custody for young persons.'

Came into force December 1, 1995.

24. These specified factors are set out as follows:

'16.2 (2) In making an order under subsection (1), the court shall take into account

(a) the safety of the young person;

(b) the safety of the public;

(c) the young person's accessibility to family;

(d) the safety of other young persons if the young person were to be held in custody in a place of custody for young persons;

(e) whether the young person would have a detrimental influence on other young persons if the young person were to be held in custody in a place of custody for young persons;

(f) the young person's level of maturity;

(g) the availability and suitability of treatment, educational and other resources that would be provided to the young person in a place of custody for young persons and in a place of custody for adults;

(h) the young person's prior experiences and behaviour while in detention or custody;

(i) the recommendations of the provincial director and representatives of the provincial and federal correctional facilities; and

(j) any other factor the court considers relevant.'

25. See for example the House of Commons Debates, May 30, 1990, at pp. 12068-9. Speaking on behalf of the official Opposition, Mr. Rideout supported the increase in maximum sentences for murder in youth court, saying 'there is no question that the change as far as the maximum period for first and second degree murder is good; up from three years to five. There is no question that early release should be more carefully monitored . . . There is no question that this legislation responds to the public outcry that has been generated by some cases.... Very serious crimes like first and second degree murder have to be dealt with, and dealt with firmly but we must be careful not to overbalance our response . . . to the detriment of the youth . . . and the young offenders . . . We must have a renewed commitment to help the youth of this country.'

26. See House of Commons Debates, May 30. One member spoke of the fundamental error in assuming that amendments to the law can better protect people from violent crime. On the theme of prevention, much was said about the need for provision of services at an early age, including family counselling, adequate housing, proper community development programmes. More fundamentally, our mental health, education and welfare systems must be made more responsive to the needs of youth.

27. In the document entitled 'The Young Offenders Act: Proposals for Amendment (Consultation Document)', Department of Justice, Canada, July 21, 1989, numerous concerns with the law in relation to murder were noted:

• Members of the judiciary faced with the daunting task of a three year sentence in youth court versus a life imprisonment sentence in adult court with no release for 25 years publicly stated in their judgements the extreme disparity and the absence of a middle ground. The late Associate Chief Justice MacKinnon of the Ontario Court of Appeal made the following comments about the disparity issue: 'There has been an unarticulated concern lurking in the background which was faced, in reply, by counsel for the appellant. Put bluntly, three years for murder appears totally inadequate to express society's revulsion for and repudiation of this most heinous of crimes. The mandatory sentence on conviction for first degree murder (with which the appellant is charged) under the Criminal Code is 25 years before being eligible to apply for parole. On conviction for second degree murder, the minimum sentence is 10 years before being able to apply ... but Parliament has legislated that three years can be appropriate in the case of young offenders.... He (Counsel) agreed the appellant should not be punished for the shortcomings of the Act . . .' *R. v M.A.Z.* (1987), 35 C.C.C. (3d) 144 at 162 (Ont. C.A.).

- The youth court sentence of three years was in the minds of many totally inadequate to express society's revulsion for and condemnation of the most heinous of crimes.
- The three year sentencing period may not provide sufficient time for necessary treatment of a given youth, taking into account the benefits of post-custodial supervision.
- The provisions governing placement rested too much on the will and resources of a given province with the result that transfer hearings became contests between the youth and the adult system and which could appropriately respond.
- The test for transfer was unclear and left too much to judicial discretion.

28. Child advocates feared the emphasis in the revised test for transfer on the paramountcy of protection of the public on the grounds that it would increase transfers to adult court but they welcomed the express inclusion of the ground of rehabilitation. A large percentage of these advocates along with members of the judiciary who privately let their views be known strongly questioned the vehicle of transfer on numerous grounds, including the conflict inherent in proceeding on an assumption of guilt.

    A significant number of Members of Parliament in the opposition ranks in 1992 opposed the Bill, viewing it as a punitive and narrow response designed to meet the concerns of that segment of the public which equates harsher penalties with better protection.

29. *R. v M.L.* (1984), 89 C.C.C. (3d) 264, 23 W.C.B. (2d) 649 (Quebec Court of Appeal).

30. [1993] 67 O.A.C. 761, Robins, Labrosse and Weiler, JJ.A.

31. Bala, Nicholas, *Transfer to Adult Court and the 1995 Amendments* (Unpublished), March 15, 1995 for presentation at a programme of the Canadian Association of Provincial Court judges in Val Morin, Quebec.

32. The Alberta Court of Appeal decision of *R. v G.J.M.* is most frequently cited for its adoption of a broader interpretation of the new transfer test, (1993) 135 A.R. 204 at 211 (Alta C.A.). See footnote 27. In this decision, two lower court judgements were being reviewed and, in both cases, the transfer applications rejected largely on the basis that the youths were sufficiently likely to be rehabilitated and therefore societal protection would be achieved. The Alberta Court of Appeal reversed the lower court decisions, emphasising the social interest in having a public hearing.

33. It should be noted that these may include some individuals who were older than 17 when the transfer occurred (1993-94 Youth Court Survey, Canadian Centre for Justice Statistics).

34. From a more preventive standpoint, there is increased authority for a court to order a medical/psychological assessment where there is

202

serious personal injury to promote more effective and timely intervention. Bill C-37 also deals with less serious offenders. It reinforces the importance of holding youth accountable in the community wherever possible so that they can make reparation to the victim or otherwise take responsibility in ways that hold out the best promise of preventing their reoffending. It specifically adds criteria to restrict the use of custody and requires judges to provide written reasons as to why community based responses are not appropriate. Records will be kept for shorter periods of time to ensure that there are no unnecessary bars to their educational and employment opportunities.

35. Proceedings of the Senate Committee on Legal and Constitutional Affairs, Thursday, June 1, 1995.

36. These changes did not attract the commentary and criticism that one would have expected given views taken by organisations previously. It is perhaps another example where individuals with polarised views supported the provisions for diametrically opposed reasons. Child advocates saw the changes as improvements for 14 to 15 year olds as it was no longer possible to order 10 years, and the 10 year mandatory period as a disincentive to transfer. Those seeking longer sentences favoured the mandatory ten years for first degree murder.

CHAPTER 24

Proposals for Change

Peter Badge

This paper attempts to give a sympathetic outsider's reaction to a series of papers which have provided a wealth of information—much of it refreshingly self-critical—from an impressively wide variety of countries and an equally wide range of professional experience. Lawyers are concerned with the presentation of evidence; judges and magistrates are concerned with determining culpability; doctors, social workers, probation officers and allied professions are concerned with how child offenders are subsequently dealt with; and academics fulfil the function of stimulating our critical facilities by making us examine closely what we have been doing for a long time without questioning whether our system is the best that can be achieved.

If those of us from England and Wales asked ourselves the question 'Are we satisfied with the way in which we deal with children who kill?', I venture to suggest that the unanimous answer would be a resounding 'No'. I nevertheless consider that we have no reason to be defensive generally about our system of justice which has many good qualities.

The concerns which have been presented to us are as follows. First, is jury trial appropriate for young offenders? In my view, it certainly is not. This was first brought home to me many years ago when I was sitting as a recorder in one of the longest Crown Court courtrooms in London and possibly in the country, and in the distance—I almost needed binoculars to see him—was a little 15-year-old charged with robbery who was not particularly well developed physically. For about a fortnight I could just see his small head appearing above the parapet of the dock. The manifest absurdity of jury trial in those circumstances struck me all those years ago and it has not left me since.

The next matter of concern is the inadequacy of our current system in dealing with such defendants individually. It is clear that you cannot generalise about juvenile killers. I was particularly interested to hear about a case in Scotland in which a youth charged with culpable homicide was referred to the reporter to be dealt with by the children's hearing system.

The third matter of concern is the rigidity of the mandatory sentence, with no period of review until the expiration of the tariff.

The fourth concern—and this relates not only to serious crime but is endemic throughout the whole of our youth court system—is the tardiness of disposal. It seems to me the height of absurdity that the courts which are supposed to deal with cases expeditiously, because this is in the interests of young offenders and especially in the interests of victims and witnesses, often take longer to deal with cases than the adult courts.

The last concern is the excessive influence of the media. It was my dubious pleasure to preside over the committal proceedings in the case of Rosemary West (convicted on ten counts of murder in 1996). I was advised by the Lord Chancellor's press officer that I should not stay in a hotel because I would get no peace at all. When I said that I was going to stay in a rented house and that my wife would probably take me to court and collect me, I was told that I could not do that either because, as the media had nothing that they could report about the facts of the case, even her activities might be of interest to them. If that put pressure on a hardened old professional, heaven knows what it must be like for a very youthful defendant.

Having been critical of our current system, I would like to say a few words in favour of our adversarial system which I think is ideal for resolving issues of fact. We may well have a youngster before the court who has myriad social and other problems, but the point of the case may be one of mistaken identity. Before one can start looking at the child as an individual, the essential matter of deciding whether the right person has been accused of the offence has to be dealt with. I think that the adversarial system is a much safer way of doing this than the inquisitorial approach. The grave danger of the inquisitorial system is that, if one is not careful, people may say consciously or unconsciously: 'It is not important what he did, let's get down to dealing with his problems.' That in my view is the appropriate concern of the family proceedings court and not the criminal court.

Other dangers of the inquisitorial system, despite its many virtues, are the blurring of issues of fact and possible conflicts of interest—for example, Reinmar du Bois has described being placed in the difficult situation as a psychiatrist of having a confession of guilt made to him and becoming a prosecution witness. That could not occur under the adversarial system. Much research is required because a system which is ideal for one country and culture could be quite unworkable in another. To compare Germany and France with Norway, Scotland and Latvia is likely to encounter all sorts of difficulties.

My proposals for change in the English and Welsh system are as follows. First, to raise the age of criminal responsibility to 14 years. An expanded form of the family proceedings court should deal with cases involving children under 14. For those between the ages of 14 and 18, special tribunals should be set up to decide guilt or innocence or other relevant issues of fact. This should be made up of a special judge and two special lay magistrates: those selected should have the right inclinations, the right experience and, above all, the correct amount of training to discharge their duties. There should be a second tribunal, a sentencing panel, consisting of a special judge, two special lay magistrates, an appropriately trained and experienced psychiatrist and a similarly trained and experienced social worker. Those aged over 18 should be tried in the adult court.

There should be a system of statutory time limits, to be policed by the special judge, who should be able to impose meaningful sanctions if his directions are not observed, to ensure expeditious trials. The idea of such defendants having to wait up to 18 months for a trial is totally unacceptable.

The press reporting restrictions applicable in magistrates' courts should prevail, with power to obtain from the High Court an order prohibiting press reporting of the trial if it would adversely affect the defendant, his or her family, or any victim or witness in the case. The High Court should be required to make such an order unless it is not in the public interest to do so.

Finally, there should be a complete overhaul of the doctrine of *doli incapax*. The Penal Affairs Consortium paper 'The Doctrine of Doli Incapax' provides a very good basis from which that consideration could take place.

Peter Badge is the Chief Metropolitan Stipendiary Magistrate, London

Appendix

Some International Statistical Comparisons

John Ogden

The statistics in this appendix relate to the incidence of crimes of murder and manslaughter committed by juveniles in a selection of European countries. The information was collected for the purposes of the British Juvenile and Family Courts Society's conference on 'Children Who Kill' in London on 24 and 25 November 1995 by John Ogden, the conference organizer.

All member states of the European Union plus Norway were requested via their embassies in London to provide limited information about grave crimes committed by children under the age of 18 years. Information was provided by eleven countries and it has been possible to present some information about each country in the following tables. In considering the figures attention is drawn to the difficulties of making inter-country comparisons of this nature. For example, the information for Germany, Italy, the Netherlands, and Norway refers to suspects, or those charged, where in other jurisdictions the figures reflect the incidence of convictions. Some countries include attempts in their figures while others do not, further increasing the pitfalls of comparison. This helps to explain the unusually high figures for Germany. For grave crimes other than homicide the problem of comparison is even greater and no attempt has been made to reproduce and compare statistics for grave crimes such as rape, arson, attempted murder, serious assaults causing bodily harm etc. because there seem to be no common definitions of these crimes.

Crimes of Murder & Manslaughter Committed by Children Under 18: Year of Adjudication 1992

Offence 1. Murder 2. Manslaughter		Age at time of incident	Under 10 years	10 years	11 years	12 years	13 years	14 years	15 years	16 years	17 years	Comments
Country												
Austria	1	At time of	*	*	*	*	*	0	0	2	1	*Under 14 years not liable under the terms of the Austrian Penal Code
	2	adjudication	*	*	*	*	*	0	0	0	0	
Belgium	1	At time of	-	-	-	-	-	-	-	-	-	Not available before 1994 when form of statistics changed
	2	conviction	-	-	-	-	-	-	-	-	-	
Denmark	1	#No crime	*	*	*	*	*	*	0	1	0	*Not criminally responsible under 15 years
	2	category of manslaughter	#	#	#	#	#	#	#	#	#	
England and Wales	1	At first	*	0	0	0	0	0	4	13	10	*Not criminally responsible under 10 years
	2	recording by police	*	0	0	0	0	2	3	5	12	
Germany (suspects)	1		1	1		2		12		52		Each figure for two adjacent years, starting 10 and 11
	2		0	0		2		25		76		
Greece	1		0	0	0	0	0	0	0	0	0	
	2		0	0	0	0	0	0	0	0	0	

Crimes of Murder & Manslaughter Committed by Children Under 18:
Year of Adjudication 1992 (continued)

Offence 1. Murder 2. Manslaughter		Age at time of incident	Under 10 years	10 years	11 years	12 years	13 years	14 years	15 years	16 years	17 years	Comments
Country												
Italy	1	minors reported	under 14	1				3	10	20	16	
	2	to the prosecutor		7				12	5	70	42	
Luxembourg	1		0	0	0	0	0	0	0	0	0	
	2		0	0	0	0	0	0	0	0	0	
Netherlands (Interrogated suspects)	1	13 cases from										Figures for murder and manslaughter for 12-17 years
	2	12-17 years										
Norway	1	persons charged						7				Figures for 14-17 years
	2	male/female						0				
Scotland	1	Culpable homicide	0	0	0	0	0	0	0	3	3	
	2 =		0	0	0	0	0	0	0	2	3	

Crimes of Murder & Manslaughter Committed by Children Under 18:
Year of Adjudication 1993

Offence 1. Murder 2. Manslaughter Country		Age at time of incident	Under 10 years	10 years	11 years	12 years	13 years	14 years	15 years	16 years	17 years	Comments
Austria	1	At time of adjudication	*	*	*	*	*	0	0	1	0	*Under 14 years not liable under the terms of the Austrian Penal Code
	2	adjudication	*	*	*	*	*	0	0	0	0	
Belgium	1	At time of conviction	-	-	-	-	-	-	-	-	-	Not available before 1994 when form of statistics changed
	2		-	-	-	-	-	-	-	-	-	
Denmark	1	#No crime category of manslaughter	*	*	*	*	*	*	0	0	0	*Not criminally responsible under 15 years
	2		#	#	#	#	#	#	#	#	#	
England and Wales	1	At first recording by police	*	2	0	0	0	2	3	3	7	*Not criminally responsible under 10 years
	2		*	0	0	0	2	1	0	5	7	
Germany (suspects)	1			0		0		18		57		Each figure for two adjacent years, starting 10 and 11
	2			2		6		36		115		
Greece	1		0	0	0	0	0	0	0	0	0	
	2		0	0	0	0	0	0	1	0	0	

Crimes of Murder & Manslaughter Committed by Children Under 18:
Year of Adjudication 1993 (continued)

Offence 1. Murder 2. Manslaughter / Country	Age at time of incident	Under 10 years	10 years	11 years	12 years	13 years	14 years	15 years	16 years	17 years	Comments
Italy	1 minors reported 2 to the prosecutor	under 14:	1 7				3 11	2 10	17 57	25 42	
Luxembourg	1 2	0 0	0 0	0 0	0 0	0 0	0 0	0 0	1 0	0 0	
Netherlands (Interrogated suspects)	1 36 cases from 2 12-17 years										Figures for murder and manslaughter for 12-17 years
Norway	1 persons charged 2 male/female						0 2				Figures for 14-17 years
Scotland	1 2= Culpable homicide	0 0	0 0	0 0	0 0	0 0	0 0	0 1	0 1	0 3	

211

Crimes of Murder & Manslaughter Committed by Children Under 18: Year of Adjudication 1994

Offence 1. Murder 2. Manslaughter		Age at time of incident	Under 10 years	10 years	11 years	12 years	13 years	14 years	15 years	16 years	17 years	Comments
Country												
Austria	1	At time of	*	*	*	*	*	0	1	4	2	*Under 14 years not liable under the terms of the Austrian Penal Code
	2	adjudication	*	*	*	*	*	0	0	0	0	
Belgium	1	At time of	0	0	0	0	0	0	1	1	3	
	2	conviction	0	0	0	0	0	0	0	0	1	
Denmark	1	Not available for 1994										*Not criminally responsible under 15 years
	2	Not available for 1994										
England and Wales	1	At first	*	0	0	0	0	0	2	1	2	*Not criminally responsible under 10 years
	2	recording by police	*	0	0	0	1	0	3	2	4	
Germany (suspects)	1			0		1		18	2	55	2	Each figure for two adjacent years, starting 10 and 11
	2			1		9		37	3	91	4	
Greece	1		0	0	0	0	0	0	0	0	0	
	2		0	0	0	0	0	0	1	1	0	

Crimes of Murder & Manslaughter Committed by Children Under 18: Year of Adjudication 1994 (continued)

Offence 1. Murder 2. Manslaughter Country	Age at time of incident		Under 10 years	10 years	11 years	12 years	13 years	14 years	15 years	16 years	17 years	Comments
Italy	1	minors reported	under 14:	1				1	7	19	19	
	2	to the prosecutor		3				16	13	55	26	
Luxembourg	1		0	0	0	0	0	0	0	0	0	
	2		0	0	0	0	0	0	0	0	0	
Netherlands (Interrogated suspects)	1	26 cases from										Figures for murder and manslaughter for 12-17 years
	2	12-17 years										
Norway	1	persons charged	-	-	-	-	-	-	-	-	-	Not available for 1994
	2	male/female	-	-	-	-	-	-	-	-	-	Not available for 1994
Scotland	1	Not available for 1994	-	-	-	-	-	-	-	-	-	Not available for 1994
	2 -	Culpable homicide	-	-	-	-	-	-	-	-	-	Not available for 1994

213

Expanded List of Contents

Part IV: The Way Forward

Appendix

Youth Justice Publications from Waterside Press

Introduction to the
Youth Court
Winston Gordon Michael Watkins Philip Cuddy
Foreword by Lord Woolf, Master of the Rolls
A basic outline of the law and practice of the youth courts produced under the auspices of the Justices' Clerk's Society for use by youth panel magistrates and other people dealing with juveniles who are in trouble with the criminal law. £12 + £1.50 p&p. ISBN 1 872 870 36 8

Introduction to the
Scottish Children's Panel
Alistair Kelly
The first basic account of this topic for 20 years. £12 + £1.50 p&p. ISBN 1 872 870 38 4

Juvenile Delinquents
and Young People in Trouble in an Open Environment
Editor Dr. Willie McCarney
An invaluable collection of comparative international materials on the law and practice of youth justice. Published in conjunction with the International Association of Juvenile and Family Court Magistrates (IAJFCM). £16 + £1.50 p&p. ISBN 1 872 870 39 2

Growing Out of Crime
Andrew Rutherford
The classic work about young people and their transition into adulthood. (Second reprint, 1995). £12.50 + £1.50 p&p. ISBN 1 872 870 06 6

The Youth Court One Year Onwards
Bryan Gibson and Others
A practitioner style work looking at the law and practice of the youth court a year after its inauguration. This book treats the subject in greater depth than *Introduction to the Youth Court* and contains statutory references and other legal authorities. £15 + £1.50 p&p. ISBN 1 872 870 20 1

Some other titles from Waterside Press

Justice for Victims and Offenders
Martin Wright (SECOND EDITION)
£16 + £1.50 p&p. 1 872 870 35 X

Criminal Classes
Offenders at School
Angela Devlin
£16 + £1.50 p&p. ISBN 1 872 870 30 9

Relational Justice
Repairing the Breach
Edited by Jonathan Burnside and Nicola Baker
Foreword by Lord Woolf
£10 + £1.50 p&p. ISBN 1 872 870 22 8

Transforming Criminal Policy
Andrew Rutherford
£16 + £1.50 p&p. ISBN 1 872 870 31 7

Capital Punishment
Global Issues and Prospects
Peter Hodgkinson and Andrew Rutherford
£32 + £1.50 p&p. ISBN 1 872 870 32 5

Criminal Justice and the Pursuit of Decency
Andrew Rutherford
£12 + £1.50 p&p. ISBN 1 872 870 21 X

Interpreters and the Legal Process
Joan Colin and Ruth Morris
£12 + £1.50 p&p. ISBN 1 872 870 28 7

Paying Back
Twenty Years of Community Service
Edited by Dick Whitfield and David Scott
£12 + £1.50 p&p. ISBN 1 872 870 13 9

Introductory books from Waterside Press

Introduction to the
Magistrates' Court
Bryan Gibson
An ideal introduction. Includes a unique *Glossary of Words, Phrases and Abbreviations*. SECOND EDITION. £10 + £1.50 p&p. ISBN 1 872 870 15 5

Introduction to the
Criminal Justice Process
Bryan Gibson
Paul Cavadino
The process of investigation, arrest, prosecution, trial and sentence. The first book to treat the subject in this easy to read way. £12 + £1.50 p&p. ISBN 1 872 870 09 0

Introduction to the
Probation Service
Anthony Osler
A highly readable account for newcomers and others. £10 + £1.50 p&p. ISBN 1 872 870 19 8

The Sentence of the Court
A Handbook for Magistrates
Michael Watkins Winston Gordon Anthony Jeffries
Foreword by Lord Taylor, Lord Chief Justice
'Excellent': *The Law*. In use for training purposes in many parts of England and Wales. £10 + £1.50 p&p. ISBN 1 872 870 25 2

Orders or enquiries: WATERSIDE PRESS, Domum Road, Winchester S023 9NN. Telephone or Fax 01962 855567. Cheques should be made out to 'Waterside Press'. Organizations can be invoiced for two or more books on request. Postage outside Europe is charged at cost.

BJFCS

Formed in 1974, the British Juvenile and Family Courts Society is affiliated to the International Association of Juvenile and Family Court Magistrates which holds consultative status to the United Nations. Overseas court contacts are available to BJFCS members.

Unique: BJFCS is the only organization of its kind representative of the United Kingdom, Isle of Man and the Channel Isles.

Objectives include:

- *educating* all persons connected in processes in relation to offending youth and young persons in need of care and control.
- *encouraging* liasion at national and international levels.
- *sponsoring* research into the causes of criminal behaviour and social maladjustment among the young.

Members: The Society welcomes ordinary (individual), associate and corporate members from the following:

- child protection officers • children's panel members • children's reporters • educators • guardians ad litem – safeguarders • health visitors • judges • lawyers • magistrates • probation workers • paediatricians • psychologists • psychiatrists • social workers

How to join
If you sympathise with the aims of the British Juvenile and Family Courts Society and wish to apply for membership please write for further details and an application form to:

The Secretary, BJFCS, 44 Queen Anne Street, London W1M 9LA.

Telephone 0171 224 3566 Fax 0171 224 3577

BJFCS Patrons: The Rt Hon Sir Stephen Brown, President of the Family Division of the High Court of Justice; Sheriff Principal Gordon Nicholson QC.